A CAMBRIDGE BICENTENARY

A
CAMBRIDGE
BICENTENARY

The History of a Legal Practice
1789–1989

by
CHRISTOPHER JACKSON
Line drawings by Peter Nuttall

Foreword by
J. MICHAEL FARRAR, M.A.
Cambridgeshire County Archivist

MORROW & CO PUBLISHERS
BUNGAY · SUFFOLK
1990

First published by Morrow & Co., Bungay, Suffolk 1990

ISBN 0 948903 08 2

Typeset by Bungay Printers, Bungay, Suffolk
Printed and Bound by The Ipswich Book Company

DEDICATION

First
to Sheila, Andrew, Fiona and Michael Jackson with love

Secondly
with profound respect to my eight predecessors
as Principals or Senior Partners of the Practice

and Thirdly
to my partners at Cambridge and Norwich
for their friendly tolerance
during the writing of this book

CONTENTS

ILLUSTRATIONS

ACKNOWLEDGEMENTS

Permission to use original source material in this work has been received from the following and is gratefully acknowledged —

The Syndics of Cambridge University Library (extracts from Romilly's Diary, University memoranda and the End Paper illustration), Cambridgeshire County Record Office (photograph of Clement Francis), Cambridgeshire Collection (photographs of the Emmanuel Street premises, Peas Hill in 1900 and E. H. Parker), J. K. Peile deceased (photograph of F. K. Peile), Peterhouse Cambridge (Archive material and bill book extracts), Jesus College, Cambridge (bill book extracts), St. John's College, Cambridge (Archive material and bill book extracts), Trinity College Cambridge (Archive material and bill book extracts), The Registrary of the University of Cambridge (Archive material relating to Fitzwilliam Museum sydicate and the Sex Viri and bill book extracts), Royal Commission on the Historical Monuments of England (extracts from City of Cambridge 1959) Hodder and Stoughton Limited (extract from The Cambridgeshire Landscape by Christopher Taylor) and Peggy Watts (extracts from Stow-cum-Quy Through Two Twenty-five Year Reigns).

TABLE OF STATUTES

ABBREVIATIONS
used in the text

BIRKS   M. Birks, Gentlemen of the Law, 1960

COOPER   C. H. Cooper, Annals of Cambridge

GUNNING H. Gunning, Reminiscences of the University Town and County of Cambridge, 1854

HISTORICAL REGISTER   Cambridge Historical Register 1910

HOWARTH T. E. B. Howarth, Cambridge Between Two Wars, 1978

R.C.H.M.   Royal Commission on Historical Monuments

V.C.H.   Victoria County History

WINSTANLEY D. A. Winstanley, Later Victorian Cambridge, 1947

PEMBERTON FAMILY TREE

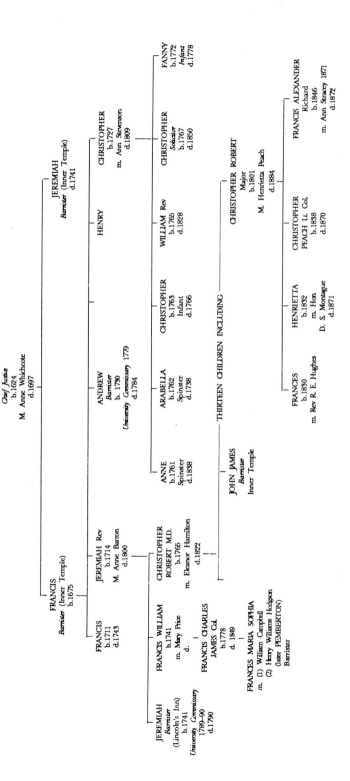

RALPH PEMBERTON of St. Albans
Gentleman

Sir FRANCIS PEMBERTON
Chief Justice
b.1624
M. Anne Whichcote
d.1697

FRANCIS
Barrister (Inner Temple)
b.1675

JEREMIAH
Barrister (Inner Temple)
d.1741

HENRY

ANDREW
Barrister
b. 1790
University Commissary 1779
d.1784

CHRISTOPHER
b.1727
m. Ann Stevenson
d.1809

FANNY
b.1772
Infant
d.1778

FRANCIS
b.1711
d.1743

JEREMIAH Rev
b.1714
M. Anne Barron
d.1800

CHRISTOPHER
ROBERT M.D.
b.1766
m. Eleanor Hamilton
d.1822

ANNE
b.1761
Spinster
d.1838

ARABELLA
b.1762
Spinster
d.1738

CHRISTOPHER
b.1763
Infant
d.1766

WILLIAM Rev
b.1765
d.1828

CHRISTOPHER
Solicitor
b.1767
d.1850

JEREMIAH
Barrister
(Lincoln's Inn)
b.1741
University Commissary
1789–90
d.1790

FRANCIS WILLIAM
b.1741
m. Mary Price
d.

FRANCIS CHARLES
JAMES Col.
b.1778
d 1849

FRANCES MARIA SOPHIA
m. (1) William Campbell
(2) Henry Williams Hodgson
(later PEMBERTON)
Barrister

JOHN JAMES
Barrister
Inner Temple

——— THIRTEEN CHILDREN INCLUDING ———

CHRISTOPHER ROBERT
Major
b.1801
M. Henrietta Peach
d.1884

FRANCES
b.1830
m. Rev R. E. Hughes

HENRIETTA
b.1892
m. Hon
D. S. Montague
d.1871

CHRISTOPHER
PEACH Lt. Col
b.1838
d.1870

FRANCIS ALEXANDER
Richard
b.1846
m. Ann Stracey 1871
d.1872

FRANCIS FAMILY TREE

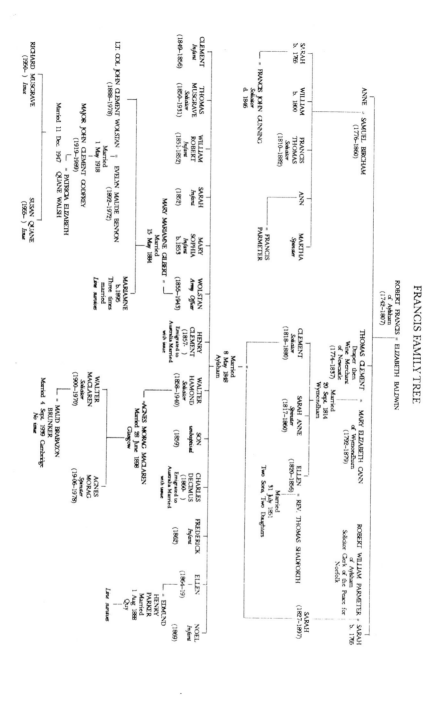

FOREWORD

It is a pleasure to dip into this book. Wherever it may be opened the attention of the reader will be caught with fascinating glimpses of times past. As an archivist, I have over the years had many dealings with Francis and Company and their records, and now find here, lovingly recorded, details of their many-sided service to Cambridgeshire and to Cambridge.

This is not, however, merely the history of a provincial legal practice, albeit the longest established in an ancient university town. In telling his story, Christopher Jackson throws light on many aspects of local history in which members of the firm have been involved. Amongst many others, these include local Parliamentary representation, the office of Clerk of the Peace, Fen drainage, the work of inclosure commissioners and the construction of railways, but most important of all the University, which the firm served over many decades. He also delights in contrasting the differences between legal methods and institutions of the past and those of the present day. Not forgotten is the story of the Francis family and their estate at Quy, where the family name still lives on.

It is particularly appropriate that this book should be published at this time, when the name of the firm has recently been extinguished as a result of a merger, though fortunately it will not be forgotten, since it will be perpetuated in the name given to the offices of the new firm, wherever they may lie.

Michael Farrar

INTRODUCTION

HIS history traces the story of a legal practice from the year 1789, when Christopher Pemberton started his career in Cambridge as an attorney, up to the present time. While some details of this story may be lost or obscured the continuous succession through different identities and at different practice addresses has never been broken. During this period the practice has been a close witness to the progress and development of Cambridge as a university town and provincial centre and a number of fascinating insights into town and university life can now be revealed. Appropriate acknowledgments are given to published sources of material but there are a number of instances where new light is thrown on otherwise well-documented episodes thanks to the surviving records of the firm and other sources hitherto unpublished.

Interest in local history has never been greater and the publication of business histories is enjoying a boom as never before. Sadly these developments were never anticipated by our predecessors two centuries ago. If some reference material still survives thanks to the acknowledged magpie tendencies of the solicitors' profession, much else has disappeared over the years and has had to be supplied from other sources. At this point it would be appropriate to acknowledge the willing help and courtesy of Mr. Michael Farrar the County Archivist and his staff at Cambridgeshire County Record Office and of Mr. Mike Petty and his staff at the Cambridgeshire Collection and to thank Dr. R. W. Lovatt, (Archivist, Peterhouse), Dr. Simeran Gell (Archivist's Clerk, Emmanuel College), Dr. Sandra Raban (Archivist, Trinity Hall), Mr. Malcolm Underwood (Archivist, St. John's College). Dr. Patrick Zutshi (Assistant Curator of Manuscripts University Library Cambridge), Mrs. D. J. Chilton of the Law Society's Records Department, Mr. Peter Emerson, Chief Archivist, Barclays Bank PLC, Officials of the Public Record Office and at the Law Society's Library, Prof. J. H. Baker of St. Catharine's College for his invaluable help and suggestions in matters of legal history, Dr. Stephen Fleet, (Registrary of the University of Cambridge), Mrs. E. Bury, Mr. D. A. Cowper, Mr. Dudley Durell for much preliminary research and for help with the last three chapters, Mr. R. D. English (Bursar's Clerk, Trinity College), Major John Francis, Miss Lucy Goodley of Trent Polytechnic, Mrs. P. Hatfield (Archivist, Eton College), Mr. A. T. Pearce Higgins, Mr. Edmund Heward (Retired Chief Chancery Master), Mrs. Sheila Jackson, Miss Jean Kennedy (Norfolk County Archivist), Mr. Ralph Phillips of British Rail, the late Mr. John K. Peile, Mr. Robin Peile, Dr. David Watkin, Miss Peggy Watts and staff members at 24 Hills Road, Cambridge, especially Mrs. Beti North, Mrs. Enid Smith, Miss Julia Mills and Miss Tracey West.

Being written by a practising solicitor, this history takes the opportunity where appropriate to dwell on half-forgotten legal practices, procedures and legislation, long since overtaken by the modern legal framework. It is hoped that these passages, necessary for explanatory purposes, may prove of interest not only to professional colleagues but to younger entrants into the legal profession who may find a comparison between ancient and modern legal practice both interesting and instructive. No apology is therefore made for including extensive verbatim passages from original source material, whether from long-repealed statutes, valedictory minutes, letters or obituaries even though the work may in places take on the appearance of an anthology. Apart from adding an authentic period flavour to the story it is felt that mere references to sources not generally available would give the reader little appreciation of their contents. The author's preferred policy has therefore been where possible to quote rather than to paraphrase. In this context it has to be recorded with some regret that not even officially preserved records escape destruction. The author made this discovery when he applied at the Public Record Office to inspect the articles of clerkship of Christopher Pemberton and several later partners. All articles earlier than the year 1840 have been destroyed as a space saving measure. This represents a sad loss of background material to any solicitors' firm investigating its early history, even if understandable in the sense that the authorities would hardly be required to authenticate the due admission of solicitors dead for upwards of one hundred years.

For the author the preparation of this history has provided a fascinating revelation of one aspect of legal practice which has changed least and of another which has changed most. It seems quite clear that the traditional concept of a professional relationship between solicitor and client, of obligations duties and confidences to be observed has changed least over the period of this history and still burns as brightly now as ever it did two hundred years ago. On the other hand, as may be expected the rate of technological progress over the last two hundred years, especially in the last two decades, has changed the conduct of a solicitor's practice very nearly (but not entirely) out of all recognition. A modern solicitor would find it difficult to run his practice without electricity or gas, without railways, cars, typewriters, telephones or copiers. Two hundred years ago transport between Cambridge and London for both passengers and letters was by stage coach, all letters and documents were hand written with quill pens (and copied out again as many times as necessary) and in those days the oft repeated bill item, "To calling upon you and finding you out," was an accepted hazard before the invention of telephones. Modern methods and equipment may have made the conduct of a practice faster and more efficient, but no one should scorn the apparently light work load and leisurely pace of two hundred years ago. Due allowance must be made for the conditions under which professional and commercial activity was then conducted.

If this history records two hundred years of continuity and change it also serves as a tribute to the founding fathers of the practice, their partners, successors and staff all of whom played a part in developing, fostering and maintaining the reputation of the oldest surviving legal practice in Cambridge.

Cambridge, 25th June 1989.

Chapter 1

THE PRACTICE BEGINS—
CAMBRIDGE IN 1789

I

 AMBRIDGE in the year 1789 still had the appearance of peaceful rural seclusion which it had enjoyed since mediæval times. Ancient college buildings, especially King's College Chapel, stood out prominently as the traveller approached across the open fields which surrounded Cambridge in every direction. The importance of Cambridge as a market town and head of navigation from the sea was largely overshadowed by the University, prompting the comment by Thomas Fuller that "Oxford is an university in a town; but Cambridge a town in an university". At this time the population of Cambridge was hardly more than nine thousand but it had a regional importance beyond its size thanks to a position which attracted trade from many directions and had led to the establishment of the ancient Stourbridge and Midsummer Fairs. The earlier importance of these fairs was, however, already starting to wane. The opening of Stourbridge Fair in 1789 was the last but one occasion at which the Mayor and Corporation officiated with full ceremonial.

It is apparent from both news items and advertisements in the "Cambridge Chronicle" that, thanks to its river borne traffic and connections with the sea, Cambridge readers in

1789 were just as interested in shipping movements at Kings Lynn and Boston as they were in parliamentary happenings at Westminster. Land transport to and from Cambridge was provided by stage coaches; it is not clear whether advertisements for stage coach services "with a guard and lighted" were intended to encourage or deter the traveller. Advertisements for cock fighting had disappeared from the front page only the previous year, working windmills were occasionally offered for sale and notices appealed for information concerning runaway servants and army deserters. On 4th July 1789 Mr. Cooper, Attorney at Law, Petty Cury, Cambridge, advertised for an Articled Clerk. On 11th July the Cambridge Chronicle announced the graduation of Christopher Pemberton's 24 year old cousin Christopher Robert Pemberton (1765–1822) in the following terms:—

> "Cambridge Commencement—Tuesday last being commencement day the following gentlemen were created to the several degrees undermentioned (inter alia) Bachelors of Physic... Mr. Christopher Pemberton of Gonville and Caius College..."

As was to be expected in an ancient University and Market Town the legal profession appears to have been already well established in Cambridge and it may be supposed that legal practitioners had been active there for many centuries. When Christopher Pemberton started practice he would have found at least sixteen professional colleagues already practising as attorneys in the Town. (see list on p. 7)

It is impossible to guess after this lapse of time whether the number of practitioners serving the legal needs of the population was excessive, inadequate or in balance. In view of the many changes in Cambridge during the last two hundred years, its tenfold expansion of population and all the changes in clients' legal needs which have occurred

CAMBRIDGE ATTORNEYS IN 1789
(taken from the Law List 1789 with augmentations)

NAME	ADDRESS (where known)	APPOINTMENTS OR POSITIONS HELD
John Bones	-	-
Thomas Bullen	-	-
Joseph Butcher	St. Andrews Street	Solicitor to John Mortlock; Agent for the Duke and Duchess of Rutland
John Cooper	Petty Cury	-
James Day	Trumpington Street	Clerk of the Peace
Edward Randall	Trumpington Street	Clerk to the Commissioners under the Act for the paving cleansing and lighting of the Town of Cambridge
John Doyley	-	-
Robert Gee	Bene't Street	Secretary, Addenbrooke's Hospital
James Gordon	-	-
John Haggerston	-	-
Thomas Lombe	-	Solicitor to the University of Cambridge
John Ingle	Trumpington Street	Steward of Manors in Swaffham Prior, Cottenham and Great Shelford
Robert White	Bridge Street	Town Clerk
Lennett Willmot	-	-
John Wood	-	Coroner
William Lenham Wilkins	-	-

during that time any comparisons may not seem particularly valid. In any case there appears to have been a heavier reliance then on public appointments as a source of income. In their time seventeen legal practitioners in Cambridge served a population, including surrounding districts, in excess of ten thousand, approximately one attorney per six hundred persons. In 1987 one hundred and seventeen qualified Solicitors served a population well in excess of one hundred thousand, roughly one per nine hundred and fifty persons.

II

Christopher Pemberton was born into an affluent and prominent land-owning family in Cambridgeshire in 1767. As the Pemberton family tree shows there were distinguished legal connections on his father's side, starting with his great grandfather Sir Francis Pemberton, Chief Justice of the King's Bench (1624–1697), his grandfather Francis Pemberton a Barrister of the Inner Temple (born 1675), his great uncle Jeremiah Pemberton a Barrister of the Inner Temple (died 1741) his uncle Andrew Pemberton a Barrister (1730–1784) and University Commissary* from 1779, and his cousin Jeremiah Pemberton a Barrister of Lincoln's Inn (1741–1790) Chief Justice of Nova Scotia (1788–89), also University Commissary (1789–90).

Christopher Pemberton was not himself a member of the University but several close relatives were Cambridge graduates of some achievement and standing as the

---

*According to the Historical Register the Commissary was appointed by the University Chancellor by letters patent. His function was to hear cases brought in the University Court. During the 18th Century the Commissary seems to have combined his office with that of Vice-Chancellor's Assessor or Deputy High Steward as the duties and salary were both small. He still had jurisdiction over such causes as remained within the cognisance of the University, with the exception of those concerning Proctors, taxes or members "in statu magistri".

following list indicates:

Christopher Pemberton (his father) M.A. 1752, Fellow of Catherine Hall 1751–60

Andrew Pemberton (uncle) M.A. Fellow of Peterhouse and University Proctor in 1777

Jeremiah Pemberton (cousin) M.A. Fellow of Christ's College

Christopher Robert Pemberton (cousin) M.D. Gonville and Caius College

Rev. William Pemberton (elder brother) M.A. 1792, Fellow of Peterhouse 1792

The Pemberton family owned two substantial landed estates in Cambridgeshire, one at Trumpington and the other at Newton. In 1789 the Trumpington estate was owned by Christopher Pemberton's uncle, Rev. Jeremiah Pemberton (1740–1800), and the Newton estate was owned by Christopher Pemberton's father, also Christopher (1727–1809).

Christopher Pemberton (Senior) married Anne Stevenson "of this Parish Spinster" by licence at Newton Parish Church on 9th June 1760, witnessed by Andrew Pemberton and John Stevenson. Christopher Pemberton was born in 1767 at Newton Hall, the family home, one of the six children of Christopher and Anne Pemberton. All six children were baptised at Newton Parish Church and of these Ann, Arabella, William and Christopher survived into adult life.

III

The route to qualification as a legal practitioner followed by Christopher Pemberton and his later partners until at least the mid-nineteenth century is worth examining in some detail because of the interesting contrast it provides with the rules and requirements for training and entry into the legal profession in force in the late nineteen eighties. Nevertheless, some word of explanation must be given with regard to the court structure then existing, within which qualification as a legal practitioner took place.

In 1789 the Courts of superior jurisdiction (or "record") in England and Wales were based in Westminster Hall and comprised the King's Bench, the Court of Common Pleas, the Court of Exchequer and the Court of Chancery. Of these the first three had concurrent jurisdiction in the application of the common law to ordinary civil actions. Dealing with each in turn:

1. *The King's Bench* was considered the superior court in dignity and power, as appeals were at one time possible to the King's Bench from the Common Pleas and Exchequer Courts, and it also enjoyed jurisdiction over lower courts, magistrates and civil corporations. Criminal cases were dealt with on the "Crown side" of the King's Bench Court and civil cases on the "Plea side". In 1789 the Chief Justice of the King's Bench was Lord Kenyon, who is said "never to have lost an opportunity for ridiculing and abusing defenceless solicitors and attorneys".

2. *The Court of Common Pleas* originated as the sole venue for civil actions. It was by 1789 sharing this jurisdiction with the Court of King's Bench save that it had exclusive jurisdiction in "real" actions, i.e. those concerned with property. Actions could not at that time be argued in the Common Pleas Court without the involvement and expense of a serjeant-at-law. In 1789 the Chief Justice of the Common Pleas was Lord Wedderburn.

3. *The Court of Exchequer* had originated as a Court where actions were brought by the Crown or officials accountable to the Crown for recovery of public revenue. By 1789 it had extended its jurisdiction beyond enforcement of fiscal rights of the Crown by means of fictitious pleadings to deal also with actions between subjects of the Crown. Here, too, additional expense

resulted from the requirement that one of the four Exchequer attorneys had to be involved in every case brought before this Court. In 1789 the Chief Baron of the Exchequer was Sir James Eyre.

4.   *The Chancery Court* administered the system of equity which had grown up as a parallel jurisdiction to the common law, providing in many cases a mitigation to the full rigour of long established common law principles. In 1789 the Lord Chancellor (head of the Chancery Court) was Lord Thurlow, "the terror of attorneys".

It was not until the Judicature Act 1873 that these four separate courts were made into divisions of the Supreme Court of Judicature. In 1880 the three common law divisions were consolidated within the High Court into the Queen's Bench Division, and the former Chancery Court became the Chancery Division.

For the purpose of comparison with the earlier system reference can usefully be made to a modern definition of a solicitor as"...an officer of the Supreme Court, who, and only who, is entitled to sue out any writ or process, or commence, carry on or defend any action, suit or other proceeding on behalf of another in any Court"—Section 18 Solicitors Act 1957. To enable a person to practise as a solicitor, he or she must nowadays serve a term as an articled clerk, pass certain examinations, be admitted and enrolled as a Solicitor of the Supreme Court and take out a yearly certificate authorising him or her to practise. By contrast, at the time of Christopher Pemberton's admission and until the passing of the Judicature Act 1873, the equivalent role was performed in the three Common Law Courts by "Attorneys" and in the Court of Chancery by "Solicitors in Chancery" (Solicitors for short). The common title "Solicitor of the Supreme Court" was given to these different practitioners by s.87 of the Judicature Act 1873. At this point the term "Attorney" was officially abandoned.

Attorneys and solicitors had been practising before the courts for many centuries prior to 1789 but there was little formal control over their admission and practising conduct until the early eighteenth century. By the year 1729 sufficient need had arisen for regulation to be imposed on practitioners some of whom had received little or no training and were virtually self-appointed. The system of binding oneself by articles to a principal, to acquire legal training already existed, though this had been a voluntary procedure followed only by those who wished to see themselves, and to be seen by their clients, as having better standing than the rest. The resulting legislation, introduced partly on the petition of the justices of Yorkshire, had the twin objects of regulating qualification and controlling what were regarded as excessive numbers.

By the Statute (1729) 2 Geo. II c.23—"an Act for the better regulation of Attornies and Solicitors" there were introduced for the first time (and for an experimental period of nine years) the following requirements:

1.　No attorney or solicitor was to be admitted before his respective Court without first taking an oath and being "inrolled". (This was the first statutory recognition of the "Solicitor in Chancery", alone entitled to practise before the Court of Chancery).

2.　The respective Courts were to be responsible for "examining his capacity" before admitting an attorney or solicitor (but no formal written examination was stipulated and none was introduced until 1836).

3.　A minimum term of five years articles had to be served before admission.

4.　A "sworn attorney" and a "sworn solicitor" could be admitted to practise before any other Court.

By the Statute (1739) 12 Geo. II c.13—"an Act (inter alia) for continuing, explaining and amending the Act made in the second year of the reign of his present Majesty, for the better regulation of Attornies and Solicitors" the earlier Act was (inter alia) continued for a further period of nine years.

By the Statute (1749) 22 Geo. II c.46—"an Act... for continuing explaining and amending the several laws for the better regulation of Attornies and Solicitors... and also for making further regulations with respect to Attornies and Solicitors...":

1.   The 1729 Act was continued for a further period of nine years.

2.   Affidavits as to due execution of articles were to be filed in the Court (evidently this supporting evidence was considered necessary to avoid fraud and other irregularity).

3.   Articled clerks were to be employed "in their proper business during the time of their contract of serving".

4.   Further affidavits were required from clerks as to their due service of five years articles.

A number of details and complicating provisions were also introduced, mainly designed to meet circumstances not previously dealt with, such as the death of the master during the course of articles, number of clerks permitted to any master at one time and certain exemptions only affecting Court officials.

No wonder the preamble to the repealing and amending Statute (1843) 6 and 7 Vic. c.73—"An Act for consolidating and amending several of the laws relating to Attorneys and Solicitors practising in England and Wales" sounded a complaining note: "Whereas the laws relating to Attorneys and Solicitors are numerous and complicated, and it is expedient to consolidate and simplify and to alter and amend the same..."

With this legal background in mind the official entries recording Christopher Pemberton's admission first as an

I. Extract from the "Roll or Book of Attorneys commencing Hilary Term 1789 ending Trinity Term 1803, Queen's Bench (Plea side)":

COUNTY	SURNAME	CHRISTIAN NAME	PLACE OF ABODE	WHEN SWORN AND ENROLLED AND BEFORE WHOM EXAMINED
Middlesex	Pemberton	Christopher the younger	Chancery Lane	25th June 1789 —Kenyon

(Christopher Pemberton was one of seven attornies admitted that day before Lord Chief Justice Kenyon)

II. Extract from the Chancery Admission Roll 1729 to 1791.

DATE OF ADMITTANCE	PERSONS NAMES, PLACE OF ABODE	BEFORE WHOM ADMITTED	WHEN ENROLLED OR ENTERED
13.2.1790	Christopher Pemberton the Younger (late of Chancery Lane but now of Cambridge in the County of Cambridge, gent.	P. Holford W. Graves*	13.2.1790

*P. Holford and Wm. Graves were two Masters in Chancery, empowered to admit solicitors in the place of the Master of the Rolls.

attorney and then as a solicitor will be better understood as reproduced on the opposite page.

Having thus survived admission as an attorney before the formidable Lord Chief Justice of the King's Bench, Christopher Pemberton had exercised his entitlement under the statutes then in force to be admitted as a Solicitor in Chancery without further examination or other formality. One further step remained, to obtain for himself an annual certificate of admission and, as a country practitioner, to pay for it the £3 duty introduced by William Pitt in 1785.

Christopher Pemberton appears to have been quick to secure the entry of his name in the Law List at the first opportunity. Seven days after his admission before the Chancery Court the Law List for that year was published (February 20th 1790) showing a last minute insertion at the end of the list of Cambridge Attorneys, and therefore out of strict alphabetical order:

"Christopher Pemberton"

Practice in Cambridge for this newly qualified twenty two year old attorney and solicitor had not only begun but was now recorded for all to see.

Chapter 2

POLITICS PREFERMENT AND
OFFICES OF PROFIT

I

HEN Christopher Pemberton started practice in Cambridge he did so as a newly qualified attorney and solicitor on his own account without joining or taking over any existing practice. Notwithstanding his family connection with eminent members of the bench and bar, Christopher Pemberton was so far as can be ascertained, the first member of his family to qualify in the junior branch of the legal profession. Many years later, when asked whether his father was a professional man he replied, "No; he was a gentleman, being in no profession".

However, if Christopher Pemberton started a practice without any clients, he did not start without valuable connections or prospects. The list of Cambridge Attorneys in 1789 serves to illustrate the point that members of the legal profession in any provincial centre, provided a ready pool of suitably qualified individuals available to accept part-time appointments in a variety of public or semi-official roles. This was long before the establishment of a career service in local government or the extension of civil service posts to regional or local level. In Christopher Pemberton's case it may prove useful to jump forward from the threshhold to the very close of his career in order to identify some of the appointments which were to come his way. This is well illustrated by the following quotation from his obituary in the Cambridge Independent Press on 26thOctober 1850:

> "Mr. Pemberton was Clerk of the Peace for the County for nearly sixty years; he was also for many years Receiver General for the County; Treasurer to the Eau Brink Commissioners, Solicitor to the University and a very large number of Colleges; Steward of upwards of thirty manors, he also many times served the office of Under-Sheriff".

It cannot be denied that patronage of various kinds played a part in the allocation of such posts and a description of the political influences at work in Cambridgeshire in the late eighteenth century is necessary if the reader is to understand the workings of this system.

II

It has been written (Murphy—*Cambridge Newspapers and Opinion 1780–1850)* that prior to 1780 "Cambridge was not a pocket borough", but the parliamentary history of two of the three Cambridge constituencies, Borough, County and University nevertheless discloses very deep-seated traditions of financial influence, widespread bribery and abuses of all kinds. The Mayor and Corporation had long dominated the freemen of the Borough and hence the outcome of parliamentary elections. Political allegiances at this time followed recognised leaders rather than sharply defined party policies although the Whig and Tory labels were already well established for the main political groupings in Parliament. The Tories were generally ascendant in Cambridge during the early part of the eighteenth century and their domination of the Borough and County constituencies (two members in each) was complete between 1715 and 1741, thanks to the influence of Sir John Cotton of Madingley Hall. Towards the end of this period the Cotton influence over the Mayor and Corporation began to wane and their allegiance was transferred in 1741 when two Whigs, supporters of Lord Newcastle's administration were returned. Secret payments of £550 per annum from Newcastle's office ensured solid constituency support for Whig members between 1754 and 1762. In 1740 the first earl of Hardwicke who was Lord Chancellor and a leading member of Sir Robert Walpole's Whig administration, in the years 1721–42, had moved to Wimpole Hall in Cambridgeshire. Lord Hardwicke felt constrained, perhaps reluctantly, to exert his influence in retaining the Borough for the Government. This responsibility and the title passed to the second earl when he succeeded his father in 1764.

Hardwicke power was considerable. "As Lord Lieutenant of the County, High Steward of the University and joint Patron of the Borough, the Lord of Wimpole was a lesser providence to whom all matters must be reported; any action taken without reference to him was a sort of treason" (VCH VOL.3 P.71).

Meanwhile, significant forces were again assembling on the Tory side. A powerful coalition started work to wrest all three constituencies from Whig control; William Pitt the Younger, with his eye on a University seat, John Mortlock seeking one of the Borough seats and John Henry Manners, Second Duke of Rutland, seeking to gain control of both Borough and County constituencies for the Tories. Of these three, Mortlock (John Mortlock II, founder of the Cambridge banking business in 1780) was soon to gain control of the Borough, and with it some notoriety in the history of Cambridge. As Mayor himself, or through nominees and successors, from 1788 onwards Mortlock rule was absolute, enduring even beyond his own death in 1816 until 1833, a continuous period of forty five years. After 1780, when this alliance first took formal shape, what would elsewhere have been spoken of as "The Whigs" and "The Tories" became personalised throughout Cambridgeshire as "The Hardwicke interest" and "The Rutland interest".

John Mortlock had considerable financial influence among the County families, and by September 1780 one County seat and one Borough seat had fallen to the Rutland interest. Lord Hardwicke was evidently not prepared to counter such powerful forces, the financial stakes having by then been raised far too high by his opponents. As part of the preparatory division of spoils Pitt was able in 1782 to secure Lord Hardwicke's appointment of Mortlock to the Receiver-Generalship of the Land Tax for Cambridgeshire, "a valuable asset for a provincial banker" (VCH Vol 3 P. 73). This represented a political setback for the Hardwicke interest, but the choice apparently resulted from family pressure exerted on Lord Hardwicke by his nephew by marriage, one Robert Manners, from the opposite Rutland camp. Mortlock held this office for two years until 1784. Then, desiring to stand as one of the Parliamentary candidates for the Borough constituency, and needing to divest himself of this office of profit, he again managed to secure enough persuasive pressure to achieve the transfer of the receivership to his banking partner Samuel Francis. This manoeuvre was a sufficient gesture to result in the return of Mortlock and his fellow candidate, General J. W. Adeane, unopposed for the Borough Constituency though there were many in Cambridge, Mortlock's supporters among them, who thought matters had gone too far. County and University interests displayed their disapproval by staging a run on Mortlock's Bank in May 1784 which the business only just survived. According to Lord Hardwicke's informant in Cambridge, Dr. Ewing, "The University have called in all their money from Mortlock's shop and are to order their tenants to take no more of their bills". Pitt refused to renew Francis's appointment for the following year, 1785. Worse scandal followed Mortlock in May 1786, when a complaint was made to the House of Commons that the list of Land Tax Commissioners in the Borough had been tampered with, and he narrowly escaped a vote of censure.

Mortlock was nevertheless unassailable, either by public opinion or parliamentary hostility, by virtue of his deeply entrenched position in the constituency and in the borough itself. Less than two years later he retired from Parliament in good order, transferring the seat and his parliamentary votes to the Rutland interest in return for remunerative positions, first as Commissioner of Salt and later as Receiver General of the Post Office. Rutland money also helped finance a series of court cases which were to leave Mortlock in sole and undisputed control of the Corporation.

If the Rutland interest had achieved political ascendancy in the Parliamentary constituencies, Lord Hardwicke still had a means at his disposal to appoint a successor more acceptable to the County interests than Samuel Francis. In fact he had only to look among his fellow members of the Cambridge County Club to find a candidate known to and accepted by all the influential County gentlemen. As the entry in the Treasury Register of Bonds, given by Receivers General for 1785, shows, his choice fell on one of the members elected only three years previously:

"Cambridge—Christopher Pemberton of Newton in the County of Cambridge Esq., (Bond also given by Philip York of New Cavendish Street in the Parish of St. Mary le Bone Benjamin Keene of Charles Street Berkeley Square both in the County of Middlesex and William Nicholl of Hinxton in the County of Cambridge)".

Further light is thrown on the appointment of Christopher Pemberton (Senior) if it is explained that Philip Yorke, who supported the Receiver's Bond, was nephew of the Earl of Hardwicke, and was to succeed to the title as Third Earl in 1790. This indeed was a copper-bottomed endorsement by the Hardwicke family. No less a valuable asset in the hands of a county gentleman, the post of Receiver General appears thereafter to have acquired considerable stability in Cambridgeshire and ceased to be treated as a political pawn or plaything. Christopher Pemberton Senior continued in office as Receiver General for the next twenty-one years, the only change to be noted is in the identity of his three bondsmen when in 1790 "Philip Yorke" changed to "Philip Earl of Hardwicke". Christopher Pemberton Senior was succeeded in office by his son Christopher Pemberton in 1806. This event and a detailed study of the post will be dealt with in a later section. (see p. 34)

III
Clerk Of The Peace

Christopher Pemberton had four years to wait from the commencement of his practice for the first of his paid appointments. This was announced in the Chronicle for 21st December 1793 in the following terms:

> "Cambridge December 20. The Right Hon. The Earl of Hardwicke Lord Lieutenant of this County has appointed Christopher Pemberton, Attorney at Law, of this place to succeed the late Mr. James Day as Clerk of the Peace for the County."

The appointment was further recorded in the minutes of the Quarter Sessions for the County of Cambridge held in the Shire Hall Cambridge on 28th December 1793:

"This day Christopher Pemberton Gent produced to this Court an appointment under the hand and seal of the right Honble Philip Earl of Hardwicke Custos Rotulorum for this County dated 10th day of December 1793 appointing the said Christopher Pemberton Clerk of the Peace for the said County and the said Christopher Pemberton was thereupon admitted to the said office, and in open Court took the Oath of Office."

This appointment did not appear to be regarded as a political gift or reward, but its connection with the membership of the Cambridge County Club is too close to be entirely overlooked.

The Clerk of the Peace is an officer of very ancient origin in the English counties. His duties in the fifteenth century were, according to Sir John Vaughan* "to assist the Justices of the Peace in drawing their indictments, in arraigning their prisoners, in joining issues for the Crown, in entering their judgments, in awarding their process and in making up and keeping their records". In effect the Clerk of the Peace was the Clerk of the Quarter Sessions for the County but sixteenth and early seventeenth century legislation added to his list of responsibilities "recording proclamations of wages, enrolling the discharge of apprentices, keeping registers of the licences of badgers**, drovers and various traders and of persons licensed to shoot in guns, recording presentments of absentees from church and certificates of the oath of allegiance, certifying into the King's Bench transcripts of indictments, outlawries attainders and convictions before the Justices of the Peace and enrolling deeds of bargain and sale of lands within his County".

In the absence of any other local government framework

---

*Quoted in Sir Edgar Stephens, "The Clerks of the Counties 1360–1960", 1961.
**A hawker, especially of provisions.

the administrative functions of the Justices of Peace increased considerably from 1500 onwards and Quarter Sessions became, according to Maitland "not merely a Criminal Court for the County, but also a governmental assembly, a board with governmental and administrative powers" (Constitutional History of England 1908). Quarter Sessions had the existing machinery of county, hundred and parish to assist in the exercise of their functions, but all the consequential administrative work, the drafting of orders, the issue of instructions and communications with central government fell upon the Clerk of the Peace. Up to the passing of the Local Government Act, 1888, the Clerk of the Peace was the principal and in some cases the only administrative officer of his County, and his responsibilities extended beyond the purely legal functions associated with the General and Quarter Sessions. Successive pieces of legislation imposed duties on the counties in relation to such matters as highways, bridges, diseases of animals, weights and measures, coroners districts, polling districts, reformatories, stage plays and county rates. A different responsiblity was added by the Statute (1837) 1 Vict.c.83. By s.2 of this Act Clerks of the Peace and Town Clerks were required, at all reasonable hours of the day, to permit all persons interested to inspect during a reasonable time, the documents thereby directed to be deposited with them respectively, on payment by each person to the Clerk of the Peace or Town Clerk of one shilling for every such inspection, and the further sum of one shilling for every hour during which such inspection should continue after the first hour, and after the rate of sixpence for every hundred words copied therefrom. Any Clerk of the Peace or Town Clerk not complying with the provisions of that Act was liable to a penalty of £5.

Among the records deposited with Christopher Pemberton for public inspection, were fair copies of the enclosure awards for all Cambridge parishes under the Enclosure Acts, and all plans of land in the county to be acquired by railway undertakings. Virtually every conveyance of such land during Christopher Pemberton's time in office incorporated a reference to the land conveyed as being "described in the map or plan and book of reference of the said railway deposited with the Clerk of the Peace for the County of Cambridge".

Ever since the Statute of Cambridge (1388) 11Ric IIc.12 the Clerk of the Peace was entitled to receive two shillings for each day he attended Quarter Sessions. Apart from this his remuneration for the office depended upon the fees he was able to charge. Some fees had been established by statute for specific duties but the rest had long been set by custom and it was said that "fee taking became indiscriminate, involving everyone whose business, whether of his own seeking or not, brought him into the Clerk's office, paupers only being in some cases excepted". Controversy led to inquiries in certain counties and during the seventeenth century several commissions were established to investigate the level of fees charged. As a result it became more common for a scale of fees to be fixed between the Justices and the Clerk of the Peace, examples being, in Middlesex, 2s 4d for a recognizance of the peace for good behaviour, 2s for an indictment of trespass or felony at common law, 3s 4d for an indictment of riot or forcible entry. However, as the County business both of the Quarter Sessions and the Clerk of the Peace increased during the eighteenth century, the fee opportunities became ever greater and more remunerative, largely at the expense of the County rate. No records survive to indicate the level, or the basis on which, Christopher Pemberton charged for his services as Clerk of the Peace, until returns were made to Parliament from 1834 onwards (see below);

but there is no doubt whatever that the post would have been remunerative in late eighteenth-century terms, and this is adequately borne out by the decision which Christopher Pemberton must soon have made, to build for himself in Cambridge a residence and office in keeping with his newly-acquired standing in the county.

The first occasion on which the fee Income of Clerks of the Peace was made public knowledge was in the year 1834, being contained in the Commons Report from the Select Committee on County Rates—13th July, 1834. The figures relevant to the County of Cambridge are contained in Appendix I Part III under the heading

"Amount received by the several Clerks of the Peace for England and Wales for the several years ending 1831, 1832 and 1833

Cambridge	1831	1832	1833
	£487 5s 6d	£526 16s 4d	£492 2s 6d"

Parliament again turned its attention to the question of the remuneration of Clerks of the Peace in 1845. That year saw the publication as a House of Commons Paper of "An Abstract Return relative to the Clerks and Deputy Clerks of the Peace in every County of England and Wales, stating their names, profession, dates of appointment, fees and emoluments from 20th January 1841 to 20th January 1845; together with the names etc., of persons appointed by them to draw Bills of Indictment during the same period"—28th May 1845.

The Return showed, for the County of Cambridge (excluding the Isle of Ely)

Name	Christopher Pemberton.
Profession	Solicitor.
Date of Appointment	13th December 1793.

By what Lord Lieutenant
Appointed or Sanctioned   Earl of Hardwicke
Amount of money received
From the County Rate for
the years ended 20th
January,   *1841*   *1842*   *1843*   *1844*   *1845*
        £453.7.2   £437.2.2.   £454.2.9.   £471.2.2. £523.18.6.
From other "(The Clerk of the Peace is unable to state the amount
sources.   received from "other sources" during these years, which,
            however, he believes exceeded £100 per annum)"
Total £453.7.2.   £437.2.2.   £454.2.9.   £471.2.2. £523.18.6
Deputy Clerk
of the
Peace   -   -   -   -   -
Persons employed
by Clerk of Peace
to draw Bills of
Indictment
Name   William Thrower.
Profession   Solicitor.
Amount paid to
them. £130.0.0.   £130.0.0   £130.0.0.   *.   *
*Up to Michaelmas 1843 Mr. Thrower was allowed £130.0.0. per annum
for the assistance he rendered in drawing Bills of Indictment etc.; that
arrangement ceased on his entering into partnership with the Clerk of
the Peace.

The figures given in the Return covered all the counties
of England and some brief comparison between
Christopher Pemberton's remuneration and those of
neighbouring Clerks of the Peace is therefore possible as
follows:

Isle of Ely—Hugh Jackson.
    £461.11.6   £454.1.0.   £487.7.6.   £735.4.4.   £669.12.5.
Norfolk—Robert William Parmeter*
        -              -   £391.0.9.   £1314.19.4.   £1202.9.8.

*Father of Sarah, father-in-law of Clement Francis — see p.97.

Total for				
England and				
Wales £53,726	£55,723.	£59,628.	£60,049.	£59,985.
Average of 63				
Clerks of the £852..	£884.	£947.	£953.	£952.
Peace.				

These comparisons may not be particuarly valid because Clerks of the Peace served in counties varying greatly in size and population, from the enormous urban agglomerations of Middlesex and Lancashire to tiny under-populated counties in Wales. It seems nevertheless that Christopher Pemberton by no means stands condemned by these figures.

The story of the Clerks of the Peace for the counties may be continued for the sake of the completeness beyond Christopher Pemberton's retirement from office in 1850. The Local Government Act, 1888, was to merge the position of Clerk of the Peace with the newly-created office of Clerk to the County Council, though after the Local Government (Clerks) Act 1931, the two offices could be held by different individuals. Meanwhile, the Clerks of the Peace to the boroughs continued in existence. This explains why Cambridge, whether borough or (after 1951) city, retained its Clerk of the Peace until recent times. The post was abolished, along with the Quarter Sessions Courts, by the Courts Act 1971.

IV

Treasurer To The Eau Brink Commissioners

The second public appointment to come Christopher Pemberton's way, in 1803, was that of Treasurer to the Eau Brink Drainage Commissioners.

The Eau Brink Commissioners had been created by Act of Parliament in 1795, in response to active public debate and pressure which had built up for a number of years previously, seeking on behalf of agricultural interests to improve drainage and to reduce the ever present risk of flooding in the Fens. The construction of the Old and New Bedford Rivers in the previous century had provided considerable relief but flooding was still a problem to fen farmers and Drainage Commissioners alike, and many hundreds of wind pumps were still in service (soon to be replaced by steam engines) to keep the fenland flooding at bay. The proponents of such improvements, among them Philip Yorke (d.1834) third earl of Hardwicke, advocated that many benefits would result from cutting through the final six mile long bend in the River Great Ouse just above King's Lynn. The upper point of the proposed artificial channel was at Eau Brink in Norfolk and from this the scheme acquired its name., "The Eau Brink Cut". The construction of The Eau Brink Cut was seen as a means of improving the speed of outflow of the flood waters to the sea. The main opponents of the scheme were the port and shipping interests of King's Lynn and those responsible for river traffic on the Great Ouse and its tributaries. Theirs was an ever present problem of silting up of the lower river and the harbour from sand and mud constantly carried downstream. They were little impressed by the 'drainage' argument that river traffic would benefit from an improved tidal flow through the new channel and that the shoals and sandbanks constantly forming in the slowly moving waters of the great river bend would no longer provide an obstruction to vessels. If river outflow was to be speeded up they feared that the silting up process would be accelerated as well.

After spirited and acrimonious debate through Parliament, especially in the committee stages, the Eau Brink Act (1795) 35 Geo III, c.77 eventually found its way into the statute book. The long and fully descriptive title of this controversial measure was

"An Act for improving the drainage of the Middle and South Levels,
Part of the Great Level of the Fens, called Bedford Level, and the Low
Lands adjoining or near to the said Levels; as also the Lands adjoining
or near to the River Ouze, in the County of Norfolk, draining through
the same to Sea via the Harbour of King's Lynn, in the said County;
and for altering and improving the Navigation of the said river Ouze
from or near a Place called Eau Brink, in the parish of Wiggenhall St.
Mary, in the said County, to the said Harbour of King's Lynn; and for
improving and preserving the Navigation of the several rivers
communicating with the said river Ouze" (19th May 1795).

In brief, the Act created Commissioners and gave them
powers to implement these objects. It is however worth
looking in detail at some of the 116 sections of the Act
because they provided the framework within which
Christopher Pemberton became involved in the
Commissioners' activities, among them:
The Preamble which referred to 132 parishes or townships in
the Counties of Huntingdon, Cambridge, Suffolk, Norfolk
and the Isle of Ely containing 300,000 acres or upwards and
to the drainage being defective, flooding and navigation
being uncertain difficult and dangerous; and that a great
improvement might be made by deserting the present
channel of the *river Ouze* between Eau Brink and King's
Lynn, by erecting a dam or dams across the said channel and
by making a new River or Cut, from or near the said Place
called Eau Brink to or near the Town or Port of King's Lynn.
The following provisions were contained in Sections
I–XVI of the Act:
Appointment of Commissioners for Drainage. Every person
having 200 acres of land "in any area liable to tax" (whether
owner trustee committee or guardian) and every rector
impropriator or vicar for the time being of any of the said
parishes or townships and the Mayor of Lynn for the time
being were appointed Commissioners for the purposes of
drainage.

Deputy Commissioners of drainage could be appointed by every owner of 500 acres of land liable to tax.

Appointment of Commissioners for Navigation. All Aldermen, Mayors, Burgesses, Town Corporations, the Vice-Chancellor of the University of Cambridge, the Conservators of the River Cam, the Lord Lieutenants of Counties, land owning nobility and 229 named individuals and their successors (any successor to a named individual to have land to the yearly value of £50, or personal estate of £1,000) within the designated area were constituted Commissioners for the purposes of Navigation. Among the named individuals was Christopher Pemberton (though not apparently appointed by virtue of his position as Clerk of the Peace).

Quarterly Meetings (for the Drainage and Navigation Commissioners respectively) were to be held at King's Lynn on the third Thursday after the passing of the Act, and thereafter at March (second Thursday in July) King's Lynn (second Thursday in October) Cambridge (second Thursday in January) and in Ely on the Tuesday after the first Sunday following 11th April.

Advertisement of Meetings was to be made in "the Cambridge and Norfolk Newspapers"; five Commissioners were to be a quorum at meetings.

The Commissioners were given power to appoint one or more Treasurers, Surveyors, Clerks, Collectors or other Officers.

These Officers were to keep accounts and the Commissioners were given power to distrain or commit any Officer failing or neglecting to account for sums received.

Sections XVII–LVII defined in detail the works which were to be carried out and gave powers to the Commissioners for Drainage to execute them.

Section LVIII required all lands within the boundary of the Act to pay 4d per acre annually for ten years beginning on 24th June 1795.

Section LIX allowed apportionment (i.e. adjustment) of tax within districts according to the benefits to be derived from the works.

Sections LX and LXVIII contained provisions for assessment collection and liability for the tax.

Section LXXIX contained provision for tolls to be collected from all vessels passing or navigating on the new river or cut for 10 years from the opening date; these tolls were to be collected by the Commissioners for Navigation, one quarter to be retained by them for maintaining and improving the navigation and the remaining three quarters to be paid to the Commissioners for Drainage.

Section LXXXIX empowered the Commissioners for Drainage to borrow money on the security of taxes payable by virtue of the Act.

Sections XC to CXV contained various powers relating to finances enforcement of powers and proceedings by the Commissioners.

Lastly, Section CXVI declared it to be "a Publick Act".

As passed, the 1795 Act may be seen as an unhappy marriage between the conflicting, if not irreconcilable, drainage interests and navigation interests. Even though by definition a number of individuals found themselves appointed both as Drainage Commissioners and as Navigation Commissioners the powers of the latter were seriously handicapped by the requirement that three quarters of the navigation tolls were to be paid over to the Drainage Commissioners who undertook the greater part of the works. The Eau Brink Commissioners were nevertheless to remain an active body for the next 70 years or more, by which time the railways had reduced river traffic on the Great Ouse to insignificance. During that time Christopher Pemberton was to serve 55 years as a Navigation Comissioner (1795–1850) and 45 years as Treasurer to the Drainage Commissioners (1803–48).

The following extracts from the Minutes of the Eau Brink Drainage Commissioners throw an interesting light on Christopher Pemberton's connnection with their affairs:

1795—4th June (being the third Thursday after the passing of the Act) the first meeting of the Eau Brink Drainage Commissioners was held at the Dukes Head in King's Lynn. Mr. William Lemmon of Downham Market (a practising attorney) was unanimously appointed Clerk to the Commissioners.

9th July—at the second meeting of the Commissioners held at the White Hart in March (being the second Thursday in July) Messrs. Gurney Birkbeck & Co. were appointed Treasurers for the North Division land Mr. William Fisher (Banker) of Cambridge Treasurer for "the Middle and South Levels".

1797—2nd February. At a meeting held at The Rose Inn Cambridge (not unfortunately the second Thursday in January) Mr. Christopher Pemberton attended "as Deputy for the Earl of Hardwicke".

1801—8th January. At a meeting held at The Rose Inn in Cambridge Christopher Pemberton again attended for the Earl of Hardwicke. It was Ordered that Mr. Pemberton be requested to apply to the Commissioners of the Swaffham and Bottisham Districts "...for the diversion of taxes". (This evidently pointed to an accrued build up of arrears due to the Commissioners by bodies themselves tax payers as well as tax gatherers).

1803—3rd January at a meeting held at The Rose Inn in Cambridge the opinion of the meeting was expressed that "a Treasurer should be appointed for receiving all monies collected and to be collected on account of the Commissioners... Resolved that Mr. Christopher Pemberton be appointed Treasurer to the Commissioners he giving Bond with sufficient sureties to the satisfaction of the Comissioners in the penal sum of £5000 for due performance of the said office And that all monies collected be paid into the hands of the said Christopher Pemberton to be by him accounted for as required by the said Act, and that the said Christopher Pemberton be allowed a salary of 50 gns. p.a. for his trouble in executing the said office". (It is evident that this appointment was made necessary by the somewhat slow and intermittent performance of the two banking firms appointed in 1795; clearly they regarded themselves as receivers but not as collectors of the taxes).

This was a relatively modest post for Christopher
Pemberton compared with his appointment as Clerk of the
Peace. On the face of it, there was not much immediate
prospect of legal work for him from this source, seeing that
another practising attorney had already been appointed as
Clerk. On the other hand, the Commissioners evidently
viewed Mr. Lemmon's appointment primarily as Clerk and
only secondarily as lawyer, and the minutes show that in
1805–6 a Mr. Mylne was employed as solicitor in tax recovery
proceedings. However, in matters of greater moment the
Commissioners must have felt it appropriate to seek a wider
legal involvement. At the Commissioners' meeting on 4th
August 1815, it was resolved to instruct Mr. Lemmon and
Mr. Pemberton to assist in the promotion of a bill before
Parliament "for recovering arrears of taxes". This minute
refers to one of a series of additional Eau Brink Acts passed
in 1805, 1816, 1818 and 1819, with the object of imposing
further taxes for additional periods of time. These were all
made necessary by the increasing estimates of the cost of
carrying out the Eau Brink works, between the original Act
of 1795 and the eventual starting date in 1818, coupled with
the successive expiry of periods during which the taxes
could be collected. The works had suffered from
considerable delays and procrastination, largely due to
emergency conditions during "the war with France" and
would not be completed until 1821.

On 5th November 1816 Mr. Lemmon was instructed to
take legal proceedings against the Corporation of Lynn for
recovery of rents...

However, at the Commissioners Meeting held on 15th
April 1817 it was ordered "that the suit with the Corporation
of Lynn be conducted jointly by Mr. Pemberton and Mr.
Lemmon".

When more business with a parliamentary flavour was
required at their next meeting on the 10th July 1817 the
Commissioners ordered:

"That necessary steps be taken to obtain an Act of Parliament to raise the funds that are necessary for completing the Cut and Works. Resolved that Mr. Pemberton and Mr. Lemmon be Solicitors for obtaining the said Bill and that proceedings for the same be conducted under the direction of Mr. Bevill, and that the regular notices be forthwith given. Ordered that Mr. Pemberton be requested to attend the Commissioners under the Exchequer Aid Act as soon as possible and that he be hereby authorised and have full power to do whatever may be required to obtain such loan, and that he request Mr. Rennie to attend the Commissioners with him".

At the meeting held on 3rd June 1818 it was noted that "Mr. Pemberton the Treasurer had advanced the contractors Messrs. Joliffe and Banks the sum of £11,076".

(It may be noted that major legal work was to be undertaken for the Commissioners by Christopher Pemberton, or more accurately his then firm Messrs. Pemberton Fiske and Hayward in the years 1823–25, as recorded in Appendix II.)

Mr. Lemmon remained in office until his death in 1835 and Christopher Pemberton until his resignation in 1848. Little else is recorded in the Commissioners' minutes to point to any further overlap of function between these two legal practitioners. However, at the meeting held on 30th November 1833 it was resolved "that Mr. Archer be requested to give his professional assistance to Mr. Lemmon, it being understood that no charge is to be made in the business for more than one Solicitor" (A somewhat equivocal attitude to the provision of professional services familiar to practitioners even to this day).

Following Mr. Lemmon's death Mr. Thomas Archer, solicitor, of Ely was appointed Clerk to the Commissioners.

Christopher Pemberton's resignation as Treasurer is recorded on a later page and it may be added in conclusion that the legal work for the Commissioners was from then onwards handled by Messrs. T. & G. Archer, Solicitors, of

Ely. The story of the Comissioners may be continued
beyond Christopher Pemberton's death by adding that by
Section 38 of the Ouse Outfall Act 1860 (23 and 24 Vic.c.88)
the responsibilities and works of the Drainage
Commissioners were transferred to the Ouse Outfall Board.
Further, by the South Level and Eau Brink Act 1893, (56
Vic.c.12) all the properties, liabilities and duties of the
Navigation Commissioners were transferred to the South
Level Comissioners.

As treasurer, voluntary financier, commissioner, lawyer
and even, for a time, as Clerk to the Navigation
Commissioners, Christopher Pemberton had played a
leading part in the establishment of the Eau Brink
Commissioners and in the performance of their tasks. By
the time of his retirement in 1848 the active functions of the
Commissioners had, too, very nearly run their course.

V

Receiver General Of Land And Assessed Taxes

Land Tax, originally introduced by the Statute (1688) 1
Will. & Mary c.3 but well established by the passing of
subsequent Acts, including the Land Tax Perpetuation Act
1798, relied for collection on an elaborate network of
Commissioners, Assessors, Collectors, Surveyors,
Inspectors, Clerks and Auditors, all locally appointed
individuals. These provided a system of collection which
could not at that time have been achieved by central
government in the absence of a host of paid revenue
officials. Central to the local structure was the Receiver
General for each county, whose appointment lay in the gift
of the Lord Lieutenant. In the days when the provincial
banking system was in its infancy, Receivers General were
charged with the task of receiving the Land Tax from the
County Collectors, and securing its transfer (or, more

literally, its transport) from the provincial centres to the Treasury Account at the Bank of England. There was direct and indirect profit for the Receiver General in respect of these transactions. In the first place he was entitled to charge poundage of 2d for each pound of tax received; secondly, he was under no obligation to remit Land Tax to the Bank of England more than once a quarter and was entitled to retain any bank interest earned meanwhile. In some cases even more imaginative modes of interim investment were chosen by the Receivers General with correspondingly enhanced profit. Evidently there was no demur if remittances were made to the Bank of England at less frequent intervals. Half-yearly payments were not unknown, with even better interest advantage.

When Christopher Pemberton Senior resigned the post at the end of the year 1805 his son Christopher Pemberton was chosen by the third earl of Hardwicke, Lord Lieutenant for Cambridgeshire, to succeed his father as Receiver General for the County of Cambridgeshire. The Treasury Register of Bonds for 1806 shows:

"Christopher Pemberton Junior of the Town of Cambridge, F. C. J. Pemberton of Trumpington, Rev. George Jenyns of Bottisham and Thos. Mellish of Lincolns Inn Coy. of Middx. £48,500."

The entries in the Treasury Register of Bonds year by year are the only surviving records giving any clue as to amounts received or financial benefits derived before 1821. In that year, a Select Committee of the House of Commons was appointed to report on the duties of Receivers General of Land and Assessed Taxes, at which a number of witnesses including Christopher Pemberton were called to give evidence. A complete transcript of Christopher Pemberton's evidence appears in Appendix I, giving an account of his methods of collection and handling of the land tax prior to the remission to the Bank of England.

In their recommendations, the Committee noted the improved state of banking and the remittance of money since the land tax collection system had been first established, and they concluded that the time had come to seek more frequent remission of the tax to the Bank of England, "so avoiding the retention of the permanent and current balances and the demanding of large and inconvenient security". They also concluded that Receivers General ought to be paid a fixed salary; that their number could with advantage be reduced from 65 to a number not exceeding 44; that receiving bankers ought to be appointed in the provincial centres (to be called "returners"); that there should be transfer of land tax balances from the Bank of England to the Exchequer at least once in every week, and finally, that the salaried posts should be offered to the existing Receivers or their deputies.

It is evident that most of these reforms were implemented and that Christopher Pemberton accepted a salaried appointment himself, as is to be seen from the next Parliamentary Report on the subject of Land Tax Collection, issued by the House of Commons on 11th March 1830,

"An Account of the Salaries and Expenses paid to the several Receivers General of Land and Assessed Taxes in England in the last year; stating when and how the money collected is remitted to the Exchequer; also, a statement of the dates two which the last accounts of each Receiver General had been audited and the discharge given".

The report contains tabulated returns from each of the Receivers General in England and Wales (by then reduced to 49 in number). The details for the County of Cambridge are listed as follows:

Name of Receiver General: Christopher Pemberton
Amount of salary: £500
Amount of allowances and
expenses: £52.19.0
Name of remitter: Thomas Mortlock

Time allowed for payment into the Exchequer—21 days.

Dates to which last accounts have been audited and the discharge given:

Land Tax   5th April 1828
Assessed Taxes   ditto

The House also showed an interest in results, producing a further Report on 29th March 1830,

"An account of the Gross Amount of Land and Assessed Taxes received by each of the Receivers General of Taxes in England and Wales."

For Cambridge the Report showed
Name: C. PEMBERTON
Year Ending 5th January 1830:
Gross amount of Taxes received   £56,807.
Net amount paid into the Exchequer £51,287.14.1d.

With the introduction of salaries for Receivers General, the practice of taking bonds for the due remittance of land tax was discontinued and with it the Treasury Register. No other contemporary record appears to survive to show for how long Christopher Pemberton continued to serve in this post for Cambridgeshire; it is possible that he continued to hold the position until his death in 1850.

It may be added that the office of Receiver General was abolished by Section 1 of the Public Accounts and Charges Act 1891 under which Act all functions of the Receivers General were transferred to the Commissioners for Inland Revenue.

Chapter 3

THE UNIVERSITY SOLICITOR—PART I

 EVERY Attorney or Solicitor of any standing practising in Cambridge during the eighteenth and nineteenth centuries seems to have coveted the title "Solicitor to the University of Cambridge". Among numerous appointments and offices claimed by members of the legal profession in Cambridge, evidenced by their entries in many successive editions of the Law List, the appointment of Solicitor to the University must be seen as the one most highly prized by the claimant and most envied by his professional colleagues. As the earlier quotation from his obituary shows, Christopher Pemberton was no exception in this respect. However, to university eyes the position may at times have been seen as one of lesser consequence, and certainly not intended as a permanent appointment.

Legal services for the University during the eighteenth and nineteenth centuries were provided in three ways. The University Commissary, as previously mentioned, was a formal appointment, evidently bestowed upon a member of the Bar. His function was to hear cases falling within the remaining and dwindling jurisdiction of the Vice-Chancellor's Court. One of Christopher Pemberton's uncles and one of his cousins had already served in this

41

capacity. A second formal appointment was of the University Counsel. These were in Christopher Pemberton's time generally two in number, chosen from members of the University who had achieved some distinction in the legal profession and were "retained to advise the University in matters of law" (Historical Register). Lastly, the choice, rather than appointment, of "University Solicitor" lay in the gift of the University Vice-Chancellor for the time being. In the days when provincial attorneys were somewhat localised in their practice and outlook, the work entrusted to the University Solicitor is likely to have been limited to such property transactions as may have been required, together with advice on matters of lesser moment. His function whenever matters of greater importance arose was the somewhat ministerial function of instructing one or other of the University Counsel to advise or to appear in court proceedings.

In Christopher Pemberton's time the Vice-Chancellor (chosen in rotation from the heads of colleges) served for a period of one year only. In theory, the position of University Solicitor could therefore have changed at shorter intervals than the time required to complete some of the work entrusted to him. This arrangement may have resulted in discontinuity and possible confusion, but this was by no means always the case. The heads of colleges were at that time seventeen in number and whilst some may have preferred to exercise individual choice or preference, most seem to have been content with an element of continuity. When Christopher Pemberton first started practice, Mr. Thomas Lombe appears to have been the established choice of the Vice-Chancellors for University legal business. Christopher Pemberton would surely not begrudge the inclusion of the following quotation from the epitaph of his well established and more senior colleague in St. Edward's Church, Cambridge,

"Thomas Lombe Esq.,
an eminent Solicitor of this place
who lived here many years
much respected both by the University
and the Town.
He was born at Norwich 7th January 1719
and died at Cambridge 3rd October `1800"

In the absence of any formal appointments or of any written records one can only be guided by external evidence of a succession. It appears that Mr. Lombe's place was taken by Mr. John Ingle of Trumpington Street and that he continued to receive legal work from the University, but not exclusively so, until 1823. This coincides with the point from which early practice records have survived showing that Pemberton Fiske and Hayward were receiving work from the University from 1825 onwards. However, the fact that other practitioners were also receiving work from the University at, or shortly before this time, is revealed by the records of Messrs. Gunning and Francis, which came into the possession of the practice as a result of the merger and succession described in Chapter 6.

While the obituary claim that Christopher Pemberton had acted as University Solicitor is therefore substantiated, it is difficult to say with any degree of certainty that the University work was entrusted to him continuously and exclusively from the eighteen twenties until his death in 1850. Instances of work undertaken by him for the University did however occur in the eighteen thirties and eighteen forties and so the connection continued for the best part of thirty years at least.

A later chapter will be devoted to the story of "the University Solicitor", dealing with the period from 1850 onwards.

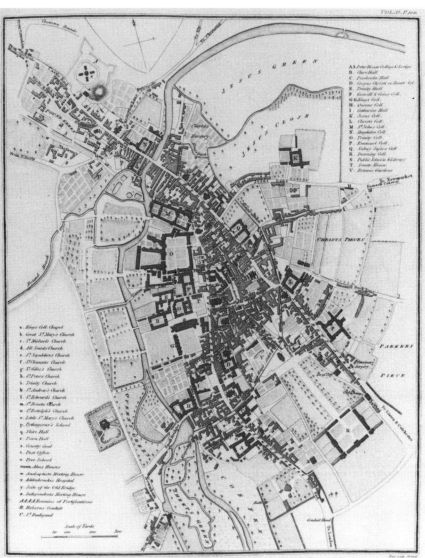

Legend (right side):

A.A. Peter House College & Lodge
B. Clare Hall
C. Pembroke Hall
D. Corpus Christi or Bennet Coll.
E. Trinity Hall
F. Gonvill & Caius Coll.
G.G. Kings Coll.
H. Queens Coll.
I. Catharine Hall
K. Jesus Coll.
L. Christs Coll.
M. St Johns Coll.
N. Magdalen Coll.
O. Trinity Coll.
P. Emmanuel Coll.
Q. Sidney Sussex Coll.
R. Downing Coll.
S. Public Schools & Library
T. Senate House
V. Botanic Gardens

Legend (left side):

a. Kings Coll. Chapel
b. Great St Marys Church
c. St Michaels Church
d. All Saints Church
e. St Sepulchres Church
f. St Clements Church
g. St Giles's Church
h. St Peters Church
i. Trinity Church
k. St Andrews Church
l. St Edwards Church
m. St Benets Church
n. St Botolphs Church
o. Little St Marys Church
p. Pythagoras's School
q. Shire Hall
r. Town Hall
s. County Goal
t. Post Office
v. Free School
www. Alms Houses
w. Anabaptists Meeting House
x. Addenbrookes Hospital
y. Site of the Old Bridge
z. Independents Meeting House
A.A.A.A. Remains of Fortifications
B. Hobsons Conduit
C. St Ruleyand

Scale of Yards
50   100   200   300

PLAN OF THE UNIVERSITY AND TOWN OF CAMBRIDGE.

Published May 1st 1807 for Gadell & Davies.

1   Cambridge in 1808

2   Grove Lodge, Trumpington Street, Cambridge — Christopher Pemberton's Residence and Office 1798–1850

3   17 and 18 Emmanuel Street, Cambridge c1913 — The Practice Offices 1850–1914

4 Elevation of 17–18 Emmanuel Street following the rebuilding of 1891–2

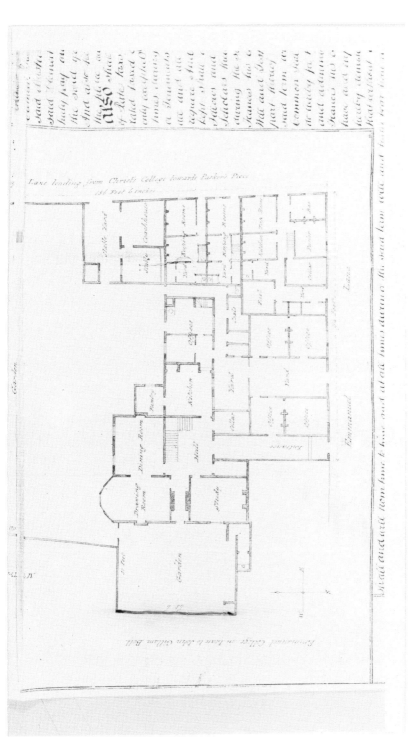

5 Plan taken from Lease of Emmanuel Lane premises dated 29th January 1850

6   Clement Francis — 1815–1880

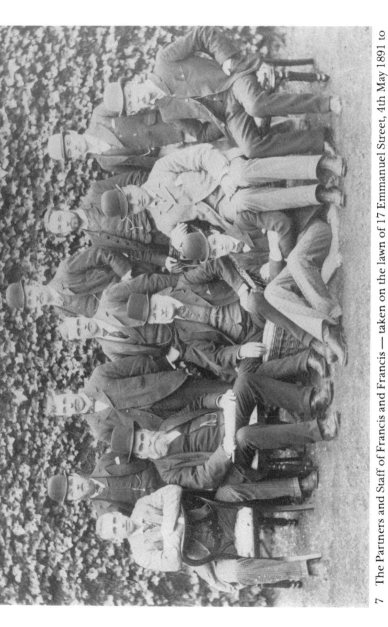

7   The Partners and Staff of Francis and Francis — taken on the lawn of 17 Emmanuel Street, 4th May 1891 to commemorate the fiftieth year of R. Looker's service

(*Left to Right*) *Standing*—T H J Porter J Collin P Barlow T Horner W S Darby C L Borissow

Seated—W H Francis E H Sanders R Looker E J Childerstone T M Francis E Juffs

8   Thomas Musgrave Francis 1850–1931

Chapter 4

GROVE LODGE—NUMBER 1 CAMBRIDGE

ROVE Lodge, Trumpington Street, Cambridge, Christopher Pemberton's office and residence from 1798 until his death in 1850, might with some justification have been given the designation "Number 1 Cambridge".* Before this house was built Trumpington Street, the main highway into the town from the direction of London, ended little more than two hundred yards south of Peterhouse in a straggle of indifferent timber-framed town cottages. There were virtually no buildings of any kind between that point and the village of Trumpington, two miles further south. An exception was the original building of Addenbrooke's Hospital which had been erected thirty-two years previously in 1766. Immediately opposite Addenbrooke's Hospital on the west side of Trumpington Street lay a close of land known as "The New Gardens". It was here that the Clerk of the Peace for the County of Cambridge chose to build his new house, Grove Lodge. At a time when many building sites in Cambridge were being corruptly disposed of at serious undervalues by the Mayor and Burgesses of the Town in return for electoral loyalty, it

*Apsley House, the Duke of Wellington's London residence, is said to have acquired the familiar name "Number 1 London", no doubt partly on account of its eminent occupant, and partly because of its prominent position immediately outside the Hyde Park Turnpike Gate.

is something of a relief to discover that Christopher
Pemberton distanced himself from activity of this kind by
acquiring the lease of his building site instead from the
Master and Fellows of Peterhouse. It may nevertheless not
escape the notice of an astute observer that Christopher
Pemberton's elder brother William was at this time a fellow
of the College.

By a lease dated 1st September 1795 Peterhouse leased to
Christopher Pemberton, of the Town of Cambridge,
Gentleman, for a term of forty years from the 10th October
1795

> "all those two third parts (to be separated from the remaining third
> part by a brick wall as hereinafter mentioned) of all that their Close
> heretofore called The English Croft and now commonly called or
> known by the name of The New Gardens the whole of which said
> Close contains by estimation seven acres (but by admeasurement only
> five acres two roods and thirty two perches more or less) and is situate
> lying and being in the Parish of St. Mary the Less in the Town of
> Cambridge aforesaid and the said two third parts thereof are
> adjoining to a certain Close of the said College called The Grove
> towards the north and on the common field towards the south one
> head abutting upon Trumpington Street towards the east and upon
> the remaining third part of the said Close called The New Gardens
> towards the west Together with the messuages or tenements
> outhouses and buildings now standing and being upon the said two
> thirds parts of the said New Gardens hereby intended to be
> demised... reserving all trees and access thereto to the College at an
> annual rent of Thirteen Pounds Six Shillings and Eight Pence"

The lease contained covenants by Christopher
Pemberton to pay the rent and taxes; to build a six foot high
brick dividing wall to separate the two thirds part from the
remaining one third; not to erect more than one messuage
or dwellinghouse; to yield up all erections and buildings or

if none then to yield up the present messuages or tenements and premises in good repair at the end of the term.

The lessee was given power to assign the lease without licence of the College; to take down "the aforesaid two (sic) messuages etc., and to convert the materials thereof to his own use for building another meassuage or tenement but not otherwise".

The lease further contained covenants by the College for quiet enjoyment and not to build anything on their retained land from whence the demised premises could be overlooked.

There were endorsed on the lease (a) a receipt for One hundred and fifty pounds fine paid for the Lease and (b) in Christopher Pemberton's handwriting "N.B. at the time executed the Counterpart of the Lease I executed bond for performing the covenants in the penalty of Three hundred pounds".

The bond was in printed form of the same date duly executed by Christopher Pemberton in the presence of William Mitchell and Joseph Smith.

As architect for the new dwellinghouse, Christopher Pemberton chose a local surveyor William Custance who is only known with certainty to have designed two houses in Cambridge,—Grove Lodge in Trumpington Street and the former Darwin family residence The Grove off Huntingdon Road. His name appears later as a Commissioner of various Enclosure Awards, but his best claim to fame is the preparation of "A Plan of the University and Town of Cambridge" (1798) on which Grove Lodge appeared prominently as the first house on the left as one entered Cambridge from the direction of London.

According to RCHM Cambridge 1959 P.354, "GROVE LODGE, house standing well back from the street in its own grounds eighty-five yards south-east of the Fitzwilliam Museum, of two storeys in part with cellars, has walls with gault brick and slate covered roofs. Christopher Pemberton took a Building Lease of the site from Peterhouse in 1795, the house is shown on William Custance's map of Cambridge of 1798; the represenatation shows a building equating with the present main E. Block the rest is a building or re-building of the second half of the nineteenth century. Further, the original part has been so arranged that entrance is now from the S. instead of under the E. portico. The house now contains lecture rooms and two flats.*

"Pemberton's Grove Lodge is a late eighteenth century Villa of simple and gracious design. The Architect was probably William Custance, surveyor and builder".

In a position of this prominence, with the stage coaches and all other traffic to and from London passing his entrance daily, it is small wonder that no contemporary letter has so far been discovered addressed otherwise than to "Christopher Pemberton, Solicitor, Cambridge".

No doubt to consolidate the tenant's position in his established residence, a further lease was executed between the same parties on 1st May, 1810, for a term of forty years from 10th October 1809, at the same annual rent of Thirteen pounds six shillings eight pence, and on the same terms as the previous lease, save that the parcels now contained a reference to "the Capital Messuage or tenement outhouse and buildings now standing and being upon the same...".

By common consent, the rutted muddy state of Trumpington Street in 1798 was a disgrace, only marginally improved by the installation of stone channels on either side to move the stream from the centre of the roadway to the margins. There must even so have been compensations for Christopher Pemberton establishing himself in this position on the edge of Coe Fen and the open fields. Wildlife would have abounded. According to Gunning, "In

*One flat being the residence of the Director of the Fitzwilliam Museum.

going over the land now occupied by Downing Terrace, you generally got five or six shots at snipes. Crossing the Leys, you entered on Cow-Fen; this abounded with snipes. Walking through the osier bed on the Trumpington side of the brook, you frequently met with a partridge and now and then a pheasant. From thence to the lower end of Pemberton's garden was one continuous marsh, which afforded plenty of snipes, and in the month of March a hare or two".

Chapter 5

GROVE LODGE—PRACTICE AND PAGEANTRY

1798-1850

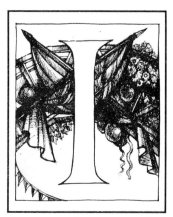 F Christopher Pemberton's long residence and professional practice at Grove Lodge was characterised by prosperity and a steady expansion on the professional side it also meant, thanks to an enviable position at the very entrance to the town, that he was witness to all the great occasions and celebrations which occurred in Cambridge during that long period. This chapter seeks to record the steady development as well as the major events.

Christopher Pemberton remained sole principal of his practice for the first twenty-four years of his professional life. Then in 1813 he took into partnership Thomas Fiske and the two partners practised for the next seven years as Messrs. Pemberton and Fiske.

Thomas Fiske was the second son of Robert Fiske (1752–1826) who had been University Proctor in 1781, Rector of Fulbourn St. Vigor's 1781–1826 and Vicar of Fulbourn All Saints 1790–1826. Robert Fiske had married in 1783 Elizabeth daughter of John Fisher, Banker of Cambridge. Thomas Fiske was born in 1785 and was admitted as an attorney in 1807. His entry in the Roll or Book of Attornies—Queens Bench (Plea Side) reads,

County	Surname	Christian Name	Place of Abode	When sworn & enrolled and before whom examined
Cambridge	Fiske	Thomas	Town of Cambridge	23rd April 1807— Ellenborough —Lord Chief Justice of Kings Bench Court

Thomas Fiske was twenty two years old when he was admitted an attorney but he reserved marriage until the year following his partnership. On 26th May 1814, he married Harriet Fisher (his cousin?) at the Church of St. Andrew the Great, Cambridge, being then twenty nine years old. Unfortunately no record survives as to where, or with whom, Thomas Fiske served his articles, but it is perhaps safe to assume that these would have been served with Christopher Pemberton and that this period had been followed by employment in the same office. Thomas Fiske died on 27th June 1829 aged forty four. His son Ernest Frederick Fiske was also to qualify as a solicitor and was employed by the practice for several years until 1843. He left to become an undergraduate at Emmanuel College graduating B.A. in 1846. He died shortly after Christopher Pemberton on 4th November 1850.

1813 was also the year in which Christopher Pemberton was elected a member of the Society of Clerks of the Peace. Having by then held office in Cambridgeshire for twenty years, Christopher Pemberton was hardly a newcomer to such position, but the Society itself had been founded only two years previously. Indeed, his relative seniority carried him to the chair in 1817 and he presided at the annual dinner of the Society held on 17th November that year at the Gray's Inn Coffee House.

Celebration in Cambridge in 1814 went considerably beyond the wedding of Thomas Fiske and Harriet Fisher. On 14th April the fall of Napoleon and the restoration of the Bourbon Dynasty in France were celebrated with illuminations in the town. The University Commencement was marked by the visit to Cambridge of the Prussian Marshal Blucher who was drawn in his carriage by enthusiastic crowds past the Grove Lodge entrance and along Trumpington Street to his reception in the town centre. Blucher's timely assistance to the Duke of Wellington at the battle of Waterloo next year joined their two names indelibly in the great victory. For the practice, 1814 was the earliest year from which the name Pemberton and Fiske survives in printed form, on "An Act for inclosing lands in the Parish of Stetchworth in the County of Cambridge" which received the Royal Assent on 17th June 1814.

A relatively early example of Christopher Pemberton's involvement in University affairs, being itself a somewhat extraordinary manifestation of the University's long running rivalry with the borough, occurred on Friday 2nd April, 1818. This was reported in the Chronicle the next day,

> "At the Town Sessions immediately after Serjeant Blossett the Deputy Recorder had charged the Grand Jury, Dr. Webb Vice-Chancellor came into Court, attended by Mr. Pemberton his solicitor, preceded by the Esquire Bedells and followed by the Proctors, and approaching John Purchas Esquire the Mayor on the Bench, demanded the seat he then occupied as Chairman of the Sessions. The Mayor stated that he conceived the Mayor had a right to the chair by long usage, that it would be an abandonment of his duty if he quitted it, and he should therefore refuse to resign it. The Vice-Chancellor then asked the Mayor if he were to understand that he positively refused him the chair. The Mayor replied, 'most positively, most unequivocally'."

The Vice-Chancellor, after saying that he did not come to have words, retired from the Court with his entourage. The following Tuesday the Corporation unanimously voted their thanks to the Mayor "for his firm and independent conduct in supporting the rights of Office as Mayor". It was also agreed to defray all expenses which might be incurred by the Mayor by reason of any legal proceedings against him by the Vice-Chancellor. No record survives of any such proceedings having being brought nor of Christopher Pemberton being involved in them. This "peaceable acquiescence", (VCH Vol 3p.56) turned out to be the last occasion on which the Vice-Chancellor was to confront the Mayor and challenge his precedence on the bench.

It seems evident that the practice continued to expand because in 1820 a third partner, William Woodcock Hayward entered the partnership and the firm changed to Pemberton, Fiske and Hayward. This alteration was reflected in the entry in Pigot's Directory 1823–4, "Pemberton Fiske & Hayward, Attorneys and Solicitors, Spital House End".

Little is known of William Hayward apart from the somewhat remarkable circumstance that he was admitted as an attorney before Lord Chief Justice Best of the King's Bench Court on 5th May, 1820, and was apparently then taken immediately into partnership with Pemberton and Fiske. His only known exploit appears to be his urgent two day journey to March and back, (including Sunday travel), on 22nd and 23rd November, 1824, to obtain the signature of one of the Eau Brink Drainage Commissioners (recorded in the Pemberton Fiske and Hayward bill book of this period—see Appendix II).

Involvement in College affairs is recorded in 1822 when Christopher Pemberton was appointed steward of a number of Manors belonging to St. John's College but he found himself on the side opposite to the University's interests two years later in 1824. In 1816 the University had received a munificent bequest, under the Will of Richard Viscount Fitzwilliam, for the foundation of a museum to contain the Fitzwilliam art collection. The University had been engaged since then in an anxious search for a suitable site on which the museum could be built. One proposal considered by the Fitzwilliam Museum Syndicate in 1824, involved the removal of Gonville and Caius College to a new site, leaving the site so vacated for building a museum intended to resemble the Parthenon in Athens. It was resolved in the Minutes of the Syndicate on 26th November, 1824, that the "Caius New Site Sub-Syndicate be empowered to ascertain from the Master and Fellows of Peterhouse whether they would be willing to dispose of the reversion of Mr. Pemberton's house and grounds for that purpose, and also whether they would be willing to dispose of the reversion in the whole of the "New Gardens"...; "and that they be also empowered to ascertain from Mr. Pemberton whether he would be willing to dispose of his present interest in that part of this estate which he holds under lease from that College".

While the records are silent, the reply given must have been clear enough. Gonville and Caius College has remained on its present site to this day, and thirteen years later the building of the Fitzwilliam Museum began on the site eventually chosen, between Peterhouse and Grove Lodge. Christopher Pemberton's response need not be seen as seriously obstructive to the University's plans. They had, after all, acquired the present Fitzwilliam Museum site in Trumpington Street in April 1823, a good eighteen months before making their acquisitive approach regarding Grove Lodge. The thirteen year delay before building work started was accounted for by the need to wait for subsisting leasehold interests to expire. It is, of course, a matter of opinion whether the site at the north end of King's

Parade would have been better occupied by a duplicate of the Parthenon than the Waterhouse building (Tree Court) erected there in 1870.

After the death of Thomas Fiske in 1829 the practice continued under the name Pemberton and Hayward. By this time Christopher Pemberton was sixty two years old and a figure of some eminence in the town. It is recorded that on 22nd January 1830 a County Meeting was held at Cambridge Town Hall convened by the High Sheriff, who presided. The meeting agreed that petitions should be presented to both Houses of Parliament drawing attention to the general agricultural distress, calling for the total repeal of duties on malt and beer and an alteration to the licensing system. Christopher Pemberton was one of the prominent citizens who addressed the meeting, as did two of his clients, Henry John Adeane and John Peter Allix.

Two years later, the Reform Act 1832, achieved long overdue re-organisation of Parliamentary constituencies and was followed by a General Election. Before the Cambridge Borough candidates were finally chosen, strong pressure had been brought to bear on Christopher Pemberton to stand as the Tory candidate, but according to his obituary in the Cambridge Independent Press "he firmly declined". Talk of this possibility had already been recorded in Romilly's Diary (22nd June 1832,

"gave whist in the study to Thomas Musgrave, Currie and Headly; Lodge came in and sat until we broke up at about one; much talk about the candidates for the Town, Pryme, Spring-Rice, Pemberton etc; Lodge in favour of Pemberton of course").

There is no recorded reason why Lodge, the University Librarian, should have felt so strongly in favour of Christopher Pemberton. George Pryme, one of the Whig candidates, and first Professor of Political Economy in the

University of Cambridge, was duly elected for the Town of Cambridge at this election, together with his political running-mate Thomas Spring-Rice. Christopher Pemberton seems to have come a long way, politically speaking, since his original advancement by the arch-Whig Lord Hardwicke thirty nine years previously.

By 1834 the railway age was beginning to dawn, perhaps more slowly in Eastern England than elsewhere. Nine years earlier, when the Stockton and Darlington Railway had been inaugurated talk of a line from London to Cambridge via Bishops Stortford had come to nothing. On 27th September 1834 Christopher Pemberton was invited to take the chair at a Public Meeting at the Town Hall, the purpose of which, according to Cooper, was "to hear an explanation from N. W. Cundy Civil Engineer, of his plan of a railroad from London to Cambridge and then to York". A committee was appointed by those present to consider the proposals further, and they reported back to a reconvened meeting held on 8th October at which Christopher Pemberton also presided.

> "At the meeting resolutions were passed that the proposed railway would be very beneficial to the County and Town of Cambridge and that Mr. Cundy's plan was the one best deserving the support of the County and Town. A committee was also appointed to promote the measure... Mr. Walker a civil engineer being called upon, said that if Mr. Cundy's plans were correct, the line was excellent and that his estimate was ample". (Cooper)

Unfortunately, Mr. Cundy's scheme, entitled "The Grand Northern and Eastern Railway" was somewhat grandiose, involving the construction of a line from North London to Bishops Stortford, Saffron Walden, Cambridge, Peterborough, Stamford, Grantham, Newark, Lincoln and Gainsborough to York. Sadly his ambition was never realised. The Great Northern Railway, as eventually constructed from 1840 onwards adopted the direct route from London to Peterborough; Cambridge only received a railway link with the capital, part of the Eastern Counties Railway from London to Norwich, in 1845. There is no mention in Romilly's diary a week later, of talk about railway matters when he went over to Abington for dinner with Rev. Charles Townley, Christopher Pemberton being also present.

In December 1834 the Duke of Gloucester died, and the Marquis of Camden was elected Chancellor of the University in his place. No time was to be lost in preparing the Letters Patent of his appointment for sealing by the University, and according to Romilly's Diary on 11th December 1834,

> "Set Roe the Artist to work in emblazoning Lord Camden's Patent; called on Mr. Pemberton to recommend a fine writer; he and Roe independently recommended to me the same man, Markham of Silver Street; I ordered Pryor the Tinman to make a box for the patent..."

> "Friday 12th. Congregation in the morning—we elected Marquis Camden Chancellor and the Orator wrote his letter—showed the patent to Master of Magdalene, he found that the garter was omitted so I immediately set Roe to work to place it round the arms..."

The installation of the new Chancellor was fixed to take place as part of the Commencement Ceremonies in July, 1835. Great excitement was caused by the arrival of the Duke of Wellington in Cambridge on 6th July to be present at the installation.

According to Cooper the Duke was

> "...received with rapturous enthusiasm. He was escorted into the Town by about a thousand horsemen. At Addenbrookes Hospital his horses were taken from his carriage which was drawn by the people to Trinity College."

These events outside his own entrance did not escape Christopher Pemberton's notice; according to Romilly's diary,

> "The Duke arrived from Lord de la Warrs at Bourn; at Trumpington he was met by a cavalcade of about five hundred; when in Cambridge the mob took off the horses and dragged the Duke in; Lady de la Warr alighted and went in at Mr. Pemberton's..."

During several more days of elaborate festivities and ceremonial, both University and Town seemed to divide their attention between the new Chancellor and the Duke of Wellington, the latter clearly the greater celebrity of the two. Christopher Pemberton was one of more than four hundred guests invited to a grand dinner at Trinity College with a profusion of dishes, toasts and speeches.

Sadder event were in store for Christopher Pemberton in the winter of 1838. By then aged seventy one, he suffered the loss of both his sisters, Anne aged seventy seven and Arabella aged seventy six, on the same day, 17th January 1838. Both sisters were spinsters who had lived together at Newton Hall ever since the death of their father in 1809 and their mother in 1815. A third death followed three weeks later, that of his partner, William Woodcock Hayward on 7th February 1838. This left him once more a sole practitioner after twenty five years in partnership. For the next five years he continued in practice either under his own name or sometimes more briefly as "Messrs. Pemberton".

Christopher Pemberton was again witness to happier events in 1842 when major celebrations took place to mark the installation of the Duke of Northumberland as Chancellor of the University, following the death of Marquis Camden. On 4th July the Duke of Wellington again arrived at Cambridge from Bourn Hall, passing the Grove

Lodge entrance "amidst the acclamations of a vast concourse of people". Notwithstanding the covenant given by Peterhouse in their lease of Grove Lodge, not to build anything on the retained land from whence the demised premises could be overlooked, the substantial structure of the Fitzwilliam Museum was already virtually completed less than 100 yards away to the North, though in its original form the Museum had no windows facing south towards Grove Lodge. Work on the structure was to continue for a further two years and the architect C. V. Basevi was not instructed to begin work on the interior until 1844. Nevertheless the University authorities took the opportunity to use the huge empty building as the venue for a Grand Celebration Ball on 6th July 1842, attended by 1,602 guests. Perhaps with a view to minimising noise disturbance to their seventy five year old neighbour the University authorities invited Christopher Pemberton to participate as one of the Honorary Stewards at the Ball.

Still greater public enthusiasm manifested itself the following year. On 25th October 1843,

"The University and Town were honoured with a visit from Her Majesty, accompanied by her illustrious Consort, His Royal Highness Prince Albert. Her Majesty and the Prince came from Windsor to Slough, thence by the Great Western Railway to Paddington and by road through Tottenham, Ware, Buntingford and Royston to Cambridge. At Royston the Queen was met by the Earl of Hardwicke, Lord Lieutenant of Cambridgeshire who accompanied by a numerous body of the yeomanry of the County on horseback escorted her Majesty to Cambridge. At the end of Trumpington Street (i.e. near to Grove Lodge) a lofty triumphal arch decorated with flowers, evergreens and flags had been erected and within the arch the Mayor and Council in their formalities waited the Queen's approach. Her Majesty escorted by the Whittlesey Yeomanry Cavalry, arrived here at ten minutes to two when the Mayor presented the Mace, which her Majesty graciously returned and the Council preceded her Majesty to Trinity College the Mayor walking by the right of her Majesty's carriage. Countless crowds were assembled to greet their Sovereign and her Prince who were received with the most rapturous enthusiasm."—(Cooper).

In the year 1843 Christopher Pemberton once more entered into partnership, his new partner being William Thrower. For the next seven years the firm was to practise as Pemberton and Thrower.

William Thrower, son of Stephen Thrower, Draper of Cambridge, had served his five years articles with the Grove Lodge practice between 1827 and 1832, being jointly articled to Thomas Fiske and William Hayward. He was admitted as an attorney of the Court of Common Pleas at Westminster on 22nd November 1832 before Mr. Justice Littledale. William Thrower seems to have shown a brief taste for independence, because in Pigot's Directory of Cambridge 1839, he is listed as practising as an attorney on his own account at 12 Kings Parade. Soon after this he appears to have rejoined Christopher Pemberton on an employed basis, and to have served for at least four years before becoming his partner.

The great political issue of the eighteen forties, the proposal for repeal of the Corn Laws, produced sharply divided reactions throughout British society. Those who saw the repeal as a means of importing foreign grain and providing cheaper bread for the working masses, found themselves opposed by others who saw this as likely to bring ruin to British agriculture. The old alignment of Whigs and Tories could no longer survive, each party being divided within itself on the issue and the more familiar party groupings, Conservatives and Liberals, were to emerge as a result.

In Cambridge on 3rd February 1844,

"A large meeting of Landowners and Farmers of the County was held

> at the Red Lion Inn, in order to oppose the Anti-Corn Law League.
> Resolutions having this object were proposed and supported by Mr.
> Edward Ball of Burwell, Mr. James Witt of Denny Abbey, H. J. Adeane
> Esquire, E. Hicks Esquire, William Leighton Esquire, Mr. S. Jonas, Dr.
> Hall of Fulbourn, Mr. Johnson, the Earl of Hardwicke, Hon. E. T.
> Yorke, Rev. F. H. Maberly and Mr. Paige Howard. A subscription was
> also opened, the Earl of Hardwicke gave One Hundred pounds, Mr.
> Yorke, Mr. Adeane, Thomas Mortlock Esquire, Colonel Pemberton
> and Christopher Pemberton Esquire Fifty pounds each"—(Cooper).

At this local level erstwhile political opponents may have found common cause together, but the opposite faction eventually won the day with the repeal of the Corn Laws by Sir Robert Peel's administration in 1846.

As has already been mentioned, the completion of the railway line from London to Norwich and the opening of Cambridge Station took place in 1845, making it possible for Queen Victoria to travel to Cambridge by train for her second visit on 5th July, 1847. She was again accompanied by Prince Albert, now Chancellor of the University. Received by all county and civic dignitaries at Cambridge Station, the royal visitors then proceeded via Hills Road and Downing Terrace, turning right into Trumpington Street where a triumphal arch gaily decorated with evergreens flowers and flags had been erected across the road between Grove Lodge and Addenbrooke's Hospital,

> "Scaffolds were erected at various points in the line of procession;
> these and the houses were crowded with spectators, and decorated
> with flowers and flags; and the streets were filled with a countless
> multitude who greeted their Sovereign with loud and long continued
> acclamations" (Cooper).

Her Majesty proceeded to Trinity College and a formal reception by the University, followed by a dinner in St.

Catharine's College. The next day the royal party visited the Fitzwilliam Museum (not yet finally completed) and next day they returned from Trinity College to Cambridge Station on their way back to London. It is not recorded whether Christopher Pemberton took any part in this great occasion or whether he witnessed the comings and goings from his residence. He was now eighty years old and his long career was drawing to a close. Symbolic too of changing times was the rapid dwindling of the stage coach traffic along Trumpington Street, supplanted by the railway service from 1845 onwards. The last stage coach service from Cambridge to London ceased to run in 1849.

Chapter 6

THE CLOSE OF A CHAPTER

 HRISTOPHER Pemberton's surviving practice records consist of no more than a single bill book covering the period August 1822 to July 1829, two client ledgers which between them span the years January 1834 to July 1850, and a deeds delivered book 1818–1850. These hardly provide adequate material for a detailed retrospective analysis but Cambridgeshire family names such as Allix, Apthorpe, Adeane, Cotton, Hamond, Kidman and Pemberton occur repeatedly among these records and among the College names, Caius, Christ's, Corpus, Emmanuel, Jesus, Peterhouse, Pembroke and St. Johns, along with occasional entries for the University.

Apart from the Clerk of the Peace, Receiver General and Eau Brink Treasurer already referred to there was a respectable collection of Stewardships of Manors and Clerkships to Commissioners of various kinds, mainly for internal drainage or for parish enclosures. Although the years 1789 to 1850 covered a period of great historical events, political and economic activity and industrial development any impact on the daily conduct of a solicitor's practice in Cambridge had been relatively slight. Not until the establishment of railway services between Cambridge and London in 1845 had the pace of communications been transformed from the horsedrawn age to the age of steam.

The reproduction in Appendix II of a complete set of entries for a matter conducted on behalf of the Eau Brink Drainage Commissioners in 1823–25 serves to illustrate the pace at which practice life was conducted and the limitations on movement and communications which today would be regarded as severe handicaps but in those days were accepted facts of ordinary life.

Early in the year 1848 Christopher Pemberton tendered his resignation as Treasurer of the Eau Brink Drainage Commissioners, an event recorded in their Minutes in the following terms:

EXTRACT FROM THE MINUTES OF A SPECIAL MEETING
OF THE EAU BRINK COMMISSIONERS HELD IN CAMBRIDGE
ON 9TH MARCH 1848

A letter from the Treasurer to the Clerk announcing the Resignation of his Office having been read—

Mr. Pemberton's Resignation

Resolved that in recording the Resignation by Christopher Pemberton Esquire of the Office of Treasurer the Commissioners deem it proper to

Resolution thereon

express the high sense they entertain of the zealous able and efficient manner in which he has uniformly discharged the Duties of Treasurership and to return him their sincere thanks for the general attention he has paid to their interests for the readiness and liberality with which he had frequently advanced considerable sums of money for their temporary purposes, and for the kindness and courtesy at all times manifested by him in his communications with them and in transacting the Business of the Treasurership during the long period of 44 years.

To be advertised   Ordered that the aforegoing Resolution be
                                      advertised in the local papers in which the Eau
                                      Brink Advertisements usually appear and that it
                                      be also printed and circulated amongst the
                                      Commissioners.

Order for   Ordered that the Recommendation of the
Security from   Committee of Management as to the Security to
Treasurer   be given by the Treasurer for the due perform-
                                      ance of his Office be adopted.

Mr. H. R. Evans   Ordered that Mr. Hugh Robert Evans Junr of
appointed   Ely be appointed Treasurer to the Eau Brink
Treasurer   Drainage Comissioners at the Salary paid to his
                                      predecessor on his giving Security for the per-
                                      formance of his Office to the satisfaction of the
                                      Committee of Management.

A similar sequence of events occurred in April 1850 when
Christopher Pemberton tendered his resignation as Clerk
of the Peace of the County of Cambridge, this event being
recorded in the Minutes of the General Quarter Sessions in
the following terms:

EXTRACT FROM THE MINUTES OF THE GENERAL QUARTER
SESSIONS OF PEACE FOR THE COUNTY OF CAMBRIDGE
HOLDEN AT THE COUNTY COURTS IN AND FOR THE SAID
COUNTY ON THURSDAY THE 11th DAY OF APRIL IN THE 13TH
YEAR ETC. AND IN THE YEAR OF OUR LORD 1850

11th April   Before The Honorable Eliot Thomas Yorke
1850   M.P. Chairman
                          The Honorable and Rev. Henry Yorke
                          George Jenyns
                          William Parker Hamond
                          William Henry Cheere
                          Thomas St. Quintin Jnr.
                          Joseph Sidney Thorp
                          Alexander Cotton
                          Samuel Newton
                          Edward Hicks

Clerks

Ebenezer Foster
Bizcoe Hile Northam
Joseph Simpson
Henry Staples Foster Esq.—Mayor of
Cambridge
The Rev. William Metcalf
Charles Townley
William Smith
William Law
John Hailstone
James Fendale

*Mr. Pemberton
Resignation of
the office of
Clerk of the
Peace*

The court resolved unanimously that the Chairman of Quarter Sessions do write the following letter to Mr. Pemberton upon his resignation of the Office of Clerk of the Peace for the County

Dear Sir,

Notwithstanding that such an event as your retirement from the Office of Clerk of the Peace was in the nature of things to be contemplated, yet until the step had been irrevocably taken by yourself, we, the magistrates of the County, were in no condition to know, or acknowledge the extent of our loss, nor to declare our sorrow at the separation.

It is, however, hoped that it may be some consolation to you to be informed how unanimous is the feeling of regret which marks your resignation, how single, and how earnest is the declaration which bears witness to your most honourable and zealous and long continued service—how sincere and heartfelt is the wish that the release from the anxious duties and responsibilities of the situation from which you have withdrawn yourself, may be the means, through God's blessing, of adding many years of happy ease to your well spent and most useful life.

In conveying, at the request of the Magistrates assembled, this public and well merited testimony of regret, that time should have made your retirement necessary, I hope I may be permitted, for myself, in a more peculiar and personal manner yet in a spirit no less sincere—to thank you for the uniform kindness and attention with which you have, at all times rendered to me very useful and great assistance. The aid of such most opportune services has obviated many difficulties, and has made a sometimes onerous duty to be performed without labor to myself, and I would fain hope, with satisfaction to the ends of public justice. The recollection of them will be long retained by me, who have now the honor of subscribing myself, for the assembled Justices and myself.

Very sincerely Yours,
Eliot Yorke
Chairman Q.S. for County of Cambridge

To: Christopher Pemberton Esq.

Mr. Thrower

The Court resolved unanimously, that the thanks of the Magistrates of the County are due to Mr. Thrower for the diligence shown by him in all matters connected with the affairs of the County, civil and criminal.

Resolved further, that the Chairman of the Quarter Sessions be requested to commnicate this Resolution to Mr. Thrower with their regret for the loss of his services.

Hugh Robert Evans Appointment as Clerk of the Peace

This day Hugh Robert Evans the Younger Gentleman produced in Court an Appointment under the hand and seal of the Right Honorable Charles Philip Earl of Hardwicke Custos Rotolorum for this County dated the

16th day of March last in the words following: (copy
appointment)
which being read the said Hugh Robert Evans
prayed that the same may be enrolled and that he
may be admitted to the said Office of Clerk of the
Peace and the said appointment is accordingly
ordered to be enrolled and the said Hugh Robert
Evans is admitted to the said office.

Even in the last year of Christopher Pemberton's life, a few
more moves remained to be played out. According to his
final client ledger, activity was recorded for only two of his
clients in 1850, but there was still his own Will to be executed
on 19th February with three Codicils dated 25th and 28th
February 1850. Furthermore, a piece of family business re-
mained uncompleted following the death of Christopher
Pemberton's second cousin, Colonel Francis Charles James
Pemberton, of Trumpington Hall, the previous October.
His will was to be proved by his four executors, Christopher
Pemberton, Major Christopher Robert Pemberton, Stanley
Pemberton and William Thrower on 19th July 1850, in the
Prerogative Court of the Archbishop of Canterbury. For
one of these executors this was only just in time. In the
Cambridge Independent Press for 27th July 1850 appeared
the following obituary notice:

THROWER At Cambridge on the 24th instant William Thrower Esq.
           Solicitor in the 39th year of his age—deeply regretted
           by his family and friends.

The death of William Thrower on 24th July 1850 also
brought to a premature end the arrangements concluded
only six days previously for the succession to the practice of
Pemberton and Thrower. These involved for the first time
Clement Francis, a thirty-five year old Solicitor then practising in Cambridge, whose origins and previous career will
be dealt with in the next chapter. A Memorandum of

Agreement dated 6th July 1850 had anticipated the establishment of a partnership between Christopher Pemberton
William Thrower and Clement Francis, the business to be
conducted "... at the offices attached to Mr. Pemberton's
residence". When Articles of Partnership were executed on
18th July they involved only William Thrower and Clement
Francis, to practise "under the firm of Thrower and
Francis". As a result, Christopher Pemberton lived the last
three months of his life in retirement.

Two months later Christopher Pemberton received a visit
from Mr. H. R. Evans junior, his successor as Clerk of the
Peace for the County. The purpose of his visit is recorded in
the Pemberton deeds delivered book 1818–1850 under the
following entry:

28th September 1850
"Received of Christopher Pemberton Esquire Commission of the
Peace for the County of Cambridge dated 28th November 1837
                          H. R. EVANS Jr. C.P."

We can only guess whether this represented a poignant
moment for the retiring Clerk of the Peace or brief relief
from his long-held responsibility.

It only remains to record that Christopher Pemberton
died at Grove Lodge on Tuesday 22nd October 1850 in his
eighty-third year. The tributes which appeared in the Cambridge newspapers the following Saturday are reproduced
below.

CAMBRIDGE CHRONICLE—Saturday 26th October 1850—
Death of C. Pemberton Esq.—Our Obituary contains an announcement of the death on Tuesday last in the 85th year of his age of
Christopher Pemberton Esq. an eminent Solicitor in this Town. He
held the office of Clerk of the Peace for 40 years; upon his resignation
in the present year he received from the Chairman of the Magistrates
in the County a letter strongly expressive of the high sense they

entertained of his merits. A member of one of the principal and oldest families in the County, he was on terms of intimacy and friendship with them all and was held by them in the greatest esteem. His clients always felt secure in acting under his advice reposing the most implicit confidence in his judgement and integrity. His friends were always sure of his sympathy; for being of a kind and tender spirit, he was ever ready to "rejoice with them that rejoice and to weep with them that weep". His dependants found in him an indulgent master, the poor a willing benefactor. It is to be feared that many will have but too great cause to lament his loss; for the extent of his private charities, though partially known, was, there is good reason to believe, far beyond the general estimate. He was moreover extremely liberal in contributions to institutions of public charity and to all objects of public advantage to this Town".

CAMBRIDGE INDEPENDENT PRESS Saturday 26th October 1850
Death of Mr. Pemberton

In our Obituary of today will be found recorded the death of Christopher Pemberton Esq. who expired on Tuesday last at his residence in Trumpington Street having attained the ripe old age of 85. Mr. Pemberton transacted business until within a short period of his decease, and enjoyed the highest respect of an extensive circle of friends; and his fame as a Gentleman of great benevolence was not confined to the Town in which he resided. He was a liberal supporter of every charitable institution in Cambridge; the loss of his public as well as his private charities will be very severely felt. Mr. Pemberton was Clerk of the Peace for the County nearly sixty years; he was also for many years Receiver General for the County; Treasurer to the Eau Brink Commissioners; Solicitor to the University, and to a very large number of Colleges; Steward of upwards of 30 Manors and in 1832 was strongly urged by the Tory Party to come forward as a candidate to represent the Town in Parliament, but he firmly declined; he also many times served the office of Under Sheriff. Mr. Pemberton never was married; his funded property was immense; he was possessed of large landed property in Wentworth and Witcham in the Isle of Ely; Newton Cambs and Sawtry Hunts"

Romilly's Diary for this period records events in a more

personal vein.

"TUESDAY THE 22ND OF OCTOBER (1850)
Our neighbour Mr. Pemberton died this morning: He had been long sinking gradually, and was of a great age.

SUNDAY THE 27TH OCTOBER (1850)
I am asked to attend the poor Provost's funeral next Tuesday...

TUESDAY THE 29TH OCTOBER (1850)
Brilliant day... at 11 to King's Comb Room for the Funeral of the Provost... I took Lucy to the Senate House... Tho she was not allowed to be present at the Provost's Funeral she had the excitement of seeing the very handsome cortege of our neighbour Chr. Pemberton, who was today buried at Newton:— the horses in one of the private carriages did not relish the slow pace and began prancing:— Lucy said that if such an event took place at her funeral and she had the power of communicating her wishes, they would be "that the pretty creatures should do just as they pleased"—very characteristic! (Whist Club met at his house)... I also asked Francis and Paget, who didn't come.

According to Cooper, Christopher Pemberton bequeathed to Addenbrookes Hospital to be appropriated to the Building Fund £500, to the Victoria Asylum £100, Cambridge Refuge £100, to the Female Servants' Training Institution on Parkers Piece £100, to the Cambridge Industrial Schools £100, for the erection of a School Mistress's House at Newton £500 (with an acre of land for the site), to the Poor of the Parish of Newton £100 and lastly Cottages and Land at Witchford for a School there.

By his Will dated 19th February 1850, Christopher Pemberton had appointed Christopher Robert Pemberton, of 37 Eaton Place, in the County of Middlesex, Esquire, the Rev. Stanley Pemberton, Rector of Little Hallingbury, Essex, Clerk, Walter Hamilton Pemberton and William Thrower to be his executors. Walter Hamilton Pemberton having renounced probate and William Thrower having

predeceased the testator, his Will, along with its three
Codicils, was proved by Christopher Robert Pemberton and
Stanley Pemberton in March 1851 in the Prerogative Court
of Canterbury.

The memorial tablet erected to Christopher Pemberton
in Newton Parish Church bears the following inscription:

SACRED
TO THE MEMORY OF
CHRISTOPHER PEMBERTON ESQ.
THE LAST REMAINING MEMBER
OF THAT BRANCH OF THE FAMILY
WHOSE MONUMENTS SURROUND HIM
HE DIED ON THE 22nd DAY OF OCTOBER 1850
IN THE 83rd* YEAR OF HIS AGE
AFTER A LABORIOUS LIFE IN THE LEGAL PROFESSION
WHICH HE PRACTISED
FOR MORE THAN FIFTY YEARS
IN THE TOWN OF CAMBRIDGE
HIS REMAINS ARE DEPOSITED
IN THIS HIS NATIVE VILLAGE
IN THE FAMILY VAULT WITHIN THIS CHURCH

ALTHOUGH NOT RESIDING HERE
HIS AFFECTION FOR THE PLACE OF HIS BIRTH
WAS EVER UNABATED
AND THE POORER INHABITANTS OF THIS PARISH
WILL BEAR WILLING TESTIMONY TO THE MANY ACTS
OF UNOSTENTATIOUS BENEVOLENCE
EXERCISED BY HIM TOWARDS THEM.
WITHIN TWO YEARS OF HIS DEMISE
HE REPAIRED AND REPEWED THIS CHURCH
AT HIS OWN EXPENCE
AND AT HIS DEATH HE LEFT FUNDS
TO ERECT AND ENDOW
A PARISH SCHOOL

*N.B. Newspaper reports stated that he was 85 when he died

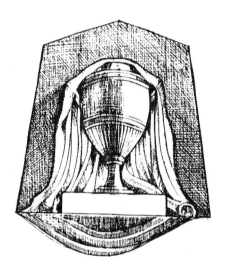

Chapter 7

FRANCIS JOHN GUNNING AND
CLEMENT FRANCIS

 RANCIS John Gunning was never himself a partner in the practice, but even so his career calls for close examination because of the important part he played in the early career of Clement Francis, acting first as his principal during articles and then as his partner in the firm of Gunning and Francis.

Francis Gunning was son of Henry Gunning (1768–1854) who is noted for having served as one of the Esquire Bedells of the University for a continuous period of sixty-four years from 1789 until his death, also as the author of *Gunning's Reminiscences*. Francis appears to have served his articles of clerkship at "Southampton Buildings; Middlesex" according to his entry in the Roll or Book of Attornies, which shows that he was admitted as an attorney before Lord Chief Justice Best, of the King's Bench Court, on 20th November 1821. He must have immediately set himself up in practice on his own account in Cambridge, occupying an office in Trumpington Street (its precise location is hard to identify because at that time Trumpington Street ran continuously from Trinity College Gateway as far as Grove Lodge, including what is today Trinity Street, King's Parade and Trumpington Street). Francis Gunning's first bill book has survived, covering the period 1821–1827. This shows that the young Gunning's practice was not slow to start, perhaps thanks to parental influence. Among 202 client matters entered during the six year period, familiar Cambridge names such as Ingle, Fitch, Beales, Martin, Musgrave and Waterbeach Level Commissioners appear. One matter was taken on for the University in June 1822 barely seven months after his admission and work for Downing College was soon to follow. However, by comparison with the surviving Pemberton Fiske and Hayward bill book of the same period Gunning's record suggests a small practice, busier in litigation matters (debt collecting and defending claims) than in conveyancing, few wills were prepared and there was no probate work. One entry on 10th December 1822 records that this young practitioner, by then admitted all of twelve months, travelled all night and attended two days in London ("Expences in London 8 shillings Coach Hire £1. 1s. 0d.") This episode can perhaps be compared with a present day newly-admitted solicitor jumping eagerly into his sports car and driving off up the Great North Road all night to attend to urgent business.

The careers and public activities of Christopher Pemberton and Francis Gunning provide an interesting contrast. One of the more senior members of his profession in Cambridge by 1820, Christopher Pemberton was to become increasingly identified with the established order of things but stopping short of outright support or involvement with the Mortlock oligarchy. By contrast Francis Gunning was closely involved in the reforming liberalising and emancipating movement which began to gain ground in Cambridge during the eighteen twenties. This reflected on a local level the trend in national politics which saw its culmination in the passing of the Catholic Emancipation Act in 1829, the Reform Act in 1832, and the Municipal Corporations Act in 1835.

Among the more immediate goals for those in Cambridge, fired with this reforming spirit, was the displacement of the solidly entrenched power of the Corporation. An unexpectedly successful instance of this challenge involved Francis Gunning and his clients Messrs. Beales and Sons, Corn and Coal Merchants of Newnham. The long established imposition of tolls by the Cambridge Corporation on the carriage of goods into the town was much resented and in 1824 a challenge to the authority of the Corporation was decided upon by local tradesmen which involved a collective refusal to pay the tolls and the launch of a fund to defray the legal expenses of those brought to Court. A first action against Messrs. Beales and Sons was heard in the King's Bench Court in January 1827. The verdict in favour of the defendants was put into suspense pending the outcome of a similar action against the Cambridge bankers, Messrs. Fisher. The eventual outcome of a second hearing in December 1829 was a final verdict against the Corporation in both actions. Francis Gunning and his allies had succeeded in proving an important point of principle. Deprived of its tolls, and faced with an unprecedented bill for legal costs, Cambridge Corporation was placed in dire financial straits and suddenly no longer able to maintain its position by the financial patronage and influence all too familiar in Cambridge in John Mortlock's day. A public dinner was held at the Red Lion to celebrate the victory, and in the course of one of the speeches Francis Gunning acknowledged "the vast and important change in public opinion in the Town since the introduction of another vehicle for giving expression to it". This reference was to the part played by the Cambridge Independent Press, and particularly its Editor, Weston Hatfield, in the promotion of liberal and reforming views in Cambridge. One may perhaps be forgiven for harbouring the suspicion that

Christopher Pemberton would have been a regular reader of the older established and opposite-minded Cambridge Chronicle.

Francis Gunning's involvement in this litigation can have done no harm at all to his practice. With six counsel involved on the Corporation's side and four appearing for the two sets of defendants the cost of the three actions over a three year period has been estimated at £8,000, the Corporation's own legal costs coming to £5,000.

Differences of political views or allegiance did not prevent the Pemberton practice and Gunning's practice from transacting legal business between each other on a perfectly normal and correct footing. One example of this occurred between November 1823 and January 1824 when Francis Gunning acted for Robert Moyse in his sale of Ward Farm, Broughton, Hunts and Thomas Fiske acted for the purchaser, St. John's College. With Pemberton and Co. quite heavily engaged for the Eau Brink Drainage Commissioners in the 1823–25 litigation, Francis Gunning acted for Messrs. Beales and Sons in the submission of "a petition to the House of Commons in favour of the Eau Brink Bill". This submission was to be dropped, as part of the general settlement of June 1825, referred to in Appendix II. Even as late as 1845, the Gunning Practice (then Gunning and Francis), was acting for J. T. Martin, and Pemberton and Thrower were acting for Magdalene College in connection with an exchange of land at Quy.

In 1828 Francis Gunning took an articled clerk, Francis Thomas Bircham, son of Samuel Bircham of Borton Hall, Norfolk. Francis Bircham was to be admitted before Lord Chief Justice Tindal of the King's Bench Court in Easter Term 1833 and he then started practising on his own account at 52 Lincoln's Inn Fields in the County of Middlesex.

Francis Gunning took a second articled clerk, Clement

Francis, who started his articles on 9th October 1832 while Francis Bircham's still had six months or more to run. As will be seen from the Francis family tree, the principal and his two articled clerks would already have been well acquainted with each other as relatives by marriage. Francis Bircham's sister Sarah was married to Francis Gunning. Clement Francis was first cousin to Francis Bircham and Sarah Gunning. Clement Francis was born in 1816, the only son and first of three children born to Thomas Clement Francis and his wife Mary Elizabeth (nee Cann). The Francis family had been long established in Norfolk, particularly in and around Aylsham, but Thomas Clement Francis, after assisting his father Robert Francis for a time in his Aylsham draper's shop then moved to Newcastle-upon-Tyne, establishing himself there as a wine merchant. This was to be Clement Francis's birthplace and childhood home before he moved to join Francis Gunning in Cambridge.

Francis Gunning wrote to Thomas Clement Francis on 4th May 1835 in the following terms:

"You mentioned in a letter received a short time since your wish to see Clement in the Summer. To this there can be one answer—viz that it will give me pleasure to promote any wish either of yourself or your son. His attention to my interests gives him every claim upon me and his attentions to his studies and endeavours to make the best return for your kindness by improving himself in the knowledge of his profession render him deserving of every indulgence on your part. His companions, as far as I can judge, are well selected. On the whole, I have every reason to be satisfied with his conduct and deportment both as an assistant in my business and as an inmate. Yours very truly FRANCIS J. GUNNING".

If Cambridge in the mid–eighteen thirties was a congenial enough place to serve articles of clerkship, Clement Francis may have begun to feel that he was missing what the metropolis had to offer to his newly-admitted cousin Francis Bircham, practising in London on his own account from 1836 onwards. Francis Bircham, too, might have felt the need for company of his own age and the letter he wrote to Thomas Francis in May 1836 on Clement's behalf advocating a move to London for the final year of his articles was judiciously balanced between the professional and the social advantages.

Letter to T. C. Francis Esq., Ellison Place, Newcastle Upon Tyne.

6th May, 1836.

My dear Uncle,

The sight of my handwriting is a matter of so infrequent occurrence to you that I suppose you at least expect that I am about to announce a birth, death, or marriage—or perhaps that I want to borrow some money of you. Of the accidents and follies which are included in the first list I have nothing to say that you have not already heard—of the latter I am (you may breathe freely again) about to say nothing more.

After expressing my gratification at the good accounts which we have lately had of yourself and family and telling you that all our late invalids in Norfolk are convalescent from my oldest ally, my mother to my comparatively recent one Kate Dalrymple, I will proceed to the more immediate object of my letter.

Master Clement desires me to state to you what I think will be his best course as to the completion of his legal education and I do so with great anxiety to serve him; I should recommend his leaving Mr. Gunning at the end of his 4th year—say October. It may be fairly assumed that he will know everything then that passes in a country office and that he will learn nothing more at Gunning's. He will come thence to me and if he do not see as much practice he will at least see a new branch of it and will have the opportunity of hearing our lectures and of spending part of his time with a pleader (a branch of his education he has hitherto been entirely without a chance of attending to). By the time he has spent a year in London he will, it is to be hoped, if anything offer, be in a fit state to take it; but I would recommend if there be then no particular inducement to begin practice, that he go to the Chambers of a Draughtsman who would (be) selected with reference to Clement's future intentions—viz. a gent of one sort of practice would be advisable if he (Clement) settled in London—and of another sort if he settled in the country.

Clement I know would prefer living with me to taking lodgings but this as matters are at present and for some time forward are likely to be, is not on the cards and he therefore asked me to say what I thought he could manage for in lodgings—and I should think not less than £180 a year—including everything of course. With that sum economically applied he may manage as you would wish a son of yours should; but you are young man enough still to know that £20 more per annum would add very much to his (reasonable) enjoyments—perhaps more than the same sum at any other period of his life—and I am sure you may safely trust Clement with any amount that you personally might incline to allow him, for he is an example of right principles and steady conduct. Further information I shall be glad to give if need be; perhaps before he finally leave Town it might be a mutual convenience that he became an inmate of mine. With kindest love to my Aunt and as kind as I may to my fair cousin Sarah.

I am my dear Sir,
Very faithfully your affec. nephew,
FRANCIS T. BIRCHAM
52 Lincoln's Inn Fields.

Francis Bircham's advocacy with his uncle had the desired effect and Clement Francis spent the fifth year of his articles in London between October 1836 and October 1837, residing at "8, Devonshire Street in the County of Middlesex".

Admission as a solicitor was no longer the easy next step following the expiration of articles. The first examination for articled clerks had been held in 1836 and already law lectures of the kind referred to by Francis Bircham had been introduced. The examinations were organised by the Incorporated Law Society and held at the Law Society's Hall; one was conducted in June for candidates seeking admission as attorneys before the King's Bench Court, and another was held in November for candidates seeking admission as solicitors in Chancery. According to Birks,

"Nobody, except maybe the candidates, regarded this examination as a serious test. It was an experiment in conducting examinations. Outside the Universities the idea of written tests was a novelty. So far as the law was concerned the thing had never been done before".

By June 1838, when Clement Francis sat his examination, the test had been made a little more difficult and instead of picking and choosing, the candidates were required to attempt all questions. Nevertheless, on 9th June 1838, less than a week later, Clement Francis presented himself for admission as an attorney before Lord Chief Justice Denman of the King's Bench Court

"...than whom no Chief Justice of England since the death of Earl Mansfield has been regarded with more personal esteem and affection...".

Clement Francis returned to Cambridge in December 1838 and by articles of co-partnership dated 1st December 1838 purchased himself a one-half share in the practice of his former principal, Francis Gunning.* The two partners then practised as "Gunning and Francis". Gunning's practice had changed somewhat since Clement Francis had last worked in his office in October 1836. The Municipal Corporations Act had received the Royal Assent on 9th September 1835. In effect, this Act was to Local Government what the Reform Act 1832 had been to the Parliamentary Constituencies. In Cambridge the old style

---

*Clement Francis paid £1,800 (three years' purchase) for his share. Practice overheads were to be shared equally, as well as profits, including "... the expenses of buying fuel and candles, pens, ink and paper... ".

Corporation of "The Mayor, Bailiffs and Burgesses of the Borough of Cambridge" had been replaced by "The Mayor, Aldermen and Burgesses of the Borough of Cambridge", with an elected Council consisting of ten aldermen and thirty elected councillors. The first councillors were elected on 26th December 1835 and the aldermen on 31st December. The Council met for the first time on 1st January 1836. After electing Thomas Hovell to be Mayor, removing the Duke of Rutland from the office of High Steward of the Town, and replacing him with Lord Godolphin, they then proceeded to remove Charles Pestell Harris from the office of Town Clerk and to elect Francis John Gunning in his place. As a result when Clement Francis returned to Cambridge in 1838 his partnership was to commence with a solicitor then engaged partly in private practice and partly in local government.

Clement Francis evidently saw the advantages to be gained from a university education and membership of the University of Cambridge. On 7th December 1838 he was admitted as a fellow commoner at Trinity Hall, matriculating in the Lent Term of 1839. He obtained a B.A. Degree in 1843 (12th of the οι πολλοι), proceeding M.A. in 1846.

It is worth noting that, according to M. A. R. Tuker, ("Cambridge"—1907 p.218) the younger sons of peers and the richer undergraduates dined at the fellows' table and were therefore called "fellow commoners".

"The advantages of this arrangement did not end with the better treatment in hall, for the companionship of the fellows and seniors of his College must have proved a welcome stimulus to an intelligent young man." "Fifty years ago... a fellow commoner required £800 a year and could not live on less than £500. These were the aristocratic days of English universities".

According to Pigot's Cambridgeshire Directory 1839, Francis John Gunning ("Town Clerk, Deputy Registrar of the Archdeaconry of Ely and Commissioner for Bankrupts in County Fiats") was recorded as practising from Cambridge Town Hall. Such, however, are the vicissitudes of elected office, that on 9th November 1840, after electing George Fisher Mayor by a majority of one vote the Council proceeded to remove Francis Gunning from the position of Town Clerk by twenty votes against seventeen and replaced him with the previous incumbent Charles Pestell Harris.

Though severed from this local government connection Gunning and Francis nevertheless continued in practice for the next seven years. During this period they and the Pemberton practice were both engaged in several categories of work which have now acquired historical interest through long obsolescence, in particular stewardships of manors and the management of Copyhold Lands, Inclosures and acquisitions of land for railway undertakings, each of which deserve separate treatment in the following chapter.

✳   ✳   ✳   ✳

A short account of the subsequent career of Francis Thomas Bircham is appropriate at this point. Apart from his family relationship with Clement Francis, a professional connection between these two former Gunning articled clerks subsisted on and off for many years. In 1837 Francis Bircham married Catherine Dalrymple, daughter of William Dalrymple of Norwich ("Kate" of his letter to his uncle the previous year). He continued to practise alone until 1844, when he took into partnership Robert Farr Dalrymple, and they practised together, first as Bircham and Dalrymple, and then with other partners in the firm which eventually became Bircham and Co. The rise of this practice to considerable eminence in the fields of commercial and parliamentary practice is clearly reflected in the successive changes of Francis Bircham's practice address—52 Lincoln's Inn Fields (1833–37), 15 Bedford Row (1837–48), 46 Parliament Street (1848–82), 60 Threadneedle Street (1867–78) 26 Austin Friars (1878–82).

By the time of his death in 1882, Francis Bircham had served as a member of the Council of the Law Society (1863–79), as President of the Law Society (1874–75), and as Solicitor to the London and South Western Railway Company. His practice became noted for its parliamentary work, notably the promotion of private acts for railway undertakings and it was in this context, as well as London agency work, that the professional connections with Clement Francis continued. Finally, their paths were to cross as fellow members of the Council of the Law Society.

Chapter 8

MANORS INCLOSURES AND RAILWAYS

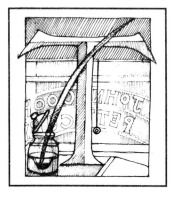 HE three areas of legal practice dealt with below are now long defunct although they were all major areas of activity throughout the nineteenth century and contributed significantly to fee income. Each requires some measure of explanation in its historical context.

I. Manors and Copyholds

Of the manors existing in Cambridgeshire at the time of the Norman Conquest, 135 were listed in Domesday Book. By reason of various sub-divisions in the intervening centuries there were at the end of the eighteenth century perhaps half as many again, approaching two hundred in all.

The customary provision of agricultural services by villein tenants in return for land occupation within the manor having long since disappeared, manors still survived in Cambridgeshire and elsewhere at the end of the eighteenth century as systems of land tenure in miniature. Occupation of land within the manor might be of equivalent status to a freehold, or for life only, or for a term of years. The essential feature of all such holdings was that entitlement to manorial lands was recorded by entry in the court roll of the manor.

This would have been closer by analogy to a modern registered title than to conventional title deeds. Every manor had its own court with its transactions recorded in a court roll. An estate in land within the manor was evidenced by a copy extract from the court roll and the land was said to be "held by copy of court roll". This became shortened in common parlance to "copy hold".

Manors in Cambridgeshire were no exception to the rest in that each had developed from time immemorial its own particular and sometimes peculiar customs applicable to the holding and transmission of an estate in copyhold land; no two manors had exactly the same customs. In virtually every case the Lord of the Manor had appointed a steward to conduct the business of the manorial court. Stewards had the threefold function first of recording changes of ownership, secondly of judging as to the application of the customs of the manor to a particular holding or to a particular transaction and last but not least of collecting rents and cash payments (known as "fines") due to the Lord of the Manor as a result of transactions in copyhold land.

Every village in Cambridgeshire had at least one manor with its own holdings of copyhold land and a manorial court presided over by a steward. The position of steward was frequently held by a solicitor or a solicitor's clerk. By the time of Christopher Pemberton's death in 1850 his obituaries recorded that he held the position of steward to upwards of thirty manors. These appointments had been largely derived from those Cambridge Colleges or County families which included manors within their land holdings. Typical of the creation of such stewardships was an appointment under the seal of St. John's College dated 5th March 1822 by which Christopher Pemberton was appointed steward "of the several manors or Lordships of Grandhams otherwise Granhams in Great Shelford in the County Cambridge, of Bassingbourne in Fordham in the same County, of Thorrington and Ridgwell Hall in the County of Essex, of Kirkbies in Ashwell in the County of Hertford, of Ramerick in the Counties of Hertford and Bedford, of Blunham in the County of Bedford and of Little Paxton in the County of Huntingdon".

Gunning and Francis also acquired a number of stewardships from their landed clients among which may be noted that of Bottisham by appointment of the Jenyns family and of Quy by the Martin family. It appears that the stewardship of certain manors was no sinecure, especially where all customs and incidents of ownership had to be proved to the satisfaction of a twelve man jury duly empanelled and sworn for the purpose. Such a requirement existed in the manor of Quy.

The system of copyhold land tenure continued undisturbed throughout the nineteenth century and beyond, being subjected to abolition by a series of Acts of Parliament commencing in 1922. By that time, various partners and clerks in the practice had convened annual manorial courts for the transaction of copyhold business in steady progression through Cambridgeshire and adjoining Counties for close on 140 years. Enfranchisement into freehold tenure by Act of Parliament meant that a substantial collection of court rolls and other manorial records became redundant. Some were to lie undisturbed in the practice strong room for the next fifty years. Then, with increasing public awareness of the value of local records, all remaining manorial court records were deposited with appropriate County Record Offices.

II. Enclosures

The process of the enclosure of the common lands of England into regular arable fields and pastures, along the modern pattern, must carry with it recollections of a sad migration of population from the villages to overcrowded towns and cities. The enclosures came late to Cambridgeshire, largely due to a reluctance on the part of the landowners to apply modern agricultural methods already successfully demonstrated elsewhere in the country. According to Charles Vancouver in his "General View of the Agriculture of the County of Cambridgeshire", in 1794 as much as 89% of the arable land in the county remained unenclosed in common fields. The advocacy of modern methods was very soon to be reinforced by the advantage of the high prices to be obtained by efficient agriculture during the Napoleonic wars. Only two years later, according to Christopher Taylor in *"The Cambridgeshire Landscape"*—1973 p. 182 a flood of Enclosure Bills started to go through Parliament:

"Between 1796 and 1850, 95 parishes in Upland Cambridgeshire were enclosed by Act of Parliament and four others by private agreement. This involved approximately 160,000 acres of former common fields and open pasture land. Never before in the history of the County had there been such a rapid alteration of the upland landscape. In just over 50 years the old common fields and the open grassland pastures were swept away and replaced by the modern geometrically shaped fields and isolated enclosure farmsteads we still have today. Even now, with our present speed of change, it is difficult to imagine the impact of the enclosure movement on the landscape. In less than a lifetime the greater part of the Cambridgeshire uplands were altered out of all recognition. After 1850 enclosures tailed off, as most of the work had been done, and between then and 1889 when the last parish, Hildersham, was enclosed, only six parishes, involving some 7,000 acres, had Parliamentary Acts passed".

There was work for solicitors in these formalities. Generally the major landlord or landowners of a parish would take the initiative for the enclosure of their parish by applying for a Bill in Parliament. Each Enclosure Act was broadly similar in form though different in detail. It would typically contain an appointment of three surveyors as enclosure commissioners to determine ownership and land interests in the parish and to award to each interested party an allotment of land deemed to be equivalent to his interest in the common fields and pastures. During the period 1795 to 1850 the Pemberton practice was involved in numerous applications for Bills in Parliament, and one or other of the partners would then be appointed as clerk to the enclosure commissioners, often a two or three year assignment before an Enclosure Award for the parish was completed. Gunning and Francis were also responsible for a number of Enclosure Acts and Awards although they came rather later into this activity. The following list, necessarily incomplete, illustrates the involvement of the two practices during this period:

PEMBERTON PRACTICE	*GUNNING AND FRANCIS*
Bottisham 1801	Stow cum Quy 1839
Trumpington 1801	Cottenham 1842
Stetchworth 1814	
Papworth Everard 1815	
Great Shelford 1824	
Chesterton 1838	
Barton 1839	
Comberton 1839	
Rampton 1839	
Willingham 1846	

The effect of the enclosures on the rural and urban population of Cambridgeshire, while serious, was perhaps not quite as tragically severe as elsewhere. Disruptive of rural communities as it was, it was also suggested that "the miserable poor might have been even more miserable had not the system of agriculture been modernised and rendered more productive". During the height of the enclosure period the population of Cambridge rose rapidly from 10,000 in the seventeen nineties to 28,000 by 1851. Overcrowded housing and insanitary conditions in Cambridge were thought by a newly appointed Health Inspector in 1849 "... to be a disgrace to humanity, and still more so to civilisation".

Neither contemporary nor subsequent accounts of the enclosures provide a particularly clear account of their effect on copyhold lands. In fact the enclosures did not provide a universal transformation of common lands into freehold interests. Taking the Bottisham Enclosure Act as a fairly typical example, the relevant section, headed "Allotments to be of same tenure as the lands in respect of which they are made" provided that

> "... the several lands, grounds and hereditaments which shall be allotted or taken in exchange, in lieu or in respect of freehold lands and hereditaments, shall, from the making thereof, be deemed freehold lands and hereditaments... and the several lands, grounds, tenements and other hereditaments which shall be allotted or taken in exchange in lieu or in respect of copyhold or customary lands, grounds, tenements or hereditaments shall in like manner be deemed to be copyhold or customary lands, grounds, tenements or hereditaments... and the lands, grounds or other property which shall be allotted or taken in exchange in lieu of leasehold lands or other property, shall in like manner be deemed leasehold..."

When the age of railways dawned, the railway lines were often to run successively through land in the same ownership but in part freehold and in part copyhold. This was the result of enclosure awards made in many cases only a few years before the Railway acquisitions reached their height.

III. Railways
It might perhaps be said that the arrival of the railways in

Cambridgeshire relieved some of the worst effects of enclosures. It was equally true that the enclosures eased the arrival of the railways. As mentioned above the movement of rural population from country districts to the town had caused severe overcrowding and housing shortages in Cambridge. Admittedly some cultivated areas within the town boundaries had themselves been subject to enclosures (St. Giles Enclosure Act 1802, Barnwell Enclosure Act 1807). Enclosed town lands readily passed into the hands of builders during the next thirty years, going some way towards meeting the demand for working class housing. Nevertheless, from 1845 onwards the railways were able to bring much needed building materials from distant sources of supply, far more rapidly than horse-drawn transport by road or barge traffic on the rivers. This in turn provided some easing of the chronic housing shortage.

As to the railways, their relatively late arrival in Cambridge could well have been delayed still further if negotiations for line acquisitions had been conducted, not with proprietors of enclosed lands, but with a sizeable proportion of the population of every unenclosed parish through which the lines were to run. The enclosures had by then brought a timely breath of modernity to land ownership through most of rural Cambridgeshire and it was only in exceptional cases that a railway undertaking had to treat with proprietors of unenclosed lands. One example of this occurred when the Ely to Newmarket Railway was constructed through the unenclosed fields of the Parish of Soham in 1878. After press advertisements convening a public meeting, a committee of five was appointed to "... treat with the promoters of the said Company for the compensation to be paid for the sale and extinguishment of all commonable or other rights..." in the open field lands of Soham, to convey title in the land to the railway and to distribute the sale proceeds among those entitled according to their fractional shares. Happily for railway development these complications were only rarely encountered in Cambridgeshire from the eighteen forties onwards.

Christopher Pemberton had been involved in various public meetings convened in anticipation of the arrival of the railways in Cambridge, yet more of the legal activity associated with the acquisition of railway lands in the eighteen forties seems to have gone to the younger, and by then perhaps more active, Gunning and Francis practice. Acquisition of land for railway construction required statutory powers, the promoters of a railway line needed a private Act of Parliament to obtain those powers. Local inquiries of the kind provided for modern motorway acquisitions were then unknown and both proponents and any objectors were obliged to appear before parliamentary committees in Westminster if they wished their cases to be heard. While environmental objections too were unknown, the arrival of the Eastern Counties Railway in Cambridge had been strenuously opposed by the University Authorities who feared a highly disruptive effect on the undergraduate population. They succeeded in having the station built in its present location, inconveniently distant from the town centre. It was not long before local interests felt the need to press for a more central position. Perhaps encouraged by this pressure, the promoters of the Cambridge and Oxford Railway submitted plans to Parliament in 1845 showing their proposed Cambridge terminus situated in Silver Street, within one hundred yards of five ancient colleges. Francis Bircham (then practising as Bircham and Dalrymple) was by this time acting for numerous railway companies including the promoters of the Cambridge and Oxford Railway. He gave instructions to Gunning and Francis to interview landowning and commercial witnesses willing to give evidence in Parliament in favour of the scheme. The full record of the activities of Clement Francis and his two clerks from January to July 1846, taken from the Gunning and Francis bill book, is set out in Appendix III. Strenuous though this activity seems to have been, it has to be said that the strong and well concerted opposition of the college and university interests eventually spared Cambridge from having a railway constructed through the Botanic Gardens, and across Coe Fen, to a station probably to have been in a riverside situation on the site where the Anchor Inn now stands. As later events were to prove, all other railway companies building lines into Cambridge were obliged to negotiate terms for a shared terminus with the Eastern Counties Railway, or its successor the Great Eastern Railway.

Apart from the objections, part justified and part predictable, as to the routing and siting of railway installations within Cambridge itself, there seems little evidence of serious opposition from individuals or groups of landowners in the rest of the county. Small villages could be skirted through adjoining farm land and wholesale demolitions were easily avoided. With agriculture suffering from a severe depression landowners were perhaps quite willing to receive the compensation paid for land acquired for railway purposes. An exception occurred in 1848–50 when the Pemberton practice was involved, for Col. F. C. J. Pemberton and Trinity College, in joint opposition to the passage of the Royston and Hitchin Railway Bill through Parliament. Opponent's legal costs were at this time paid by railway promoters and in June 1848 the minutes of the Finance Committee of the Royston & Hitchin Railway Company authorised payment of £1,063.4.1. "to Mr. Christopher Pemberton of Cambridge, costs of opposition to the Royston & Hitchin Bill now before Parliament". The Royston & Hitchin Railway, thirteen miles long, was in fact all that had survived through Parliament of the seventy three mile long Cambridge and Oxford Railway of two years before. In attempting again to make a railway connection through to Cambridge, the Royston & Hitchin had allied itself with a powerful neighbour. The Great Northern Railway was anxious to establish a route from King's Cross to rival the Eastern Counties Railway from Bishopsgate (later Liverpool Street) Station to Cambridge. The opposition of the Eastern Counties Railway was sufficient at first to prevent the Royston & Hitchin line coming closer to Cambridge than Shepreth. When this alternative route (operated by The Great Northern Railway), was opened on 1st August 1851 the seven mile gap between Cambridge and Shepreth was to be bridged by a service of four-horse omnibuses. Christopher Pemberton did not survive to see this short-lived revival of horse-drawn passenger traffic past the Grove Lodge entrance.

Chapter 9

EMMANUEL LANE

AN ENDING AND A BEGINNING

 HIS chapter traces the story of the Gunning and Francis practice, starting with its move to a new office in Emmanuel Lane in 1842, followed by the termination of the partnership with the death of Francis John Gunning in 1846, Clement Francis' years there as sole practitioner, his brief entry into partnership with William Thrower in 1850, and ending when he became sole principal of the Pemberton practice later that year.

The partnership between Francis Gunning and Clement Francis from 1839 onwards would have created a need for more office space than Francis Gunning had originally taken in Trinity Street in 1821. A solution to this problem was no doubt postponed while Francis Gunning occupied the Town Clerk's Office between 1836 and 1840. A move of the Gunning and Francis office was eventually made in 1842 to premises in Emmanuel Lane, Cambridge held under lease from Emmanuel College. The impending move was recorded in the minutes of the governing body of the College for 9th April, 1842, as follows:

"Agreed that the College seal be affixed to a licence of alienation to enable Mrs. Searle to alienate certain property held by lease (from) College to Mr. Francis John Gunning for the remainder of the term of her lease".

The lease referred to had originated in a grant on 19th February 1836 to William Searle of Chesterton for a term of forty years from Michaelmas 1835 of premises therein described as

"All That their messuage or tenement situate in or near Emmanuel Lane in the Parish of St. Andrew the Great in the Town of Cambridge with the tenement yard garden courtyard coach-house stable stableyard and appurtenances thereunto belonging abutting upon a brewery belonging to the said Master Fellows and Scholars now in the occupation of Messrs. Weldon & Co., upon the way or lane leading from Christ's College towards Parker's Piece in part and upon a piece of ground claimed by the Corporation of Cambridge in other part towards the East upon Emmanuel Lane towards the South upon other premises belonging to the said Master Fellows and Scholars in lease to Peete Musgrave in part and upon a garden belonging to Joseph Truslove in other part west as all the said demised premises are more particularly delineated upon the map or plan drawn upon the margin of these presents..."

This description referred to a site on the corner of the present day Emmanuel Street and Drummer Street, partly comprising a collection of buildings with a frontage to Emmanuel Lane and the rest consisting of the corner building, an imposing house, formerly "The White Horse" Inn.

Francis John Gunning appears to have raised money on the lease from family sources in 1845. He assigned the lease to Frederick Gunning, William Bircham the younger and Francis Thomas Bircham with three policies of assurance. These policies would have served to pay off the outstanding loan when Francis Gunning died the following year.

The move of offices brought Gunning and Francis next door to the premises of Mr. Peete Musgrave a tailor and woollen draper. His son Rev. Thomas Musgrave had been a client of Francis Gunning since the mid 1820's. Having entered Trinity College in 1804 Thomas Musgrave was to become successively Fellow of Trinity 1812–39, Senior Bursar 1825–37 and Professor of Arabic 1821–37. Thomas Musgrave had also held a Lease on a cottage two doors away in Emmanuel Lane from 1823 onwards but he had by the time of the Gunning and Francis move been appointed Bishop of Hereford and was resident in the Episcopal Palace there. Thomas Musgrave appears in this story eight years later, as will be seen below.

Gunning and Francis continued to practise in Emmanuel Lane until the partnership was terminated by the death of Francis Gunning on 5th October 1846. Clement Francis then continued the practice from the Emmanuel Lane premises as sole principal.* No doubt to facilitate the allocation of profits between himself and Francis Gunning's executor a fresh bill book and a fresh ledger were both begun in October 1846 prominently marked with the initials "C.F.". It is evident that Clement Francis also took up residence at the Emmanuel Lane premises during the following year 1847 and established his first matrimonial home there with his bride Sarah Parmeter of Aylsham

---

*By a Deed of Release dated 8th April 1848 Clement Francis paid to Francis Thomas Bircham (Gunning's executor) the sum of £300 in respect of his deceased partner's share in the practice. This payment was for the benefit of Gunning's three daughters Frances Anne and Mary. The deed recited that the partnership had subsisted between the two partners up to the decease of Francis Gunning ": but for a period of two years and upwards previously to such decease the said Francis John Gunning was wholly incapacitated by serious illness from employing himself in or attending to the business and concerns of the... co-partnership..."

following their marriage on 8th May 1848. The principal of
the practice and his wife carried on their domestic life with
all the lively distractions of a young and growing family, in
No. 17 Emmanuel Lane immediately next door to the office
at No. 18.

By the time of the Cambridge Borough Census in March
1851 the residents of 17 Emmanuel Lane were recorded as:

SURNAME	FORENAMES	AGE	BIRTHPLACE
Francis	Clement	35	Newcastle-upon-Tyne
	Sarah	24	Aylsham, Norfolk
	Clement	2	Cambridge
	Thomas M.	11mth	Cambridge

This return names the first two children born to Clement
and Sarah Francis out of an eventual total of thirteen. Five
sons and one daughter were to survive into adult life.
Clement Francis II had been born on 10th February 1849
and was baptised at the Church of St. Andrew the Great on
11th March 1849. Thomas Musgrave Francis had been born
on 3rd April 1850 and was baptised at St. Andrew the Great
on 1st May 1850. He received his Christian names as a
compliment to the client and family friend Thomas
Musgrave who had by then achieved still further eminence
as Archbishop of York (1847–60). Sadly, Clement Francis II
died on 17th October 1856 aged seven, but his brother Thomas survived to become senior partner of the firm in succession to his father.

On 29th January 1850 the Master Fellows and Scholars of
Emmanuel College granted a new lease to Clement Francis
of premises substantially similar to those leased to William
Searle in 1836, save that a handsome and detailed ground
plan of the premises was included in the lease (see
illustration 5). The lease was for a term of forty years from
Michaelmas 1849

"... paying during the said term unto the said Master and Scholars at or in the Common Dining Hall of the said College the rent or sum of £17 of good and lawful money of Great Britain at the two usual feasts or days of payment (that is to say) the Feast of the Annunciation of the Blesed Virgin Mary and the Feast of St. Michael the Archangel by two and equal portions. And also paying and delivering therefor yearly and every year at each of the two several accounts or audits holden for the said College two fat capons or in lieu thereof five shillings of lawful money of Great Britain together with the further sum of two shillings yearly to the Bursar of the said College for the time being for his trouble in writing an acquittance or acquittances for the reserved rent..."

Rebuilding of the Emmanuel Street offices for Clement Francis was undertaken by Messrs. William Bell, builders of Cambridge, between March and September 1850 at a cost of £441. Construction of a strong-room by Messrs. Lucas Brothers of Lowestoft was also undertaken between March and August 1851 and cost £342.

*   *   *   *

From 1850 until the year 1913, 18 Emmanuel Street was occupied by the practice under nine successive names,

Clement Francis	1850–1861
Francis Webster and Riches	1861–1876
Francis Riches and Francis	1876–1879
Francis and Francis	1879–1887
Francis, Francis and Parker	1887–1888
Francis and Francis	1888–1898
Francis, Francis & Collin	1898–1905
Francis, Francis, Collin and Peile	1905–1907
Francis & Co.	1907–1913

The purchase of the Quy Hall Estate by Clement Francis from Mr. and Mrs. J. T. Martin on 11th October 1855 marked an approaching end to family residence at 17 Emmanuel Street. Major work of refurbishment and improvement at Quy Hall meant that the family did not take up residence there before 1858. Even then, Quy Hall was considered quite unsuited for residence during winter time and was for several more years the family summer home with Emmanuel Street their winter one. Apart from discomfort in the Hall itself the roads around Quy were difficult to the point of impassability during the winter and this must have constituted a serious deterrent to residence there until substantial improvements to the highways were made.

Francis was a keen cyclist and often made his daily journey from Quy to the office by bicycle.

The restored Quy Hall is described by Mark Girouard (*The Victorian Country House*, 1979) as follows:

QUY HALL, nr Cambridge
By William White 1868, for Clement Francis. A modest remodelling of a gabled manor house, long and low, of diapered red brick, with minimum Gothic detail. Inside, agreeably planned along spacious pine corridors. Dining room has original furniture and stencil decoration (said to be by Gambier Parry). The staircase has an ingenious open timber roof and is spatially remarkably effective.

On 31st May 1864 the Master, Fellows and Scholars of Emmanuel College granted a fresh lease of Emmanuel Street premises to Clement Francis for a period of forty years from Michaelmas at an increased rent of £22 per annum. The signature of Clement Francis on the counterpart Lease was witnessed by "Richard Looker Clerk to Messrs. Francis Webster and Riches".

Thirty years later, after the death of Clement Francis, an Agreement dated 23rd March 1893 was endorsed on the 1864 Lease between Sarah Francis of Quy Hall Widow of the one part and the Master, Fellows and Scholars of Emmanuel College of the other part. This recited that by the Will of

Clement Francis dated 29th January 1855, he had devised and bequeathed all his real and personal estate whatsoever and wheresoever unto his wife the said Sarah Francis her heirs executors administrators and assigns absolutely and had appointed the said Sarah Francis sole executor (sic) thereof And further recited that the said Clement Francis had died on 7th March 1880 without having altered or revoked his said Will which was duly proved by the said Sarah Francis on 31st March 1880 in the Peterborough District Registry Probate Division of her Majesty's High Court of Justice And further recited that the said Master Fellows and Scholars had recently at the request of the said Sarah Francis built and made large additions and alterations to and in the within mentioned Solicitors office and premises at the cost of £750... in consideration of which it was agreed that an additional rent of £37.10s. should be payable from 29th September 1892, the rent to be thenceforth £65 per annum in lieu of £27.10s. therein reserved.

The "large additions and alterations" are well illustrated in the surviving photograph taken from the corner of Drummer Street in the year 1913 shortly before the practice moved out. The move was brought about by the decision of the Governing Body of Emmanuel College to proceed with the building of the College North Court along the north side of Emmanuel Street running westwards from the Drummer Street corner. Mr. Leonard Stokes' plans for North Court were approved by the College on 29th October 1910 and Messrs. Saint's tender for the building work was accepted on 27th May 1911. Part of North Court was finished in time for occupation in the Michaelmas term of 1913. An opening celebration fixed for 7th October 1914 never took place owing to the outbreak of the First World War. It appears that the premises comprised in the 1864 Lease were the last portion of the site to be vacated by College tenants prior to demolition. A letter from the

Charity Commission addressed to Messrs. Francis and
Company at 18 Emmanuel Street, Cambridge dated 20th
November 1913 appears to be one of the last surviving items
of correspondence addressed to the firm in Emmanuel
Street. A letter from Messrs. J. Carter Jonas & Sons, Land
Agents, to Messrs. Francis & Co., Peas Hill is dated 5th
March 1914. This seems to point to a move from Emmanuel
Street at about the turn of year 1913/1914. Mr. William
Boyce who was employed by the practice at this time, for
shorthand, typing, engrossing and entering college lease
books, described the move from 18 Emmanuel Street to
Peas Hill by hand carts with staff assistance in 1913. He
remembered the difficulty of negotiating the tramlines
along St. Andrew's Street, between Emmanuel Street and
Petty Cury.

Thus no more than thirty years after the "large additions
and alterations" had been made to the office by Emmanuel
College all was to be demolished without trace. No contemporary description of the rather striking late Victorian
exterior has survived. Along with the reconstruction of the
Emmanuel Street elevation (see illustration 4) the following description has been attempted by the author to make
good this deficiency.

18 Emmanuel Street

Two storeys without attic, walls of gault brick and tile
covered roof in Victorian Tudor style. The Emmanuel
Street elevation had three large ground floor windows with
flat brick arches and stone sills (presumed to have two
mullions and single transoms behind shutters), the semi-
circular arched office doorway placed between the east and
central windows. A prominent moulded brick string at first
floor level served as a box gutter and extended across single
storey gault brick walls east and west, each with parapet
blocking course containing semi-circular side entrance

east, and flat arch over wooden corniced door-frame to residence west. Another brick string at second floor level below a rendered eaves cornice with deep overhang. The wall plane was continued upwards by three flush semi-dormer windows with moulded brick sills, each window with two mullions and single transom finished with brick and rendered multi-curved gables of East Anglian pattern, above prominent moulded brick cornicing.

Chapter 10

CLEMENT FRANCIS
SOLE PRACTITIONER 1850–1861

 LEMENT Francis could at the start of 1851, the year of the Great Exhibition, have surveyed his practice and clientele with some satisfaction. The colleges he was now acting for comprised Downing, Emmanuel, Jesus, Magdalene, Pembroke, Peterhouse, St. John's and Sidney Sussex, among the better known town and county families were Allix, Chaplin, Cust, Huddleston, Jenyns, Martin, Mortlock, Musgrave and Pemberton, quite apart from the Cambridge Borough Charity, Babraham Charity, Pampisford Charity, William Eaden Lilley, Robert Sayle and the Commissioners for Cottenham Level, Waterbeach Level and Swaffham and Bottisham Drainage Districts. College lettings were representing an increasing volume of business for the practice, these transactions being recorded for a time in a separately designated "University Bill Book—Leases". An additional charge was made for entering leases in the College Registers, an activity which has continued to this day, but no longer at the standard fee of 6/8d.

One of the major preoccupations for Clement Francis at this time was the administration of the estate of Christopher Pemberton, a task which was to continue until final estate accounts were prepared by the London Accountants, Messrs. Kain, in 1860. As previously mentioned, Grove Lodge was Christopher Pemberton's residence as well as his office and formed part of the assets passing to his nephew and residuary beneficiary, Christopher Robert Pemberton. The residuary beneficiary was soon to take up residence at Grove Lodge, as recorded in the Cambridge Borough Census, taken 30th March 1851, by the following entry for the Parish of St. Mary the Less:

Trumpington Street: Pemberton's Residence:

Christopher Pemberton	Head	Married	50 Magistrate Middlesex London
Harriet Pemberton	Wife	Married	40 Wife Middlesex London
Frances Pemberton	Daughter	Unmarried	21 Daughter Middlesex London
Henrietta Pemberton	Daughter	Unmarried	19 Daughter Middlesex London
Christopher Pemberton	Son	Unmarried	12 Scholar at home Middlesex London
Alexander Pemberton	Son	Unmarried	11 Scholar at home Middlesex London

Together with nine servants.

A bill book entry refers to Christopher Robert Pemberton "taking the house and gardens from Peterhouse College", though this appears to have been a short term arrangement and did not prevent the execution on 16th December 1851 of an assignment of the Land Tax Redemption by the executors of Christopher Pemberton in favour of Peterhouse. After reciting a Land Tax Contract dated 24th July 1799, the last Will of Christopher Pemberton dated 19th February 1850, the appointment of his four executors, the death of Christopher Pemberton on 22nd October 1850, and the grant of probate to Christopher Robert Pemberton and Stanley Pemberton on an unspecified day in March 1851 in the Prerogative Court of Canterbury there followed an Assignment by the executors, in consideration of a payment of £167.9s 6d, of the benefit of the Land Tax Redemption on Grove Lodge. A receipt for the payment was endorsed and the document was signed, sealed and delivered by the executors in the presence of "Clement Francis Solicitor Cambridge".

Meanwhile arrangements were put in hand to invite tenders from building contractors for the erection of a new mansion for Christopher Robert Pemberton at Newton. The contract was awarded to Messrs. Bell, Builders and payment for the construction proceeded by instalments from the Executors' account until 1856.

Parliamentary work came Clement Francis's way in 1853. Acting for the Martin family of Quy, he was involved in an application for a private Bill in Parliament which was to become Martin's Estate Act (1853) 16 and 17 Vict.c.12. In the absence of specific powers conferred under a family trust, this Act enabled James Thomas Martin Esq

"... and the persons in remainder under the Will of Mary Jackson deceased, to grant Leases of parts of the estates thereby devised in settlement for the purpose of building upon and otherwise improving the same and for other purposes". (4th August 1853)

The effect of this Act was to give James Thomas Martin power to grant building leases on prescribed terms in respect of devised estates near Bristol and Clifton, comprising the Sneed Park Estate.

The Schedule of Properties annexed to this Act bears the signature of William Baker, Surveyor and Clement Francis, Solicitor.

Business for the same client was to bring about the earliest recorded use of telecommunications by the practice, as well as being the earliest example (by no means the last) of the practice being brought under anxious pressure by a land surveyor. A bill book entry on 14th March 1854 records:

> "Having received letter from Mr. Baker by this morning post requesting me to telegraph to him in London this day…"

External events may however have overshadowed this landmark even in the memories of the participants. The outbreak of the Crimean War occurred thirteen days later on 27th March 1854.

The period of the Crimean War was coincidentally to see a remarkably successful conclusion to the centuries-long rivalry and conflict between the Town Authorities and the University. As summarized in VCH Vol. 3,

> "The story of the relations of town and gown was one of endemic border warfare, with recurrent crises, the longest and fiercest being that under Elizabeth I. In the 18th century the warfare transformed itself into petty skirmishing, as administrative torpidity settled on both communities. It reopened in the 19th century with all the hostility and resentment that obsolete privilege and injured amour-propre can arouse. It was not until 1856 that peace was signed—a peace that was 'lasting because there were no victors.'"

General matters of precedence and prestige apart, the main areas of conflict were those concerning police, morals and health, jurisdiction, trade and finance. The resolution of these long outstanding issues was to require three stages. In December 1854 the University and Corporation combined to appoint Sir John Patteson as arbitrator. A hearing of the matters in issue was held at the Law Society's Hall, Chancery Lane in February and May 1855. The interested parties were represented by various counsel and solicitors, among them Mr. Clement Francis representing Magdalene College. Sir John Patteson was presented with a list of fifteen answers from the University side. After hearing representations on behalf of the interested parties the Arbitrator closed the hearing on 18th May and published his Award on 31st August 1855. The Award contained a seventeen point programme for reconciling and reconstituting the management of the Borough of Cambridge and these recommendations were carried into the Statute Book by Parliament the following year in the Cambridge Award Act 1856. "It was a triumph of common sense over feeling". (VCH Vol. 3).

If a treaty of peace had been brought into effect, a barrier between the two communities still existed, members of the University being unable to hold office or vote in municipal elections. This barrier was eventually removed in 1889 when six seats on the Borough Council were allocated to University and College representatives.

It may be assumed that the involvement of Clement Francis in the arbitration proceedings would have enhanced his reputation and strengthened his standing among the Colleges and the University.

Among property purchases for the Colleges involving the practice in the late eighteen fifties and early eighteen sixties that of Crumps Farm in the Isle of Thanet by St. John's College in May 1860 is worth mentioning, this being preceded by a sale to the East Kent Railway in November 1858. According to J. S. Boys Smith ("Memories of St. John's College Cambridge 1919–1969") agricultural land had been the traditional, and in early times the only, form of College investment and little land had been sold off. In the nineteenth century important sales to the new railway companies and to public authorities had taken place, resulting in large sums becoming available for investment. The sale to the East Kent Railway Company helped provide the purchase money for Crumps Farm and other large purchases of land mainly on the north coast of Kent and in Thanet. Crumps Farm and the nearby Shuart Farm were to become names familiar in the practice as succeeding generations of partners, assistants and clerks dealt with a variety of conveyancing and tenancy business affecting these holdings.

By 1860, Clement Francis had acquired the positions of Clerk to the Conservators of the River Cam and Under Sheriff of the County. Among University-connected clients the Cambridge Union Society and the University Rifle Corps had by then both appeared in his bill books.

In 1861 Clement Francis took into partnership two solicitors who had already been associated with him for some years, Thomas Webster and Alfred Smith Riches. The practice assumed the name Francis Webster and Riches for the next fifteen years.

Thomas Webster (1832–1913) had read classics at Trinity College (B.A. 1855), he had then been called to the Bar at Lincoln's Inn in 1856 and became a fellow of his college in 1857. Relinquishing a career at the Bar he served articles of clerkship in London and was admitted as a solicitor in 1861. He immediately became a partner in the Francis practice. For the next fifteen years he remained actively involved in the University, whether as law lecturer, examiner or member of the Moral Sciences Syndicate. However, his college fellowship ceased on his marriage in 1863.

[It should be added at this point that on 30th October 1861 instructions were first received by the practice from Trinity College.]

Alfred Smith Riches (1810–1879) was a Norwich man who had been articled to George Jay of the City of Norwich for five years on 5th November 1827 (his father Henry

Riches of the hamlet of Carrow acting as surety). He was admitted before the Court of Common Pleas on 22nd January 1833 and practised in Wymondham Norfolk, according to Law List entries, from 1833 to 1839.*

*Clement Francis notified his clients of this development in the following printed circular:

Cambridge, February 1st 1861

Dear Sir

I have the pleasure of informing you, I have this day taken into Partnership Mr. Webster, M.A. Fellow of Trinity College & Mr. Riches, who has held a position of confidence in my Office.

I am, Dear Sir,
Yours truly,
Clement Francis

Chapter 11

CLEMENT FRANCIS IN
PARTNERSHIP 1861–1880

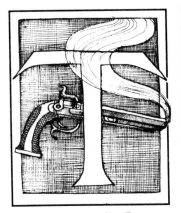

HE practice records from this period provide a picture of solid and established Victorian respectability, the principal clients drawn in roughly equal parts from Cambridge colleges and county families. Occasionally episodes were recorded which also give illuminating insights into contemporary happenings.

The Great Coprolite Boom

In a period otherwise marked by agricultural depression the discovery that coprolite could be processed into artificial fertiliser and increase agricultural productivity led to the Great Coprolite Boom of 1860–1890, the first known example of open-cast mining in Britain and the production of the first known chemical fertiliser. A broad seam or stratum of these hard phosphatic nodules ran diagonally across Cambridgeshire from Royston in the south to Soham in the north, only a few feet below the surface. The economic benefits resulting from this exploitation were to spare Cambridgeshire from some of the worst effects of the agricultural depression.

The boom did not however proceed everywhere at the same beneficial pace, as the following bill book entry for 1864 indicates:

"April 8th, Having heard from Mr. Hales that Mr. Wallis had not yet commenced digging your estate, writing Mr. Wallis thereon.

"April 9th, Attending Mr. Wallis when he informed us that the Mill and machinery which he expected had not yet been delivered pursuant to the Contract and he promised to commence the work immediately.

"July 20th, Writing Mr. Wallis requesting him to call at our office on Saturday 23rd instant on the subject of a letter received from Captain Hatton.

"July 23rd, Attending Mr. Wallis when we expressed our surprise he had not yet commenced operations and requested to be informed the cause hereof and he stated that the extremely low price that ruled in coprolite market, coprolite coming in any amounts being sold at a price not exceeding 30/- ton and some at 29/- made it impossible for him to work your land at a profit and therefore deemed it essentially necessary to remain inactive until the present time when coprolites had reached about 34/- and he was about to take immediate steps for commencing operations and he showed a letter he had received from Captain Hatton subsequent to that which he had addressed to us in which he expressed himself satisfied at the explanation and his offer to complete the tender in two years, we therefore felt outselves excluded pressing the matter further."

Clement Francis himself, his acquisition of the Quy Hall Estate having conferred upon him the position of Lord of the Manors of Quy and Fen Ditton, experienced greater success. He granted a licence to John Eaden and others to dig coprolites at various sites for a return of £50 per acre per year. These workings took place either in marginal land of little use for agriculture or in better land where nevertheless the return from coprolite working was better than from farming. In certain areas, such as Reach and Stow-cum-Quy the value of the coprolite mined was greater than the potential cost of restoring the land to cultivation. Some restoration never took place and water filled workings remain visible in these parishes to this day.

The coprolite boom was to reach its peak by the eighteen seventies, production contributing in 1874 a greater value to British exports (£628,000) than tin (£605,000) of which Britain was then a major producer. The decline which became noticeable from the mid-eighteen eighties was due in part to exhaustion of deposits but in far greater measure to a steady build up of lower priced imports of artificial fertilisers from foreign sources. A few Cambridgeshire workings continued but none remained by the year 1900.

Turnpike Roads

Although railways had by this time taken over the bulk of passenger and goods traffic, turnpike roads still existed in many parts of the country including Cambridgeshire. The following bill book entry in February 1864 records an episode involving the Hauxton Turnpike Trust:

"February 5th, Attending Mr. Carr on his informing us that Mr. William Coulson's steam engine had passed through his tollgate at Hauxton at half-past five o'clock pm on Saturday last, and taking down his evidence and afterwards attending him at Mr. Barley's office instructing him to issue a summons against Coulson.

"February 13th, Attending at the County Courts when evidence adduced that defendant's engine passed through the Hauxton gate at half-past five o'clock in the evening of Saturday the 30th January last, and the engine driver Shadrack Jacobs proved that he was in the employ of William Coulson and that the engine was the property of the said William Coulson but the magistrates decided that it was necessary to prove the order given by Coulson to the driver to use the engine before he could be convicted and they dismissed the complaint on Mr. Garret (the defendant's solicitor) undertaking not to repeat the offence whilst the present order is in force."

It was the practice of turnpike trusts to let their tolls to the highest bidder on an annual basis. The Arrington Turnpike Trust suffered a temporary reverse in November 1864:

"November 24th, Attending a special meeting at the Lion Hotel when tolls put up to be let failing to obtain a bid beyond £602.0.0 the present rent, they remained not let and receiving instructions to give notice of meeting on the 29th December next, to put the tolls up again.

"December 29th, attending special meeting of trustees when the tolls were let to Mr. Joseph Barrell at £594.0.0 for 1 year, to fill out the contract and obtain Mr. Barrell's signature for the same."

Attendance at Completions

One entry served to underline the fact that until very recent times a purchaser's solicitor would, without exception, attend at the vendor's solicitors office to complete a purchase of property. Sometimes however, this took place on neutral ground:

"December 6th 1864, "Special journey to London to meet Mr. Barker and Mr. Lovegrove at the Law Institution (now Law Society's Hall, Chancery Lane) when the purchase was completed and the Title Deeds were handed over to us on our giving an undertaking to deliver them up to the purchaser of the advowson..."

Railway Construction

Although the main railway network was complete throughout the country by 1864 certain minor branch lines were still under construction, among them in Cambridgeshire the Ely, Sutton and Haddenham Railway. The work undertaken on this line might not have been conducted to the same standard as elsewhere. An episode in November 1864 prompted the following entry:

"Attending you with reference to the proposed taking by the Ely, Haddenham and Sutton Railway Company of a portion of your land at Thetford when it was arranged that the matter should be put into the hands of Mr. Bidwell.

"Writing Mr. Wheeler the Company's solicitor for a tracing of the land taken and with reference to your complaint that the company had cut the fences of the adjoining field and that your land lay exposed to the inroads of your neighbour's stock.

"December 12th, Attending Mr. Bidwell when it appeared he was already employed on behalf of the Company. Writing you, informing you thereof and suggesting the appointment of Mr. Carter-Jonas to act as your surveyor…"

The Judges of Assize

In October 1864 a meeting with the Master of Trinity College, Rev. Dr. William Whewell, resulted in the following entry:

"October 24th, Attending you when you stated that it was your intention to consult Counsel with respect to the right of Judges of Assize to use Trinity Lodge during the Winter Assize and generally as to their rights in the matter and conference thereon.

"October 29th, Attending at the Chronicle Office examining newspaper files from 1818–1829 inclusive as to the accounts of HRH the Duke of Sussex visits to Cambridge found that he went to the Sun Hotel up to 1828 and 1829 when he stopped at the Hoop Hotel making notes of same."

(Preparation of the case to Counsel followed)

"October 31st, Writing agents therewith and instructing them to lay same before Sir Fitzroy Kelly, Sir Hugh Currie and Mr. Fitzjames Stephen for a joint opinion. Attending at the Cambridge Chronicle, searching file of newspapers of 1835 for a report of where HRH the Duke of Cambridge and HRH the Duke of Cumberland resided on their visit to the public installation of the Marquis of Camden as Chancellor of the University but could not trace it.

"November 17th, Counsel having required copies appointment of several Masters of Trinity attending you thereon when you stated that

no appointment nor copy was in your possession except your own and
it was arranged that such as were necessary should be bespoke from
Record Office.

"December 6th, Agents having telegraphed for a copy of Cooper's
Annals for the use of Counsel attending booking and despatching
same, although Mr. Cooper's account showed him that no special
commission of Oyer and Terminer had ever sat in Cambridge"

Perhaps embarrassingly for his fellows, when the
Counsels' Opinion was received, it showed that the Master
had been legally correct in resisting the suggestion
(originating from the Home Office), that a legal and
enforceable custom to lodge Her Majesty's Judges at Trinity
College had been established through long usage.
Nevertheless, according to Winstanley this opinion
produced some consternation among the seniority who
feared the loss of the exceptional prestige and privilege they
had enjoyed over the centuries, acting as hosts to the Judges
of Assize. Clearly the issue could not remain unresolved
indefinitely. On 12th June 1866 a Corporate Act was sealed
by Trinity College allowing Her Majesty's Judges of Assize
the use of all apartments and all offices which had usually
been appropriated to them for Spring and Summer Assizes
"whenever they should hold Courts of Assize or Jail
Deliveries for the Town and County of Cambridge".
    This being in the nature of a perpetual invitation rather
than a legal and enforceable grant, Winstanley was
prompted to comment:

"... so the controversy remains unsettled. But it is not likely to arise
again, and probably never would have arisen but for Whewell".

The solution proved to be stable and enduring, no
further controversy or confrontation occurring during the
next one hundred and five years. As a result of the Courts

Act 1971 the Assize Courts were abolished and the judges' visits to Trinity College were discontinued. More recently the practice has revived as Crown Court judges once more visit the College.

The Cambridge Union Society

Founded as an undergraduate debating society and reading club in 1815, at first frowned upon by the university authorities on account of its intellectual and liberal flavour, the Union Society had by the eighteen sixties achieved a respectable and established position in the life of the University. Meetings had hitherto been held in "a low ill-ventilated, ill-lit gallery at the back of the Red Lion Inn— something between a Commercial room and a District Branch Meeting House"—(Lord Houghton). By 1863 the need for more permanent and more commodious premises was clearly felt. Starting on 23rd October 1863, bill book entries record visits from the Senior Treasurer of the Society, various trustees and undergraduate officers and instructions being given to Mr. Wentworth the Surveyor to consider suitable properties for freehold purchase. The alternative of remaining where they were was ruled out in November 1863 when it was found that "the owners of the present Union Society building were not disposed to lower their price". By the Spring of 1864 a list of eligible sites had been reduced to three in number, first the Hoop Inn and adjoining premises in Peas Hill, secondly "certain property belonging to St. John's College, Sidney Street" and thirdly "premises owned by St. John's College held under lease by Mrs. Edwards". Mrs. Edwards' premises were not considered further when it was found that St. John's College were not willing to sell the freehold reversion. Attention quickly switched to a fourth site when the President of the Union announced on 18th March 1864, as a result of an interview with the Master and Bursar, that St. John's College were willing to sell the freehold interest in a tenanted property variously described as "abutting on Holy Sepulchre Churchyard" and "at the rear of St. Sepulchre's Church". The Society was clearly attracted by this opportunity and the rest of 1864 and the greater part of 1865 were occupied with procedures which would today be described as site assembly, involving negotiations for the purchase of the freehold interest, for the acquisition of the interests of several occupying tenants and for additional land adjoining to complete a site on which the Union Society Premises were to be built. The architect Mr. Alfred Waterhouse (Manchester Town Hall; Natural History Museum) had been brought into the discussions by March 1865, the conveyancing formalities were completed soon afterwards and the Building Contract signed on 14th July. Financial considerations prompted an entry on 26th October 1865

> "Attending a meeting of the New Building Committee when the scheme of raising a loan upon debentures was approved of and we were instructed to prepare the requisite declaration of trust by the trustees and a form of debenture and to get same settled by Mr. A. G. Marten so as to submit them to a further meeting of the committee".

The Society moved into its newly completed building in 1866 and has remained there in dignified seclusion ever since, behind the Church of the Holy Sepulchre.

The Union Society's accommodation problems did not disappear overnight. Once the new building had been completed neighbouring owners, including a Mr. Eakin, began to complain about interference to rights of light. This had already been forecast in an entry for 16th February 1866...

> "Attending meeting of the Society this day on the same business at which Mr. Waterhouse was present and it was agreed to resist any

proceedings that might be taken on the part of Mr. Eakin and we were directed to reply to Mr. Foster's correspondence..."

Lockers in Mr. Francis' Room

Visitors to the practice premises over many years have either admired or been intrigued by the storage cabinets generally located in one of the senior partners' rooms, all neatly painted with an arresting display of notable clients' names.

Although the origin of these cabinets seemed doubtful until quite recently, it is now firmly established by the discovery of a pencil note in the 1864 Bill Book, inserted at the conclusion of a transaction "Papers are in Downing College locker in Mr. F's room", that these lockers were an installation dating from the early years of the firm's occupation of 18 Emmanuel Street.

The Case of John Frederick Mortlock

John Frederick Mortlock was involved in a long running *cause celebre* in Cambridge which began in 1842 and only ended with his death forty years later. As eldest grandson of John Mortlock the banker he held obsessively and with tenacity throughout this period to the unshakeable conviction that he had been defrauded of a share in his grandfather's fortune by the legal machinations or manoeuvres of his uncles Thomas Mortlock and Rev. Edmund Mortlock. Frustrated to the point of outrage he had in 1842 discharged a firearm at his Uncle Edmund in his room at Christ's College, fortunately causing little injury. For this crime he was convicted and sentenced at Cambridge Assizes in 1843 to transportation for twenty one years. For premature return to England he was sentenced to one year's imprisonment at Cambridge Assizes in 1858. On completing this sentence he was returned to Australia to complete the remaining five years of his original twenty one year sentence. He eventually returned to Cambridge a free man in 1864. His obsession undimmed by years of hardship and privation, he then set about a single-handed campaign to recover his family fortunes from his surviving Uncle Edmund and the executors of his deceased Uncle Thomas. His campaign partly involved the publication of a copious series of autobiographical pamphlets and polemical outbursts against his uncles for their supposed wrongdoings. The somewhat limited sales of these pamphlets nevertheless helped finance a series of unsuccessful court applications and proceedings which John Frederick Mortlock conducted in person from 1865 onwards, only setting down his campaigning pen shortly before his death. Needless to say his uncles' lawyers (especially, "Clement F-.") were part victims of his scathing remarks, being characterised as accessories in the conspiracy against him. Since the first appearance of Mortlock's detailed autobiography "Experiences of a Convict" in 1865 his story received a certain amount of attention over the years, more recently in a biography written by his first cousin, the late Dr. A. E. Clarke-Kennedy (*"Cambridge to Botany Bay"*—1982) and a subsequent television dramatisation. Notwithstanding his obsessive conduct Mortlock remained an attractive character throughout, managing to acquire some passing sympathy, even regard, from those who felt admiration for his determination in adversity. The bill book entries for the period 1867 onwards are more prosaic and yield nothing to support Mortlock's darker suspicions.

Mortlock's first move in May 1865 was to commence proceedings against his Uncle Edmund. These proceedings came to nothing when the Attorney General refused to sanction them with his fiat in September 1865.

Next in March 1866, Mortlock started an action to eject

his Uncle Edmund and his first cousin Edmund John Mortlock (son and heir of his late Uncle Thomas) from their property, claiming it as his. Once the trial had been fixed for a hearing at Cambridge Assizes on 31st July the bill book entries show that efforts had to be made to obtain a copy of the Will of John Mortlock (the Grandfather) dating from 1816. As the attesting witnesses were themselves long since dead evidence had to be obtained as to their burial (in the days before death certificates) and witnesses found to vouch for their signatures. Serjeant O'Malley* of Counsel was briefed to appear at the hearing on 31st July

"Attending court this day when plaintiff appeared and conducted his case in person but failing to make out a case the jury gave a verdict in your favour".

Mortlock then commenced proceedings in Chancery by filing a bill of complaint against his Uncle Edmund and cousin Edmund John on 21st March 1867. Rev. Edmund Mortlock was now eighty years of age and in poor health. He resided in the village of Moulton, beyond Newmarket, and the bill book records several journeys made there between April and June, conferring at considerable length as to the answers given to the bill of complaint, telegrams passing between London and Cambridge calling for copies of the bills to be sent down to Mr. Hall of Counsel. On April 2nd,

"On receipt of letter from Mr. Hall stating that our agents could not obtain copies of Bills and requesting to be furnished with those left with us attending at the railway station and delivering parcel to the guard of the express train and arranging with him to send a

---

*Serjeant O'Malley is not listed in Prof. J. H. Baker's comprehensive "The Order of Serjeants-at-Law" 1984 but J. F. Mortlock's own account of the proceedings also refers, less directly, to "Serjeant O'M-".

messenger with it to Mr. Hall.

"Preparation of telegram to agents that we had sent out copies of both Bills to Mr. Hall and requesting them to call on him and see what course he recommended and to attending at telegraph office therewith."

Considerable activity appears to have been necessary in order to compile answers to the complaint from family papers and records, some of which were no longer available. Concern over the filing date seems to have prompted an entry on 31st May:

"Preparing telegram to agents requesting them to inform us of the last day for Rev. E. Mortlock to put in answer and directing them to telegram in reply".

Rev. Edmund Mortlock seems to have been in no mood to stir himself on account of his litigious nephew. On the same day:

"Having received telegram from agents that answer was due this day and asking for affidavit of the medical attendant of the Rev. E. Mortlock, instructions affidavit to be made by a Mr. Richard Faircloth Surgeon, Newmarket as to the Rev. E. Mortlock's state of health and that he was unable to attend to the matter."

"Journey to Newmarket and attending Mr. Faircloth who consented to make the affidavit and sign the certificate and the only two commissioners at Newmarket being from home, it was arranged that Mr. Faircloth should go to Cambridge for the purpose of being sworn."

"Writing agents with affidavit and certificate and urging them to obtain ten days at least further time."

Evidently further time for preparing the answers was

obtained but Mortlock filed a replication in July 1867 to which further answers were required. Rev. Edmund Mortlock evidently felt sufficiently recovered by 2nd August:

> "Attending you on your bringing a large number of letters received by you from various members of the family, going through and selecting some to form the First Schedule of your affidavit but after being engaged several hours we found this inpracticable and he left them with us to arrange and select."

On August 3rd:

> "Engaged several hours arranging and selecting the letters left by you and making Schedules thereof."

The case eventually came on for hearing in the Rolls Court in December 1867.
On 6th December:

> "Writing you informing you that you would not be required to attend in Court unless you wished to do so."

On 9th December:

> "Journey to London for the purpose of attending consultation at Mr. Baggallay's Chambers tomorrow morning at 9.30 but upon arriving in town we found the case had been part heard and that the Master of the Rolls had taken the papers home, requesting that the Deeds might be in Court tomorrow."

On 10th December:

> "Attending consultation at Mr. Baggallay's Chambers this morning and afterwards attending Court when the Bill was dismissed with costs."

Difficult though it might be to see what other decision the Court might have reached, Mortlock remained dissatisfied with the outcome and made four further unsuccessful attempts to commence proceedings during 1868 and 1869. The award of costs against him in December 1867 had, however, placed Mortlock in dire financial straits. His uncle and cousin had after all been put to considerable inconvenience and had incurred sizeable legal costs as a result of these proceedings. It may well have been more for motives of protection against future proceedings than of vindictiveness or exasperation that the taxation of their court costs went forward in February 1868. On February 29th:

"Writing agents not to lose any time in enforcing payment of the costs herein after taxation."

The bill of costs being duly taxed, presented and remaining unpaid, on 14th April 1868,

"Having received notice from Registrar of County Court of examination of plaintiff J. F. Mortlock as a bankrupt described himself as a bookseller so as to get out of jail at the end of a fortnight as a trader instead of two calendar months as a non-trader. Writing agents informing them thereof and with copy notice and requesting them to see Mr. Capron and enquire if we could oppose the examination on the ground that he was not a trader."

In the event Mortlock was imprisoned for non-payment of costs and declared a bankrupt. His own version of this experience appeared in yet another pamphlet, "How I Came To Be A Bankrupt" by John Frederick M-, (London 1868).

[Leaving the treatment of individual subjects this chapter now moves to a chronological account of the period]

By 1867, the seventeen year old Thomas Musgrave Francis, eldest surviving son of Clement Francis, had completed his schooling at Eton and came up to Trinity College as a pensioner in the Michaelmas Term. He was to graduate B.A. in 1871 and M.A. 1874. With the possible exception of Thomas Webster, whose early career path seems less clear cut, Musgrave Francis must have been the first solicitor in the practice to take advantage of the dispensation permitting graduates of the Universities of Oxford, Cambridge, Dublin, Durham and London to serve three years articles instead of five (Solicitors Act 1843). In the absence of any surviving evidence it must be assumed that Musgrave Francis served his three years articles with his father, being admitted as a solicitor in 1874. He was, however, certainly the first solicitor in the practice to have faced an examination in book-keeping and trust accounts in addition to the legal subjects, this requirement having been introduced in 1862. He then served as an assistant solicitor in the practice until his admission to the partnership in 1876.

Bill book entries for the year 1872 note the appearance, for the first time as clients, of Rev. J. V. Durell, Rector of Fulbourn St. Vigor's, Vicar of Fulbourn All Saints (grandfather of Dudley Vavasour Durell a future partner in the practice), the Trustees of the Cambridge Savings Bank (later to become the Cambridge Trustee Savings Bank and eventually part of the TSB Organization) and Messrs. Peak Frean the biscuit manufacturers. This last and somewhat unexpected connection seems to have involved a reorganization of the firm's Camberwell premises following their acquisition from the Martin family and was not of long duration.

In 1873 an entry records what at that time was a rare occurrence, the acquisition of a domestic residence for a client. For many years previously and for some years to come, private residences appear to have been mostly taken on lease and anyone occupying their own freehold residence would have either inherited the property (as a member of the landed gentry) or would have purchased a plot on which to have their own house built. The purchaser in 1873 was John Willis Clark the eminent architectural historian, later to become University Registrary. The subject of his purchase was a leasehold interest in 1, Scroope Terrace. Later in the year this same Mr. Clark was to become the unfortunate victim of a cheque forgery, one of his cheques on Mortlock's Bank being presented and cashed in the sum of £200 by one Merry. Acting for the Bank as well as its customer, Clement Francis had to advise both parties with some caution. The restitution to Mr. Clark's bank account was postponed until the offence of forgery was proved at the next assizes. The entitlement to restitution would have been immediate if section 24 of the Bills of Exchange Act 1882 had been in force.

References to educational provision for ladies first appeared in the year 1874, one involving St. John's College in a building agreement described first as "for Ladies Hall", later being identified as "the Newnham Hall Company Limited". Between March and May in the same year a site was acquired for the Trustees of Eden Street Higher Grade School for Girls.

In May 1874 the practice received joint instructions from St. John's College and Trinity College for the preparation of an agreement "... for the construction and maintenance of a footbridge to connect the grounds of the two Colleges", half the costs of the matter being paid by each College. This related to the installation of the iron footbridge between the Backs of these two Colleges, well known ever since to countless Cambridge visitors.

During the summer of 1874 Storey's Charity, the University of Cambridge, Gonville and Caius College and

Trinity Hall were acquired as clients by the practice in quick succession. This appears to have resulted from an untoward professional incident involving a Mr. Crane, described in one entry only the previous year as "the University Solicitor". John William Howard Crane had been admitted in 1844 and was by 1874 practising at 13 Free School Lane. No explanation for this sudden transfer of clients is recorded but two years later the Governors of the Perse School expressed concern over the rent owed to them on the Free School Lane premises by Mr. Crane "in view of his financial difficulties", and negotiations were concluded with Messrs. Peeds the solicitors then acting for him for a surrender of his lease to the landlords.

Some long distance railway travel was enjoyed by one of the clerks to the practice in July 1875 following the death of a member of the Cust family. One of his Executors, the Earl of Mount Edgcumbe was required to swear the probate papers and had to be followed first to Ashburton then to Oakhampton then to Ilfracombe where he eventually "proved the Will".

A concert at the Corn Exchange on 8th November 1875 was the scene of an undergraduate disturbance involving young gentlemen from Christ's, Caius, St. John's and King's Colleges, all of whom had to be defended in Court on breach of the peace charges and worse still, in one case, for "damage to a pair of Trowsers". Meanwhile Mr. Robert Sayle was to increase his growing Cambridge property empire by the purchase of additional premises in Petty Cury with the aid of a mortgage from Clement Francis.

Partnership changes occurred in 1876 with the retirement of Thomas Webster after fifteen years. Musgrave Francis then aged twenty six joined his father and Alfred Riches in partnership and they practised together for three years as Francis Riches and Francis.

Thomas Webster's withdrawal from the partnership at

the age of forty four was not the end of his professional career. It appears that he may already have been practising on his own account from an office in London and it was there that he continued his full-time practice, until his death in 1913 aged eighty. There were numerous occasions after his move when Thomas Webster was entrusted with business to be attended to in London, particularly if the client was Webster's own College, Trinity. To an extent Thomas Webster was overshadowed by his wife Mrs. Augusta Webster (1837–1894) the poet, later accorded an entry in the Dictionary of National Biography. This considered that her verse "... entitles her to a high place among English Poets... she was a warm advocate of women's suffrage... and she sympathized with all movements in favour of a better education for women". Unfortunately Augusta Webster's poetry does not appear to have found its way into any modern anthology.

On 14th February 1876, Clement Francis's third surviving son Walter Hamond Francis, having completed his schooling at Repton, was admitted as a pensioner at Trinity Hall at the age of eighteen. He graduated B.A. in 1880 and proceeded M.A. in 1883. He was to commence his three years' articles with the practice in 1880.

The threat of a new railway line to be constructed through the western side of Cambridge was to pre-occupy the practice and a number of its clients during 1876 and 1877. This was a proposal by the Great Northern Railway Company to build a railway from Shepreth (on their Royston—Cambridge line) northwards as far as March. An urgent request was received by the practice on 17th November 1876 from Messrs. Johnston Farquhar and Leach to complete the Book of Reference for the 15 mile stretch between Shepreth and Cambridge "... by Wednesday next". These instructions involved site visits to identify the land owners along the route of the proposed railway from Shepreth through Haslingfield, Granchester, Histon and Impington to Cottenham. In reporting their findings, considerable misgivings were expressed, according to a bill book entry, on behalf of clients affected by these proposals. Particular mention was made of the closenesss of the proposed line to the Rifle Range and University Observatory "… and the necessity of providing a commodious station". Principal among these concerned clients would have been the University and in March 1877 "our Mr. T. M. Francis" was recorded as having attended at Westminster to lodge a petition in Parliament against the Bill for the Shepreth to March line, only to hear that the Bill had been rejected by the Committee on Standing Orders. Nothing more was to come of this proposal and the vision of a commodious Cambridge West Station (perhaps located in Madingley Road in the vicinity of the present day Churchill College) was lost for ever.

Alfred Smith Riches resigned on 31st December 1878 (after eighteen years) on account of ill-health and died on 2nd June 1879 aged 69.* Clement Francis and his son Musgrave continued together in partnership for a short time under the name Francis and Francis.

The practice was involved from May 1879 on behalf of the University in a dispute with Mr. Bell, the builder of the recently completed Museum of Comparative Anatomy. On cost grounds the floors of the building had been made of concrete instead of wood. The Architect Mr. W. M. Fawcett M.A. declined to issue his final certificate for the building by reason of "… specifications for asphalte floors not having been used". Mr. Bell issued a Writ against the University in respect of his unpaid final instalment on 23rd January 1880. Further negotiations were impeded by the death of an agreed umpire, Mr. Barry, but negotiations involving an

*Two letters were exchanged to record this resignation. The one from Riches began "My Dear Sir," the other from Francis began "My Dear Riches".

arbitrator continued during that year, eventually being settled on the basis that the University, Mr. Bell and Mr. Fawcett were each to contribute one third of the cost of "replacing the concrete floor". This episode is recorded more dramatically by J. Willis Clark (Architectural History of the University of Cambridge 1886) who mentions that part of the roof, also of concrete, suddenly collapsed carrying with it the floors beneath it. As a result of "this deplorable accident…" the concrete floors throughout the whole of the new building were removed and replaced by wood.

Clement Francis had served as Under Sheriff to a number of High Sheriffs of the county during the course of his career. He assumed this position for the last time in 1879 on the appointment of his client W. Parker Hamond as High Sheriff. This involved an attendance on 10th November "… on the Lord Chief Justice on his arrival on Friday evening the 7th instant until his departure this day".

Conspicuous by their absence in the 1879 Bill Book for the first time in 29 years were any entries relating to the Pemberton family. Christopher Robert Pemberton was by this time an invalid and had moved from Newton Hall to take up residence at Fredville Park Kent. In the process he appears also to have changed his Solicitors to a London firm Messrs. Hopgood and Co.

＊　　＊　　＊　　＊

The new decade opened with a sad and unexpected blow for the practice. Clement Francis died from an acute attack of bronchitis at Quy Hall on 7th March 1880 aged 64. This event was recorded in the following press reports.

THE TIMES WEDNESDAY 10TH MARCH 1880
The death is announced of Mr. Clement Francis M.A. the Solicitor

to Cambridge University which occurred somewhat suddenly on Sunday at his private residence Quy Hall, near Cambridge. The deceased was admitted as a Solicitor in Trinity Term 1838. He subsequently graduated at Trinity Hall, proceeding M.A. in 1846. In addition to being Solicitor to the University, Mr. Francis was also the legal adviser to the majority of the various Colleges, and among other public appointments he held was that of Clerk to the Visitors of the Cambridgeshire and Isle of Ely Lunatic Asylum and also Clerk to the Conservators of the River Cam. He was a Deputy Lieutenant for the County of Cambridge and a member of the Council of the Incorporated Law Society. The deceased, who had been ill only a few days, died from an acute attack of bronchitis. He was in his 65th year. The appointment of Solicitor to the University is in the gift of the Vice-Chancellor. Mr. Francis was held in much esteem by his numerous clients.

CAMBRIDGE INDEPENDENT PRESS SATURDAY 13TH MARCH 1880
DEATH OF MR. CLEMENT FRANCIS
We regret to have to record the death of Mr. Clement Francis, M.A., which occurred on Sunday at Quy Hall, after an illness of very short duration. The deceased gentleman has for many years been one of the leading solicitors of this town. He was admitted a solicitor in Trinity Term, 1838 and afterwards entered as a student at Trinity Hall, where he graduated B.A. in 1843 proceeding M.A. in due course. For many years he has enjoyed a lucrative practice, being professional adviser to a majority of the colleges and a few years since was appointed solicitor to the University. Among other public appointments, he held the clerkship to the visitors of the Cambridgeshire and Isle of Ely Lunatic Asylum, and was clerk to the Income Tax Commissioners, and clerk to the Conservators of the Cam. He was a deputy-lieutenant for the county and a member of the Council of the Incorporated Law Society. On several occasions he acted as Under-Sheriff for the counties of Cambridge and Huntingdon. The post of Solicitor to University is in the gift of the Vice-Chancellor. The deceased gentleman was in his 65th year. The funeral took place at Quy on Thursday. The procession left the hall at half-past two. The coffin, a polished oak one, was placed on a wheeled bier and drawn by two of deceased's carriage horses. No pall

was used, but the coffin, besides having beautiful wreaths of flowers, was strewed with snowdrops, violets and other flowers. Next the bier came the deceased's three sons and two daughters, the Rev. T. Shadforth (brother-in-law) his son, F. Parmeter, Esq., (another brother-in-law), the domestic servants, the clerks, and a large number of personal friends of deceased, amongst whom we observed T. Webster, Esq., (formerly a partner with Mr. Francis), the Hon. and Master of Magdalene College, the Rev. the Master of St. Peter's College, Dr. Westmorland, the Rev. A. Rose and Dr. Perkins, bursars of Jesus, Emmanuel and Downing Colleges, Mr. Bumpstead (medical attendant). C. P. Allix, J. H. Wilkinson, E. Shuckburgh, G. Ainslie, C. Mortlock, Esq., the Rev. J. Martin (Cambridge), Messrs. W. C. Ambrose, J. King, Collett, R. Ellis, and other tenants of deceased. In this order the mourners walked through the long avenue in front of the hall, and on emerging from the park they were joined by a very large number of villagers to pay their last respects to deceased, and proceeded to Quy Church. The building is now in progress of restoration, principally through the instrumentality of the deceased, who has taken great interest in the work which he was not permitted to see carried out. Arrangements were, however, made for the coffin to be taken inside the church, where the Funeral Service was read by the Rev. E. Ventris. Much sorrow was visible on all present. The coffin rests in the same vault as that of deceased's aged mother, who died about three months ago. Mr. Sayle, of Cambridge, was the undertaker.

E. H. PARKER, J.P.,

Mayor of Cambridge.

9   Edmund Henry Parker 1858–1928

10   Frank K Peile 1871–1927

11   Number 10 Peas Hill, Cambridge — Practice Office 1914–86

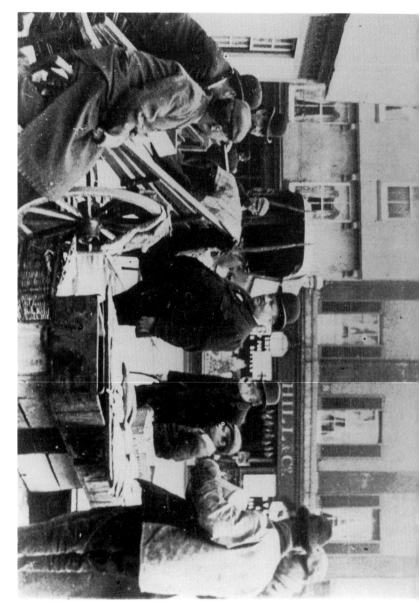

12 Fish market in Peas Hill 1900 — 10 Peas Hill in background

13   The Partners and Staff of Francis & Co. — taken in the garden at 10 Peas Hill, 26th September 1938
(*Left to Right*) *Standing*—P G Wheeler W J Collins R D Charter H G Collin W M Francis D V Durell H Martin A Flack
Seated—J D Pipe S J Dunn J Collin W H Francis C E Woods F Hale S H Hirons

14   The Partners and Staff of Francis & Co. — August 1981 taken in the Fellows Garden at Peterhouse to mark the retirement of B W Cox

Back (L to R)—D Smith P Hallinan J Ladds C E H Jackson D A Cowper D Winning A T Pearce Higgins D C F Hutchinson R Broom R Buttress

Middle (L to R)—Mesdames E Smith D Westwood J Brett P Whitby C Houston B Benton J Walker J Haws L Williams

Front (L to R)—Miss J Nicklinson Miss A Goldstone Mrs D Cant B W Cox D V Durell Miss S Bland Miss L Carter Mrs V Wilson

15   24 Hills Road, Cambridge (Francis House I) — Practice Offices 1986–89

16   112 Hills Road, Cambridge (Francis House II) — Practice Offices from 1989

Chapter 12

PROFESSIONAL INVOLVEMENTS — I
(NINETEENTH CENTURY)

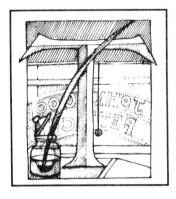

HIS chapter examines the various ways in which members of the practice participated in the life and activities of their profession whether by receiving professional appointments or taking a part in the activities of professional bodies. The two appointments referred to below, being long since defunct, call for lengthy explanation.

Christopher Pemberton—Master extraordinary in Chancery

In his Law List entries from 1796 onwards, Christopher Pemberton was described as "Master Extraordinary in Chancery". This office was a very early forerunner of a Commissioner for Oaths. Masters Extraordinary had acted from time immemorial in the administration of oaths to persons making affidavits for Chancery proceedings. They were appointed to act outside London and as well as taking oaths they sometimes took evidence in the country.

By the end of the 18th century the qualification for a Master Extraordinary was similar to that later required of a Commissioner for Oaths. Gentlemen in the county had to certify that the candidate was a person well qualified for the appointment, well affected towards the Government and that there was a need for such an appointment in the county. This certificate was sent to the Lord Chancellor's secretary who obtained the fiat of the Lord Chancellor. The commission of appointment was then prepared by the Clerk of the Crown. The fee levied on the appointment of a Master Extraordinary at the end of the eighteenth century was £7.0.0. The commission was prepared by the Clerk of the Crown which had to be sworn by the applicant together with an oath of allegiance. According to Edmund Heward, retired Chief Chancery Master writing in 1988,

> "All the early Masters were civilians but after about 1650 barristers were appointed. The Masters Extraordinary were also usually barristers and I am surprised that a solicitor was appointed as early as 1790. Perhaps there were no suitable barristers in Cambridge!"

By 1848, Victorian reforming zeal had caused enquiries and examinations to be made into all aspects of court procedure. According to the Minutes of Evidence before the Select Committee on Fees in Courts of Law and Equity, on 7th January 1848, Mr. Pearce William Rogers (11th Clerk to the Registrars of the Court of Chancery) stated

> "I might also mention that the suitors are frequently occasioned much inconvenience in the country districts, by reason of there being so few Masters Extraordinary for taking affidavits in Chancery, which arises from the fees now levied on the appointment of Master Extraordinary being so high as £8.15s; if this fee was reduced to £1.1s the number of Masters Extra would soon be increased. The fee of 2/6 now taken by them for each Oath might then be reduced to 1/- as at common law".

Christopher Pemberton's appointment remained undisturbed during his lifetime but by the Statute (1853) 16 and 17 Vic c. 78 "An Act relating to the Appointment of Persons to Administer Oaths in Chancery and to Affidavits made for

Purposes connected with Registration [15th August 1853], Section 1 prescribed that

> 'Masters Extraordinary in Chancery shall cease to be so styled and they and all persons hereafter appointed by the Lord Chancellor to administer Oaths in Chancery in England shall be designated; 'Commissioners to administer Oaths in Chancery in England...'".*

The Statutory Declarations Act 1835 had created a new variety of declaration enforced by statutory penalty, but no reform in the administration of statutory declarations was made until the Commissioners for Oaths Act 1889. This allowed the Lord Chancellor to appoint

> "practising solicitors or other fit and proper persons to be Commissioners for Oaths with power in England or elsewhere, to administer any oaths or take any affidavit for the purpose of any Court or matter in England..."

Most partners in the practice held the appointment of Commissioner for Oaths from then until commissioners were themselves rendered largely obsolete by S.81 Solicitors Act 1974 which permitted qualified solicitors holding a practising certificate to exercise the same powers as a Commissioner for Oaths without a formal appointment.

Clement Francis—Perpetual Commissioner

Clement Francis' Law List entries indicate that he held the appointment of Perpetual Commissioner under the Fines and Recoveries Act 1833 and the Married Women's Reversionary Interests Act 1857. "Proper persons" were

---

*Clement Francis had also been admitted as a Master Extraordinary in Chancery on 17th December 1838 and was therefore affected by this change of designation in 1853.

appointed under both acts by the Lord Chief Justice for the purpose of examining any married woman who executed a deed, "separately and apart from her husband" for the purpose of ascertaining and certifying that such woman had executed the deed voluntarily and of her own free will. Acknowledgments by married women were abolished by Section 167 Law of Property Act 1925.

Cambridge Law Society

This society of Cambridge attorneys and solicitors was founded on 1st April 1830 as a meeting point for members of the legal profession. Initially there were nine members, Messrs. Hayward, Twiss, Randall, Foster, Gee, Randall, Harris, Gunning and Cory. The first Chairman of the Society was Mr. Robert Gee and the Treasurer Mr. Foster laid out 8d for a copy book for resolutions and 3d for an account book. The annual subscription was £2.2.0 and fines of 5/- were levied "for inattendance at meetings". In 1831 subscriptions amounting to £18.18.0 were received and fines represented another £14.4.0. Clement Francis joined the Society in May 1842, membership then being only eight and he was already auditing the Society's accounts the following February. Apart from William Woodcock Hayward (d. 1838) Francis John Gunning and Clement Francis the only other member from either practice was William Thrower who joined the Society in 1844. By 1834 the subscription had been reduced to £1.1.0 and subscriptions were not collected at all after 1849, investment income from accrued subscriptions apparently being adequate to pay outgoings, including 7d or 8d for notices to members and two magazine subscriptions.

In 1850 the Society was responsible for sending out eighty three circulars to local solicitors convening a meeting at Cambridge Town Hall on 3rd October "to meet the secretary of the Metropolitan and Provincial Law Association".

This was clearly a meeting intended to canvass support for an association formed three years previously for the purpose of campaigning in the defence of solicitors' rights and interests. Its role at the height of the age of Victorian law reform may be compared to that of the present day British Legal Association, being entirely independent of the activities of the Law Society.

There is little record of activity by the Cambridge Law Society between 1850 and 1866. On 3rd August 1866 the Society was dissolved and the final balance of the Society's funds amounting to £113.3.11d was divided among the five surviving members, H. H. Harris, Clement Francis, John Eaden, H. Gotobed and Ebenezer Foster.

Cambridgeshire was to remain without a local law society until 1871.

The Cambridge and District Law Society

The first General Meeting of the Cambridge and District Law Society (later to be called "The Cambridgeshire and District Law Society") was held at the Lion Hotel, Cambridge, on 8th May 1871 with Mr. Clement Francis in the chair and sixteen other members present. Clement Francis, then a relatively senior solicitor in the Town, aged 56 and admitted for 33 years, was appointed first President of the Society.

At the second Annual General Meeting of the Society held at the Lion Hotel Cambridge on Monday 13th May 1872, Mr. Clement Francis presented his presidential report to the other eighteen members present, the text of which was as follows:

REPORT

It is with much pleasure that I present to the members a report for the past year the first of this Society's existence.

The Society was founded under asupices not all together favourable, some thinking that such an Association was useless and some that it would not be found to work well but I trust that the fact that 48 solicitors out of the 180 (about) within the area have already joined the society is itself sufficient evidence of the general opinion that such an institution is not without its usefulness. In consequence however, of several requests during the year having been received from the Incorporated Law Society of the United Kingdom, the Associated Provincial Law Societies and others to send representatives to meetings in London upon various subjects of great importance, some of which I will hereafter refer to and of the extent and character of the correspondence with members of the Society in different towns within its district to ascertain as far as practicable the opinion of members before taking responsibility of representing them, I have been induced to believe that the advantages of such a Society as this may be further developed by the formation of a Committee, and a scheme on the subject will be laid before the Society for its consideration.

The finances of the Society are I am happy to say in a flourishing state, there being a balance of £75.13.11. in the hands of the Treasurer.

During the past year several questions of importance to the profession have been extensively and prominently discussed. The first of these related to professional remuneration. It will be within the recollection of members that at our first meeting in May last this question was considered and a resolution was passed approving of the scale of the Incorporated Law Society but without recommending it for general adoption. Subsequently to that meeting the Associated Provincial Law Society propagated another scale of rather a lower character which I thought should be circulated and I caused a copy to be sent to every Solicitor in the district. Those Associated Societies moreover invited this Society to send a representative to a Deputation from Provincial Societies, which it was proposed should wait upon the Lord Chancellor to represent to his Lordship the desirability of altering the system of taxing costs; and on 22nd July I as such representative attended the interview with the Lord Chancellor who received the deputation very favourably and promised to give the matter his consideration. The proposals submitted to the Lord Chancellor may be shortly stated as follows:—

First the costs as "between party and party" should be taxed upon the principle now applicable to costs "as between solicitor and Client"

Second, the time of solicitors should be paid for on a more liberal scale than at present.

On the 17th November the Lord Chancellor returned an answer to the statement expressing his disapproval to the proposals so laid before him, but pointing out that the full effect of recent legislation upon the relations between the solicitors and their clients should be allowed more time to develop. The whole question therefore remains exactly where it was at the last General Meeting but the Associated Law Societies' scale is worthy of careful consideration and I think the principles upon which it is based are slowly but gradually making their way into practice.

The foundation of a Central Law University for the Improvement of Legal Education has occupied much of the time of the Law Society of the United Kingdom as well as of various other legal bodies and I attended several meetings at the Law Institution during the discussion of the question where I found an opinion that it would be a very difficult measure to carry into practice, if indeed it was practicable at all. In consequence however, of the defeat of Sir Ronndell Palmer's motion in the House of Commons in the early part of this session, the question is postponed for a time and probably a long time to come and I need not further refer to it now.

The Attorneys' and Solicitors' Act 1871 has partially repealed the provisions which disqualified members of the profession from being appointed County Magistrates but I trust that before long the disqualification of Solicitors for various offices will be still further removed.

The Incorporated Law Society having proposed to increase the numbers of the members of the Council and to double the numbers of Country Members thereon, that the relative proportion of London to Country Members on the Council should more perfectly represent the members of the Society, I attended a meeting at the Institution in support of such a measure so conducive to the interests of Country Solicitors and had the pleasure of assisting to carry a resolution in its favour.

The Court of Chancery Funds Bill is now under the consideration of Parliament; it does not seem to me to be a necessary measure or one which will conduce to the interests of suitors but it will be for the Society to say whether they would take any action in the matter, by Petition or otherwise, for or against the measure.

C. FRANCIS (President)

After discussion the President's report was adopted unanimously and committee members were appointed for the two years ensuing, among them Clement Francis.

A proposition of thanks to the President for his exertions during the past year was carried unanimously.

Six years later, on 13th May 1879, Clement Francis was elected to serve a second time as President but did not live to complete his term of office. This event was reported to the members by the committee at the annual general meeting in 1880. "Your committee regret the loss during the past year of the President of the Society through death".

Musgrave Francis was only an articled clerk at the date of the 1872 meeting, but joined the Society upon his admission as a solicitor in 1874. In 1881, one year after his father's death, Musgrave Francis was himself elected President of the Cambridge and District Law Society at the relatively early age of thirty one.

The Law Society

Clement Francis demonstrated in his 1872 presidential address his active representation of Cambridgeshire solicitors in Law Society affairs during his year in office. In 1873 he was elected to serve as a member of the Council of the Law Society, a position he held until his death. He would have seen at first hand the culmination of many decades of activity in the fields of legal and procedural reform. This reached its peak in 1874 in the unification of all the superior courts within one Supreme Court of Judicature, divided into the Court of Appeal and the High Court of Justice. This measure was given the wholehearted endorsement of the Law Society but Clement Francis did not survive to see the implementation of a further reform which must also have received his full support during its introductory stages. The Solicitors Remuneration Act 1881 introduced a system of scale fee charges for conveyancing work which for the first time carried parliamentary blessing and which was to endure (subject to revisions from time to time) until abolished by the Solicitors Remuneration Order 1972.

One can imagine that Clement Francis also derived some personal satisfaction from sitting on the Council at the same time as his cousin Francis Bircham (Council member 1863–79) and of seeing him elected President of the Law Society 1874–75. The two Gunning articled clerks had both come a long way from the modest office in Trinity Street forty years before.

Chapter 13

THE FRANCIS FAMILY SUCCEEDS

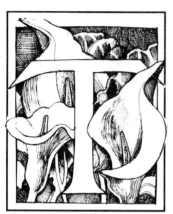

HE unexpected death of his father on 7th March 1880 put Musgrave Francis in a difficult position. By now aged thirty he had been a practising solicitor for six years, two of those in partnership. He may have acquired adequate experience and knowledge for the needs of his major clients but there must have been moments when he would have dearly wished for the greater stature which added years would have bestowed upon him, particularly in his professional dealings with clients of standing such as the University Vice-Chancellor, the partners of Mortlock's Bank and the bursars of eleven Colleges. Only two years previously this clientele had been served by a three partner firm, now Musgrave Francis was on his own and needed help. His brother Walter Hamond Francis, eight years his junior, had joined the practice the previous year but he was as yet only an articled clerk, with two years still to serve, so effective help from that direction was therefore some way off. Dr. Bond, Master of Trinity Hall, was aware of the predicament and was instrumental in introducing Musgrave Francis to an exceptionally able and highly appropriate candidate to fill the gap. This was a newly admitted twenty-two year old solicitor, Edmund Parker.

Edmund Henry Parker had been born on 21st April 1858, the younger son of a Lincolnshire clergyman. An elder brother, Robert John Parker, was a scholar of Eton and a scholar and fellow of Kings College. In 1913 Robert Parker was to achieve high judicial rank as a Lord of Appeal in Ordinary with the title of Lord Parker of Waddington. Edmund, too, achieved some academic distinction as a scholar of Westminster School but was then articled for five years with a solicitors' firm in Lincoln, his fifth year being spent in a London office. Edmund Parker dearly wished to achieve the same academic distinction as his elder brother but could only take up a place at King's if he found employment to support himself during his undergraduate studies. Thus employment in the practice by Thomas Musgrave Francis in 1880 allowed Edmund Parker to matriculate in 1882 and to enter King's College in 1883. In June 1885 he was equal First in the First Class list of the Law tripos and was elected a scholar of King's College. Musgrave Francis must have greeted the arrival of this young assistant with relief and would have quickly recognised his manifold abilities.

The title to this chapter also reflects a further family involvement in the practice following the death of Clement Francis, who, as has already been mentioned, by his Will appointed his wife Sarah to be his sole Executrix and universal beneficiary. She inherited the Quy Hall Estate but was also now possessed of the Emmanuel Street premises, continuing as tenant of Emmanuel College until her death in 1897. There are no signs of untoward matriarchial influence, but the fact remains that the senior partner of the practice did not have any recognisable legal interest in the premises for a period of seventeen years until he inherited the lease from his mother.

It must stand to the credit of Musgrave Francis and those who helped him carry on, that the practice was quick to recover from the severe blow of bereavement, apparently without loss of clients, yet this would not have been possible without a loyal and sympathetic clientele. By the start of the year 1881 this included the University and eleven colleges, Downing, Emmanuel, Gonville and Caius, Jesus, Magdalene, Pembroke, Peterhouse, St. John's, Sidney, Trinity and Trinity Hall, as well as Mortlock and Co., Bankers, the Visitors of Fulbourn Asylum and the Conservators of the River Cam.

For the next seven years the practice continued under the name Francis and Francis, although a bill submitted to the Vice-Chancellor in 1880 following a bye-election in the University Parliamentary constituency bore the name of the sole principal "Mr. T. Musgrave Francis".

Musgrave Francis soon had to assume a senior role. In 1880 St. John's College became involved in a dispute with railway promoters undertaking the construction of the Hundred of Hoo Railway from the existing London–Rochester line at Higham Junction in Kent through college land to Port Victoria and Allhallows on Sea. The College disputed the adequacy of accommodation works to be provided through their lands and in October that year Musgrave Francis and the Senior Bursar journeyed to Rochester to attend a meeting of the Higham Common Commmissioners to discuss matters still at issue. In March the following year a writ was issued against the Railway Company claiming specific performance of their fencing obligation.

However, after long negotiations between the parties a settlement out of Court was reached in 1882 based on a repositioning of a culvert. Exchanges of correspondence were, however, still continuing in December 1882, seeking to complete the sale and release the money.

As a result of the introduction of the Copyhold Enfranchisement Bill in Parliament in June 1881 Musgrave Francis visited a total of eight College Masters or Bursars with reference to this Bill and informed each of them

> "... that in our opinion it was very prejudicial to the rights of manorial property and we proposed a Petition to Parliament against it". (Petitions were duly drawn up and presented). "... the Bill was subsequently withdrawn".

In the same year the Food Reform Stores of Cambridge were threatened with proceedings for infringement of the trade mark "Keiler and Son" on certain marmalade. Arrangements had to be made for an apology to be given together with an undertaking not to repeat the infringement. This appears to be the earliest recorded instance of the practice dealing with a threatened passing-off action concerning what would now be described as "intellectual property".

In 1882 Walter Hamond Francis aged twenty-four, completed his articles, passed the Solicitors final examination and was admitted to the Roll of Solicitors. He worked in the practice as an assistant solicitor for the next five years before being taken into partnership. In the same year work started on the last railway line to be built through Cambridgeshire, linking Cambridge with Mildenhall. The line passed through the Quy Estate and the Bill Book for this year records a sale of land by Mrs. Francis to the Great Eastern Railway, also mentioning the possibility of a station and the need to seek a level crossing. Both these items were to be provided, according to Peter Turner (*By Rail to Mildenhall*, 1978),

"Stow cum Quy Station... was some considerable way from the village, one mile north from the centre in fact. Outside Quy Station was another level crossing. The station itself possessed only one platform which was looped onto the line. A dock or bay was at the back of the platform, used mainly in latter years for loading sugar beet".

Sales to the Great Eastern Railway by various owners along the Mildenhall line continued during 1883, the first section of the line between Cambridge and Fordham being opened for passenger traffic on Monday 2nd June 1884. In the same year the four-year old dispute between St. John's College and the Hundred of Hoo Railway in Kent was finally concluded.

Activity for Mortlock's Bank during the year 1884 included the completion of a mortgage advance to Selwyn College which had been founded two years previously and the buildings for which were then in course of construction.

Robert Sayle, a long-standing client of the practice also died early in 1884. His Cambridge properties, mostly located on the west side of St. Andrew's Street and including the site of the present day department store were sold by public auction at the Red Lion, Petty Cury on 3rd June 1884, Musgrave Francis attending at the auction with two clerks to assist him in the completion of the contracts. Twenty-three of the twenty-four lots offered were sold for a total of £14,452. Most of the properties were leaseholds held either from Jesus or Corpus Christi Colleges and among the successful purchasers of these premises appear Cambridge Permanent Benefit Building Society and Messrs. Joshua Taylor, Cole, Chalk and Thoday. Upon the completion of these sales bills were delivered to the executors on the basis of charging newly introduced in 1881, "according to scale fee".

Robert Sayle's own drapery and outfitting business was sold, following the grant of a licence to assign to Mr. Clarke and Mr. Porter of "the Messuage, Shops Warehouses and Premises in St. Andrews Street, Cambridge", for a consideration of £145,000. The sale was completed in July 1885 but the purchasers returned on 30th September complaining

> "... that they suffered much inconvenience by Mr. G. M. Sayle using the title of R. Sayle and Son whereas they had purchased the goodwill of the business for £5,000... we recommended a friendly letter should be first written him on the subject and if that did not produce the required effect a carefully worded circular should be issued to the trade and your correspondents generally".

A century later the successors to Robert Sayle's business do not appear to have suffered any serious consequences from this initial name rivalry.

The practice was also involved the same year for Jesus College in the grant of a lease of a builders yard and premises in Station Road and Hills Road, Cambridge for forty years from 25th March 1885 to George Kett and others. This lease related to the yard and works of the long-established Cambridge builders Messrs. Rattee and Kett, the site later being occupied by the modern Kett House. Rattee and Kett were to commence work the same year on a well-known Cambridge landmark, the Catholic Church at the corner of Hills Road and Lensfield Road.

Advice was called for by Messrs. Mortlock and Co. in June 1885 concerning one of their Bank clerks who

> "... had informed them of his intention to marry a widow who was believed to have considerable property and that they had taken Mr. Whitmore's house at Trumpington but that it had been found just before the marriage proposed took place that the lady would lose her

money if she married again and that they nevertheless had gone to
live together and that she had driven him down to the Bank in her
pony and carriage and we advised that this misconduct entitled you
to dismiss the clerk without notice".

The dismissal took place and caused protests "from the
clerk and from his solicitor Mr. Lyon"who appeared to have
gained the impression that his client had been dismissed for
having taken too large a house. One of the Bank's partners
Mr. Ainslie was at some pains to explain that

"the reason given for his dismissal was not for living in too large a
house but was for living with the lady in question which he did not
deny and we advised that as he had been engaged to be married as he
himself had stated to you and as he was living with the person to whom
he was engaged the only inference to be drawn in our opinion was
quite sufficient to entitle you to discharge him at once...".

Embarrassment of a different kind must have been
caused the same year when the Bank reported that another
firm of solicitors Messrs. Fosters and Lawrence had exceeded their permitted overdraft and had been asked for
the provision of additional security. The practice was asked
to investigate the properties available for the purpose and
the situation was saved partly by additional mortgages and
partly from proceeds of sale. Such close examination of the
financial affairs of a competitor practice must have been of
more frequent occurrence in the days of single-branch
Banks with only one firm of solicitors acting for them.

*Under Sheriff for Cambridgeshire and Huntingdon**
Musgrave Francis was appointed Under Sheriff for the
counties of Cambridge and Huntingdon on 12th March

*Alone among the counties of England and Wales, Cambridgeshire and Hunting-
donshire had long shared a single High Sheriff.

1885 by the High Sheriff John Carbery Evans of Hatley Park. Christopher Pemberton and Clement Francis had also held this appointment before him and his nephew Walter Maclaren Francis was to serve as Under Sheriff as recently as the year 1958. The detailed surviving record of his activities provides a useful insight into the requirements and demands of the office and deserves close examination.

At the start of his year, Musgrave Francis was involved in the preparation of formal appointments for himself and his High Sheriff, the appointment of Sheriff's Officers for Huntingdon and the Isle of Ely, preparation of a Power of Attorney from the High Sheriff to authorise the execution of his duties and filing these appointments with the Clerks of the Peace for Cambridge, Huntingdon and the Isle of Ely. Lists of jurors had to be compiled and selected for the needs of three levels of Court and at three separate locations—the Assizes, the Quarter Sessions and the Petty Sessions at Cambridge, Huntingdon and Ely; the Assizes and the Quarter Sessions sat four times a year in each location and they required juror provision accordingly; the appointment of a Sheriff's deputy in London had also to be made and Messrs. Cole and Jackson, the London Agents for the practice at this time, were selected for the purpose; arrangements for the arrival, lodging and departure of the Assize Judges in the three towns had to be attended to at quarterly intervals; in the case of Cambridge this required advance notice to the Vice-Master of Trinity that the accommodation in the Master's Lodge would be required, arranging for the Judge's Service at Great St. Mary's Church and for "footmen buglers and bellringers" to be in attendance, quite apart from the personal attendance of the Under Sheriff throughout; further duties during the year involved the receipt and posting of Royal Proclamations issued from time to time; one of these involved "calling out the Reserves and Militia", another referred unaccountably to "A New Coin for British Honduras". Other notices announced the prorogation and dissolution of Parliament. The failure of the parties to agree to compensation for acquisition of land for railway purposes at Ramsey led to the provision of a special jury for the purposes of attending an enquiry and determining the compensation. At least Musgrave Francis was spared attendance at the County Gaol in Cambridge to witness a hanging during his year in office. His successor was not so fortunate and was required to attend the execution of one Robert Browning on 14th December 1886.

Over and above all these activities the Under Sheriff was fully engaged in the preparation, conduct and aftermath of the General Election called for 1st December 1885. Musgrave Francis had overall responsibility for four county constituencies and immediate responsibility for three in Cambridgeshire—The Western or Chesterton Division, The Eastern or Newmarket Division and the Northern or Wisbech Division. Responsibility for the Huntingdon constituency was allocated to a deputy Mr. Bird. The General Election of 1885 was the last in which the Under Sheriffs of counties acted as registration officers and held responsibility for making all electoral arrangements. Three years later with the creation of county councils, for the first time the function of registration officer passed to the Clerks of the County Councils—(Local Government Act 1888).

Musgrave Francis needed all the help he could get between August 1885 and the December polling day to engage poll clerks, presiding officers, counting clerks and to hire polling stations and screens in numerous village locations throughout the three constituencies. This was the third General Election in which secrecy was observed in voting since its introduction in 1872. A high demand for screens as well as for village polling stations resulted from the extension of the Parliamentary vote to all householders in County constituencies without a property qualification in 1884. For the first time agricultural labourers were able to vote. At Castle Camps, a remote corner of South East Cambridgeshire, the Under Sheriff recorded

"Journey to Castle Camps for purpose of engaging polling place and poll clerk when we found there was a good school room but no schoolmaster to act as poll clerk, there being only a school mistress".

Furthermore, the Corrupt Practices Act 1883 had for the first time introduced severe restraints upon all irregular electoral practices from personation through bribery to excessive expenditure. The Under Sheriff too was faced with a very exact set of requirements to be observed with regard to locked ballot boxes, numbered voting papers and supervision at all stages from polling stations through the transport of the filled ballot boxes to the count. Even printing of ballot papers could provide a headache, as recorded on 21st November,

"Attending printer on his bringing ballot papers when we found the spaces for the two candidates names were uneven and we informed him we could not accept them unless the agent who represented the lower name consented to do so; attending Mr. Wayman when he considered the unevenness would act against Mr. Hall and he could not take the responsibility of consenting to them. Attending printer informing him of our interview with Mr. Wayman and giving instructions to have ballot papers printed afresh".

The Under Sheriff was also required to attend at the delivery of nominations for candidates and to receive their deposits (£275 at that time) these being paid into an election account at Mortlock's Bank.

The result of the 1885 General Election was a defeat for Mr. Gladstone and his Liberal administration by a narrow margin. The Conservatives briefly assumed power with

Lord Salisbury as Prime Minister. Mr. Hall, the successful Conservative candidate, entered Parliament for the first time as M.P. for the Chesterton Division of Cambridgeshire, perhaps thankful that the ballot papers had been "printed afresh".*

✳   ✳   ✳   ✳

Advice given to the University Vice-Chancellor in July 1885 concerned the remaining criminal jurisdiction of the University. This foreshadowed the serious controversy concerning this issue which six years later was to shake the

---

*The staff of Francis and Francis also appeared satisfied with the whole episode as the following testimonial indicates:

TO T. Musgrave Francis Esq.,
              Solicitor,
                      Cambridge
Sir,

We the undersigned your Staff of Clerks beg you to accept the accompanying Inkstand as a small token of our heartfelt regard towards you and in gratitude for the many kindnesses we all acknowledge to have received at your hands from your first becoming the head of the Firm and especially for the great liberality shown to us in the recent Parliamentary Election which kindness and liberality will never be forgotten by any of us.

Some of us have had the honour as well as the pleasure of having served for many years under your late lamented Father than whom no finer Gentleman (in all that is embodied in that name) ever existed and we are thankful that his Mantle has fallen on a Son so well worthy to wear it and may you long continue head of that Firm honoured and respected as it ever has been and with our fervent wish for your future health and happiness and for all bearing the name of Francis.

              Believe us to remain,
              Yours ever faithfully,
                      Richard Looker
                      Edward Heath Sanders
                      Thos. H. J. Porter
                      Edwin Juffs
                      Willm. S. Darby
                      F. A. Hook
                      C. E. Levett
Cambridge   24th December 1885

accord between town and university to its very foundations,

> "July 11th—Perusing and considering letter to the Vice-Chancellor from the Home Secretary in respect of the criminal jurisdiction of the Vice-Chancellor of Oxford and draft bill to amend the summary jurisdiction of the Acts of '79 and '84 in relation to the Vice-Chancellor's Court. Also a short memorandum on the subject and draft of proposed bill.
> "Engaged the whole morning investigating the magisterial powers of the Vice-Chancellor. Attending at his lodge advising that the eighteenth section of the Award Act had taken away his powers in all matters in which either party was not a member of the University but powers of imprisoning prostitutes were conferred by Charter and confirmed by Statute in the reign of Queen Elizabeth and these Powers remained in full force as we showed in the case of Kemp v. Neville but we pointed out that they were exercisable by the Vice-Chancellor not as a Magistrate but as a University Officer though we thought a clause might be introduced into the present Bill to the effect that nothing contained in the two Acts referred to should control or affect the powers of the Vice-Chancellor and it was decided that we should express our opinion by letter. Writing the Vice-Chancellor long letter accordingly."

The year 1886 saw the first of many attempts by the trustees of the late Rev. J. Hailstone to sell Anglesey Abbey. Nowadays a well-known National Trust house just outside the village of Lode, this remnant of an ancient priory had been purchased by the Vicar of Bottisham, Rev. John Hailstone in 1861 and had been restored and converted for use as his residence. Following his death in 1871 the house was clearly too large for his widow who eventually moved to 11 Scroope Terrace, Cambridge, in 1887. The bill books from 1886 onwards record various attempts to dispose of the empty and steadily deteriorating mansion but considerable reluctance seems to have been displayed both by the trustees and various intending purchasers to agree a satisfactory price. Eventually the property was purchased in 1926 by an

American millionaire, Huttleston Broughton (later Lord Fairhaven), who spent the next forty years in a lavish restoration of the house and grounds to their present state. Anglesey Abbey passed to the National Trust on the death of Lord Fairhaven in 1966.

Much consternation was caused to several land-owning clients in 1886 by the proposal of the Cambridge Town and University Water Works Company to obtain parliamentary powers for the establishment of a one hundred foot deep well at Fulbourn to improve the water supply for the Town of Cambridge. The practice was engaged on behalf of four clients, the Visitors of the Lunatic Asylum, Mrs. Francis, Mrs. Hailstone and the Surveyors of the Parish of Fulbourn in unsuccessful opposition to the passage of the bill through Parliament. Then negotiations took place with the Company's Solicitor Mr. Peed to obtain modifications and variations to the proposed works or for compensation in lieu. In the case of the Quy Estate this claim was based on Mr Bidwell's opinion

"... that if the water was diminished to a great extent injury to the simple and marketable value of the estate would amount to some £1,000".

Eventually the company was prevailed upon to pay £1,200 and expenses to Mrs. Francis on the footing that the bill would be allowed to pass through Parliament unopposed.

The advancing powers of local authorities in the later nineteenth century were reflected in their financial demands on ratepayers. This trend was illustrated in 1886 when a request for advice was received from the University as to the rating of the "Mechanical Museum". Advice was given to the effect that

"... if a profit was made from the works it would be necessary merely to include such a profit with those of the Press and Local Examinations. Probably the building would be exempt if used as a workshop; ... the Fitzwilliam Museum not being a Museum of Science but Art was rated £1,000 but the Archaeology Museum being considered a lecture room was exempted from rates...".

In February 1886 Trinity College sought advice as to an allegation received from the Post Master General's department that the messenger service provided by Trinity and many other colleges was infringing the monopoly of the General Post Office:

"... attending at Library searching Law Lexicons and other books endeavouring to find some legal definition of the term letter; instructions to Counsel Sir Richard Webster to advise... 5th April travel to London... 5th June considering Opinion of Sir Richard Webster...".

The advice received from Sir Richard Webster and Mr. Graham, after a full review of the statutory authorities, was that

"there was no doubt or difficulty in placing this interpretation on the act now that postal districts post offices and letter boxes have been so multiplied and having regard to the ambiguous language used and the serious nature of the penalties we could not advise the College to continue the collection and distribution of letters without first obtaining a judicial decision upon the point which might be done by stating a special case and we think the College would be quite justified in submitting this for the decision of the Court if they desire to contest the question on the above basis".

This opinon was considered by a sub-committee of representatives from Trinity, St. John's, King's, Christ's, Caius, Emmanuel, Pembroke, Corpus, Trinity Hall and Selwyn Colleges. They felt it inadvisable to submit a special case for the decision of the Court as suggested by counsel. However, they noted counsel's suggestion that much of the need for an inter-college messenger service would be removed if members of colleges were encouraged to use the full address (Court, Staircase, Lodging etc.) of each addressee, leaving the Post Office to make their own deliveries direct to individual rooms. They further recommended that a list should be published on an annual basis containing full addresses of resident members, to be undertaken by a local printer "as a matter of business and without expense to the Colleges".

As a result the full messenger service provided for all college members throughout the University was substantially curtailed. The legal costs of £55.7.0d. incurred were split between those ten Colleges involved in this legal consultation.

The reader is left to speculate as to the precise role played in this episode by one of the University M.P.'s, Rt. Hon. Henry Cecil Raikes M.A., himself a member of Trinity College, who commenced a five-year period in office as Postmaster General in 1886.

On 1st January 1887 Walter Hamond Francis and Edmund Henry Parker, both 29 years old, were admitted into Partnership with Thomas Musgrave Francis and the three partners practised together for the next year and nine months as Francis, Francis and Parker.

In 1882 fellows of all Cambridge Colleges save one were permitted to marry without forfeiting their fellowships, the exception being Gonville and Caius College, whose fellows had been permitted to marry from 1860 onwards. In consequence there was a perceptible increase in the demand for family homes in Cambridge. One sign of this, in 1887, was the involvement of the practice in procedures for the laying out of Tenison Road for Jesus College "in conjunction with the Town Surveyor". Meanwhile St. John's was involved in the grant of a building lease of 1.5 acres of building land at the end of Thompson's Lane. Fifty homes were to be built at a cost of not less than £120 for detached and £100 for terraced houses. An even more extensive tract of open land in West Cambridge was to be set aside by St. John's College for residential use, resulting in the development of Mount Pleasant and a rectangle enclosed by Madingley Road, Grange Road, Herschel Road and Wilberforce Road.

Mysteriously coded entries appeared in the bill book between 17th May and 15th August 1887. Under the heading "M. and A.", entries such as "attending M", "telegram to C", "journey to London" and "attending Mr. C. receiving three boxes" all refer to an unfortunate and potentially damaging dispute which had arisen between the two partners in Mortlock's Bank, Edmund John Mortlock and Gilbert Ainslie. In a matter so sensitive to the fortunes of the Bank the highest degree of secrecy was essential. Matters clearly went from bad to worse for M. and A. By 28th April 1888 it was noted

"Attending at the Bank the greater part of the day owing to threatened run. Journey to London to obtain cash from S. P. and S"

(this being Smith Payne and Smith's Bank at 1 Lombard Street, Mortlock's London agents).

The remaining entries relevant to this episode record further time spent at the Bank on 2nd and 3rd May, a visit to the Cambridge Chronicle Office, a journey to London to interview Mr. Casson, and two weeks later an attendance to all the formalities necessary for the dissolution of the partnership, affidavits being sworn and notices inserted in the newspaper and the London Gazette. The events which followed this serious blow to the standing of Mortlock's Bank were recorded in a memoir on Edmund Henry Parker published after his death in the Cambridge Review (12th October 1928),

"In 1888 Mortlock's Bank was in some difficulty and Mr. Mortlock decided to determine his then partnership and seek a new partner; he asked Mr. Francis to join him but the latter suggested Edmund Parker, whose great banking career thus began. He shortly afterwards married Ellen Francis. They lived for some time over the Bank, and his close attention to its affairs speedily raised it to a position such that when in 1896 it was absorbed in the great joint stock undertaking of Barclay & Company, he became one of the original twenty Directors of that concern".

Edmund Parker's move from the law to banking appears to have taken place on a date convenient in accounting terms to both partnerships—1st October 1888. Edmund Parker soon adapted to his new role as an important client of the practice. By 17th October that year he had evidently formed a view of the standard banking forms employed by his Company,

"October 17th Attending Mr. Parker on his giving us instructions to prepare three forms of security to retain at the Bank viz

a)   Memorandum of Deposit of Title Deeds to secure account current etc.
b)   Ditto Bonds and Stock Certificates.
c)   Assignment of Policy of Assurance.

Drawing three forms accordingly; fair copies thereof.

November 10th Attending Mr. Parker therewith when it was decided they should be printed and he would let us know how many copies".

Thus separated from Edmund Parker by his retirement from the partnership yet closely allied to him by family ties and daily business contacts, the two Francis brothers were to continue together in partnership for the next ten years, reviving once more the use of the firm name Francis and Francis.

Chapter 14

A TRIO OF PARTNERS'
WEDDINGS 1888–98

I. EDMUND PARKER

HE crisis in the affairs of Mortlock's Bank in the early part of 1887 took place during the period of Edmund Parker's engagement to Ellen Francis, a sister of his two partners Musgrave and Walter Francis. Their wedding was celebrated at Quy Parish Church on 1st August 1888. This event was reported in the Cambridge Chronicle the following Friday

MARRIAGE OF MISS E. FRANCIS OF QUY HALL

On Wednesday last Miss Ellen Francis of Quy Hall was married to Mr. Edmund Henry Parker of Cambridge the third son of the late Rev. Richard Parker of Claxby Rectory, Lincolnshire. The ceremony was fixed for 2 o'clock at which hour the bridegroom accompanied by his best man Mr. Harman arrived from Cambridge but owing to the delay with regard to the bride's and bridesmaids' bouquets which had to come from London, the service was not commenced until nearly a quarter to three. Beautiful arches of evergreens and flowers had been placed by Miss Ellis, Miss Collett and other kind friends over the gate of the avenue leading to Quy Hall and over the entrance to the Churchyard while the inside of the Church was also prettily decorated by the same ladies, a noticeable feature being an arrangement of lilies and maidenhair ferns inside the centre arch of the chancel screen. The bride who wore a handsome dress of plain ivory cord silk and a tulle veil fastened with orange blossom, her only ornaments being a diamond pin (the gift of the bridegroom) and a pearl pendant (the gift of her brother) was accompanied to the Church by her Mother, Mrs. Clement Francis who gave her away. The carriage was met at the churchyard gate by Mr. T. Musgrave Francis and Captain W. Francis and the bride was conducted by the former to the chancel steps being joined at the porch by her four bridesmaids— Miss Parker (sister of the bridegroom) Miss Sawrey-Cookson, Miss Mabel Hichens and Miss Mortlock. The bridesmaids were dressed in cream coloured surah silk with bonnets to match and carried bouquets of Marechal Niel roses and brown leaves presented by the bridegroom. The Church was crowded in every part with invited guests and with the parishioners, places being reserved for Mrs. Alexander and the other servants from the house who arrived in a Break and who wore bouquets supplied from Cambridge. The service which was partly choral Miss Ellis playing the harmonium, was conducted by the Vicar, the Rev. S. Watson and the Rev. J. S. Warren of Willoughby Rectory, Lincolnshire, the latter giving a short telling address in lieu of the usual exhortation. On leaving the Church the bride and bridegroom were preceded to their carriage by a selected number of school children who strewed the path from the porch to the gate with flowers and rose-leaves, the rest of the company following them to Quy Hall where light refreshments were served. They left for Cambridge at 4 o'clock to catch the 4.45 G.E.R. train for London en route for Scotland where the honeymoon is to be passed. Before they started a good photograph of the wedding group and of several of the guests was taken by Mr. Stearn of Cambridge. The bride's travelling dress was of grey cloth tailor made with a light bonnet. After the departure of the bride and bridegroom the guests proceeded to inspect the numerous wedding presents which were laid out in the upper part of the house, and of which a list is subjoined.

At half past six the villagers were entertained at tea by Mrs. Francis and about 300 persons sat down to an excellent repast served by Mr. G. Apthorpe of Cambridge in a large marquee which had been provided for the purpose. In the course of tea a letter was read from the bride (whose bouquet was placed on the centre table) conveying her warm thanks for the dining room clock which had been presented to her on Monday evening by "the cottagers of Quy". The letter was responded to by three hearty cheers for Mr. and Mrs. Edmund Parker. After tea the Fordham Band played a good selection of music and there was some dancing on the grass which however was not in very good condition for the amusement owing to the wet. The proceedings were brought to a close with a brilliant display of fireworks at 9 p.m. after which the band played God Save the Queen and the company separated with three cheers for Mrs. Francis.

The weather throughout the day was not propitious but the rain which had fallen heavily in the morning stopped just before the bride arrived at the Church and the evening was fine though cold."
[The wedding presents included:—

Mr. J. Collin	2 tall glass vases.
Mr. R. Looker	
Mr. E. H. Sanders.	
Mr. T. H. J. Porter.	
Mr. T. Horner.	
Mr. E. Juffs.	
Mr. W. S. Darby and	
C. Levett, the Staff	
at 17 Emmanuel Lane,	4 Handsome silver dessert spoons.
The servants at 17 Emmanuel Lane	
Mrs. Clement Francis	A pair of vases.
(to the Bride)	A gold watch and a piano;
(to the Bridegroom)	A gold watch-chain.
Mr. T. Musgrave Francis.	A pearl pendant and gold chain, a gold snake bracelet and a Dinner Service.
Captain and Mrs. W. Francis.	A gold bracelet and a silver Muffineer.
Mr. W. H. Francis.	A revolving breakfast dish and four silver salt cellars.
Mr. E. H. Parker (To the Bride)	Diamond ring.

Among the numerous other donors of wedding presents were local solicitors Mr. J. Eaden, Mr. Evans, Mr. Peed, Mr. Whitehead and Mr. Guy W. Stanley]

II. JOHN COLLIN

Among the guests at the wedding at Quy on 1st August 1888 was a twenty-one year old articled clerk from the practice, John Collin. Born in Cambridge on 10th October 1866, he was the son of William Collin, coal, deal, timber and slate merchant of 54 Castle Street and his wife Anne (nee Garrett). Educated at the Perse School he then entered St. John's College, matriculating in 1884, graduating B.A. in 1877 and proceeding M.A. in 1891. A keen oarsman, Collin had stroked Lady Margaret 1st VIII in the May Races in 1886 and 1888, rowing bow in 1887 and stroking the eight which won the Thames Cup and the Ladies Plate at Henley in 1888. He was also a leading member of one of the town clubs, the Rob Roy Boat Club and acted as their coach for a number of seasons. His involvement with the Rob Roy Club and the Cambridgeshire Rowing Association lasted for nearly sixty years.

John Collin appears to have started his articles with the practice in January 1888 and after serving three years he was admitted as a solicitor in 1891. It seems safe to assume that he was articled initially to Edmund Parker and that he was left without a principal when Edmund Parker retired from the practice to join Mortlock's Bank in October 1888. This would certainly account for the execution of further articles of Clerkship with Walter Hamond Francis on 20th February 1889 and these were submitted for registration accompanied by a petition supported by a statutory declaration. The London agents were asked to ascertain whether having regard to the note in the margin of the further articles it would be possible for Mr. Collin "... to go in for his intermediate in June". The marginal note no longer survives but is likely to have mentioned the unexpected retirement of his principal which would have resulted in a technical loss of several months service under articles.

After his admission in 1891 John Collin remained with the practice as an assistant solicitor, joining the partnership on 1st January 1898. The practice name was then changed to Francis Francis and Collin.

The wedding of the newly admitted partner took place that spring as reported in the Cambridge Chronicle on 29th April 1898,

The marriage of Miss Kate Tearle younger daughter of the late Reverend Tearle vicar of Gazeley and Kentford and rural dean with Mr John Collin M.A. of the firm of Francis Francis and Collin took place on Thursday 14th April 1898 at St. Mary's Church, Barton Mills. The service was performed by Rev. Tullett. The church was filled with friends and well-wishers. The bride who was given away by her brother wore a gown of cream satin brocade with tulle veil and real orange blossom and white heather. She carried a lovely shower bouquet and wore a pearl and gold necklace, the gift of the bridegroom. The three bridesmaids were Miss Tearle, Miss Munt and Miss Hammond the best man was Mr. Loftus Bushe-Fox.

The bride and bridegroom left at 4.45 for London en route for South Devon. The bride travelled in a coat and skirt of electric blue with vest of cream mousseline de soie and lace black straw hat trimmed with pink hyacinths.

[Among the wedding presents were

    W. H. Francis Silver tea pot

    T. M. Francis Silver Salver and sugar basin]

III. WALTER HAMOND FRANCIS

The path of Walter Hamond Francis to the altar closely matched that of his articled clerk John Collin, his junior by nine years. He married two months after John Collin in 1898. Walter Francis was also keenly involved in a spare time activity of his own, that of a volunteer soldier. In following his father Clement and his elder brother Musgrave into the legal profession, Walter Francis may have been no less attracted by the example of his next elder brother Wolstan, three years his senior, who after leaving Eton had chosen a military career. By 1888 a captain in the Duke of Cornwall's Light Infantry he had already seen active service in the Egyptian campaign of 1882, including the battle of Tel-el-Kebir. During his University career the activities of the University Rifle Volunteers must have caught the attention of Walter Francis and he enrolled as a member. The University Rifle Volunteers and their town equivalent the Cambridge Rifle Volunteers had both originated from an earlier organisation, the Cambridge Rifle Club. This had been formed on 6th May 1859 during a wave of patriotic fervour which had swept the country during the late eighteen fifties. Following the Indian Mutiny in 1857 it was realised that Britain's small regular army needed support in a home defence role from trained part-time volunteer forces. Clement Francis had been present at the meeting in Cambridge Town Hall in 1859 when the Rifle Club had been founded and had taken part in the proceedings. By 1888 Walter Francis had acquired a commission in a Militia unit, the 4th Battalion Suffolk Regiment, which was to become part of the Territorial Force in the army reforms of 1908. He later rose to the rank of Captain in this Battalion, attending their drills, parades and summer camps for a number of years, eventually being promoted to the rank of Honorary Major. He again became active in this Battalion during the First World War.

As a bachelor, Walter Francis resided first in the family town house at 17 Emmanuel Street, later finding himself rooms at 4a Kings Parade. By 1895 he was resident in a terraced house, 107 Hills Road, and was still living there at the time of his marriage three years later.

The wedding of Walter Hamond Francis to a Scottish bride took place north of the border on 28th June 1898 and was recorded in the Cambridge Chronicle on 1st July 1898, as follows:

The Marriage of Mr. Walter Francis and Miss A. P. Maclaren was solemnized on Tuesday at Claremont Church, Glasgow. Mr. T. M. Francis and Mr. Walter H. Francis left Cambridge on Monday morning early and stayed the night in Edinburgh at the home of Mrs. Urquhart, sister of the bride, proceeding to Glasgow by train on Tuesday morning. Miss Francis went to Glasgow direct from London and stayed at Dr. Maclaren's residence. The ceremony was fixed to take place at 2.30 and the bride arrived to the moment, the bridegroom being in his place one minute before. The church was tastefully decorated with flowers, the hymns used were The Voice that Breathed O'er Eden to a special tune—O Perfect Love. The service was conducted by Rev. Dr. McEwen assisted by the Rev. Dr. Boyd uncle of the bride. A reception was held immediately afterwards at Dr. Maclaren's house.

The bride's dress was of white satin trimmed with real Brussels lace and she carried a shower bouquet of white lilies and white carnations the gift of the bridegroom.

The bridesmaids were Miss E. and Miss M. Maclaren, Miss Paton and Miss K. Boyd, their dresses were of white muslin with lace insertion. They carried shower bouquets of pink roses and each wore a gold bracelet also gifts of the bridegroom.

Mr. and Mrs. Walter H. Francis left at 4.20 for Callander the bride's going away dress being of violet and blue canvass over silk of the same colour and hat to match trimmed with parma violets. The honeymoon is to be spent in the Highlands. The wedding presents were both costly and numerous. Appended is the list up to the time of going to press:—
(inter alia)

Bridegroom to Bride	—	Gold bracelets, watch etc.
Bride to Groom	—	Scarf pin etc.
F. K. Peile	—	Drums of the Fore and Aft. (a picture?)
Mr. Francis	—	Cheque.
Miss Francis	—	12 Silver Fish Knives and Forks.
Major and Mrs. Francis	—	Chippendale Wardrobe—inlaid.

Mr. & Mrs. E. H. Parker	—	Chippendale Sideboard—inlaid.
Servants at		
4 Kings Parade.	—	Flower bowls.
Clerks at		
Emmanuel Street.	—	Silver sugar caster.
Officers 4th Battalion		
Suffolk Regimemt	—	Silver Beer Jug
Mr. & Mrs. John Collin	—	Postal letter balance.
Vice-Provost of Kings	—	Silver salt cellars

Mr. and Mrs. Walter Francis took up residence in an imposing newly built house Romanhurst No. 3 Grange Road and were to remain there for the rest of their married life. Two children were born to them, Walter Maclaren on 2nd August 1900 and Agnes Morag on 25th October 1906.

When Walter Maclaren Francis joined his father and uncle in the practice in 1925 he represented the third generation of the Francis family to enter the legal profession.

Chapter 15

THE UNIVERSITY SOLICITOR
PART II (1850 onwards)

HIS chapter deals with the continuing story of the University Solicitor following the death of Christopher Pemberton. Pemberton was not himself actively engaged in University work at the time of his death, nor is there any record of Clement Francis having undertaken work for the University before 1874.

According to a memorandum retained in the University Archives a meeting of the Vice-Chancellor and Heads of other colleges took place on 21st October 1850 at the Master's Lodge Christ's College, by coincidence the day before Christopher Pemberton's death. At the meeting a letter was read from Mr. Twiss, resigning the business of solicitor for the University. It was agreed that Mr. Hyde be employed as his successor by the Vice-Chancellor for the time being, with the understanding that the Vice-Chancellor should hold himself at liberty to employ a solicitor in London whenever the interests of the University appeared to him to require it.

This resolution seems to have reflected what already tended to occur in practice. In 1847/48 Messrs. Twiss and Marshall of Cambridge had been involved in the initial stages of litigation for the University but by 1849 when the proceedings had become more demanding Messrs. Currie, Woodgate and Williams of 32 Lincolns Inn Fields were on the court records as "attorneys for the Chancellor, Masters and Scholars of the University of Cambridge".

According to Winstanley, the University Solicitor, Mr. Hyde was too unwell to attend to business in 1860 when the notorious University Spinning House Case, Kemp v. Neville was in prospect. Sensing danger the University appointed a syndicate to overhaul the proceedings of the Vice Chancellor's court, which in October 1860 sought the advice of a London solicitor Mr. F. J. Fuller of 12 Regent Street (Middlesex). Mr. Fuller acted on behalf of the defendant University Vice-Chancellor when Kemp v. Neville and an associated case Ebbon v. Neville were heard by the Court of Common Pleas in 1861.

There is also preserved in the University Archives a note book containing "sundry memoranda respecting Cambridge", being a miscellaneous collection of memoranda concerning the history traditions and legal powers of the University. This includes a note by the then University Registrary,

"16th December 1862—Mr Fuller gave me this book this day. Mr. F. J. Fuller was for several years solicitor to the University and to Christ's College".

No record has been traced to identify Mr. Fuller's successor unless this was Mr. John William Howard Crane (admitted Michaelmas 1844) who by 1873 was practising at 13 Free School Lane, Cambridge, and was then using the designation "University Solicitor". By June of the following year, as has already been mentioned, this appointment passed suddenly to Clement Francis. If a hurried choice had to be made by the University Vice-Chancellor (who in 1874 was the Master of Emmanuel College) it seems at least understandable that he would have chosen the solicitor already acting for his own college. After holding the position for six years, Clement Francis died leaving his son Musgrave Francis as sole principal of the practice. Musgrave Francis' obituary in The Times (7th March 1931) referred to the appointment continuing "... with the exception of a brief interval after the death of Mr. Clement Francis." In fact the practice records show this interval to be fairly imperceptible and it can therefore be said that Musgrave Francis served the University as their solicitor for a continuous period of fifty years between 1881 and 1931. Among the more noteworthy episodes which occurred during this period and which are referred to elsewhere in these pages were the imprisonment of Kate Elsden and Daisy Hopkin (1891–2), the deprivation of degrees held by Dr. Scott Sanders (1895–6) and above all the Haldane case of 1925–6.

After 1931 the University work was handled in part by John Collin but increasingly from 1935 onwards by Hugh Collin and Dudley Durell. Conditions were however much altered since Clement Francis had first taken on this responsiblity. The adoption of new University statutes in 1926 and the establishment of the Regent House as the effective legislative body meant that the functions of the University Vice-Chancellor were changed. Permanent officials were appointed to handle much of the day to day business of the University and the role of the Vice-Chancellor began to bear a closer resemblance to the chairman of a company than to its managing director. By the time Musgrave Francis died it was no longer the case that the appointment of the University Solicitor lay in the gift of the Vice-Chancellor any more than the University looked exclusively to one solicitor or firm of solicitors to provide all its legal services. The world was becoming an altogether different place, though a letter dated 28th November 1956 written by the senior partner of King Metters and Harrison of Cambridge to Walter Maclaren Francis (by then senior partner of the practice) may have been written without full appreciation of these changes and probably arrived twenty years too late,

"Dear Mr. Francis,
I was recently casually glancing through Butterworth"s Empire Law List 1956 and noticed the insertion for Cambridge under the name of your firm. I see that you have included, probably by mistake, the following entry... "Solicitors to the University of Cambridge...".
"While there can be no possible objection to the inclusion of public appointments in such a publication I do feel that reference to the clients of a firm, especially such clients as the University of Cambridge, could well be construed to constitute direct advertising..."
"You will appreciate that this letter is written in the most friendly way and whilst bearing in mind the happy relationship which has always existed between our firms, both my partner and I feel that the words in question do give a professionally undesirable advantage to your announcement as against our own which appears immediately underneath. I do hope that I shall hear from you that in the new Edition, such words will not appear. Yours sincerely, M. J. H. HARRISON"

This chapter effectively concludes the story of the University Solicitor as an appointment though it by no means marks the termination of the practice involvement in the legal business of the University.

Chapter 16

TOWARDS A NEW CENTURY

O celebration or commemoration seems to have taken place to mark the centenary of the practice in 1889. If this may be explained partly through lack of appreciation of their antecedents the main reason for this oversight must be the major pre-occupation of the two continuing partners, Musgrave and Walter Francis, in meeting the needs of their important clientele.

An instance of this kind had occurred on 2nd July 1888 when a hearing took place before the Universities Committee of the Privy Council, consisting of the Lord Chancellor, the Lord President of the Council, Lord Derby, the Duke of Devonshire and the Master of the Rolls. The purpose of this hearing was to adjudicate on an unprecedented dispute between the fellows of St. John's College as to the adoption of a new College statute. In December 1886 a majority of the fellows had approved the sealing of a proposed Statute No. 54, intended as a convenient means of meeting calls on the College towards the University Contribution by permitting any vacant Fellowship of the College to be declared suspended. Hitherto the share (or dividend) from the college revenues due to a vacant fellowship had been paid into the College Pension Fund, and the purpose of Statute 54 was to direct that share of dividend to be paid instead as part of the

University Contribution. Two fellows opposed to the statute, Mr. Webb and Mr. Foxwell, engaged the services of
Messrs. Eaden and Knowles to petition the Privy Council to
have the new statute set aside. Francis and Francis were
instructed to appear through counsel at the Committee
hearing on 2nd July and on 19th August they received the
following notification from the Clerk to the Privy Council:

Gentlemen,
    With reference to your letter of 15th inst. I am directed by the Lord
President of the Council to inform you that Her Majesty at the
Council held on the 13th inst was pleased to approve of the report of
the Universities Committee dismissing the petition of Mr. R. R. Webb
against the Statute made by the governing body of St. John's College
Cambridge on 6th November 1886 (suspension of vacant Fellowship
Statute 54) and directing that the Statute be laid before Parliament.
The Statute will be so laid when Parliament reassembles in November
next.
    I am, Gentlemen, your obedient servant C. L. PEEL.

Another ripple disturbed the calm of the academic world
during 1887–8, caused by 'proposed scheme for granting
degrees to physicians and surgeons'. A petition to the
Queen in Council against this proposal was prepared on the
instructions of the University in February 1887 but not filed
with the Privy Council for another year, in February 1888.
The pressure on Parliament, evidently well concerted
within the academic world, succeeded in its object. The
medical qualifications* awarded by the Royal College of
Surgeons and the Royal College of Physicians have never yet
acquired the status of degrees.

A benefaction to the University in 1888 by the widow of
Professor James Clerk Maxwell resulted in advice and assistance being sought from the practice. Professor Clerk

*(Licenciate; Membership; Fellowship)

Maxwell (1831–79) was the first Professor of Experimental Physics at Cambridge and had been responsible for organising the Cavendish Laboratory. He was the first to show that electro-magnetic waves travel close to the speed of light and in 1861 he had laid the theoretical foundation for colour photography by discovering the three image additive principle. The gift to the University by his widow consisted of her residence at Dunoon on the Firth of Clyde. Concern over the disposal of such a distant property within the jurisdiction of the Scottish legal system led Musgrave Francis between 5th and 9th October to travel to Edinburgh, Glasgow and by the paddle-steamer "Iona" across the Clyde to view the property, then engaging Edinburgh solicitors, Messrs. McKenzie and Black, to undertake the sale. Travel to Scotland and accommodation for four nights cost £10 18s 9d.

Continuing expansion in the provision of buildings for scientific studies and research in the University was reflected in advice given to the Vice-Chancellor in March 1888. This concerned the documentation for building greenhouses at the Botanic Gardens by Messrs. Boyd & Son of Paisley. The following year instructions were received to consider a draft contract between Mr. William Sindall and the University for the erection of the Physiological School next to the Museum for Human Anatomy in Corn Exchange Street for the sum of £4,496. The Town Council resolved that they would not take any step with regard to the infringement that would be caused by this new building on condition that they would be treated the same way by the University if they raised the height of their buildings on the other side of the street.

Another sign of progress was noted in November 1889 when an agreement was concluded between Christ's College and 'the Telephone Company' to permit telephone wires to cross the College premises. However, it would be some years before the practice itself would be connected to the telephone service provided in Cambridge by the National Telephone Company. Another sign of the times was recorded in the Cambridge Daily News of 14th October 1888 as follows,

> "The typewriter, after years of labour has been brought much nearer to perfection, and it is now to be found in many of the leading Business Houses in England, and in America its use is taught in some of the public schools."

> "In most of the large towns of England typewriting offices have been established where authors and others can have their MSS typed at a very low figure. As will be seen in our advertisement column one of these offices has been opened at number 5 Alexandra Street, Cambridge".

Some years were to elapse before the practice was to purchase its first typewriters and engage its first (male) typists. Far too much habit, tradition and custom was bound up in handwritten letters, hand-engrossed documents and hand-entered ledger entries for any such change to be contemplated on more than an exceedingly gradual and cautious basis.

Business for Mortlock's Bank continued actively during this period, undoubtedly thanks to the invigorating influence of Edmund Parker. Little more than three months after his move to the bank more cryptic entries for Mortlock and Co. appeared in the practice Bill Books under the coded designation 'BK'. Judging by the individuals named and the amount of travel involved to and from London these entries coincide with the incorporation of the Mortlock and Co. partnership as a limited liability company, John Mortlock and Co. Limited. Virtually every provincial banking business had until then been formed as a partnership, the private assets of the banking partners constituting the working capital and the reserves of the business.

Edmund Parker's financial situation was clearly different, as has been seen from his need to take employment during his undergraduate studies. It was undoubtedly this financial factor which prompted Mortlock's Bank, noticeably ahead of some of its contemporaries, to seek the protection of incorporation under the Companies Acts 1862–1886.

The subscribers to the Memorandum and Articles of Association of John Mortlock & Co. Ltd, on 29th March 1889 were

EDMUND JOHN MORTLOCK, Abington Lodge, Nr. Cambridge, Banker.
EDMUND HENRY PARKER, Benet Street, Cambridge, Banker.
CHARLES HALL, New Court, Temple, Barrister-at-Law.
THOMAS MUSGRAVE FRANCIS, Cambridge, Solicitor.
WILLIAM SEVERIN SALTING, 103 Piccadilly, London,
Barrister-at-Law.
HENRY CASSON, 4, Stone Buildings, Lincoln's Inn,
Barrister-at-Law.
JOHN LEES CASSON, 4, Stone Buildings, Linc. Inn, Barrister-at-Law.

Until the company merged with others to form Barclay & Co. in 1897 the practice undertook the task year by year of filing the Summary of Capital and Shareholders of Mortlock's Bank at Somerset House, the early home of the Companies Registry.

Items of Bank business during this period included a mortgage advance in May 1891 to Mr. Marcus Bradford which enabled him to take over the business of the University Arms Hotel, the security being the assignment

"... by way of mortgage unto John Mortlock and Co. Limited of the University Arms Hotel held under lease from Jesus College dated 30th October 1890."

The Hotel was to remain in the ownership of the Bradford family until 1989. Later the same year, the practice was requested by Edmund Parker to act both for the Bank and the former partner Mr. Ainslie (then one quarter in arrears on his mortgage interest due to the Bank) in the sale of his Lancashire property, the Hall Garth Estate. This involved two journeys to Lancaster to inspect the property to meet the auctioneers and to discuss the auction arrangements. Active pre-auction offers resulted in a private treaty sale being agreed on 21st September 1891 and the auction was cancelled. The mortgage debt owed to the Bank by the former partner was paid off on 31st December.

The Borough was no less active than the academic and commercial worlds in close-of-century Cambridge. Seeking to relieve congested traffic across the existing town bridges the River Cam Bridges Bill was promoted in Parliament by the Borough Council in 1889 to obtain powers to construct additional road bridges across the Cam. The practice, acting for the Conservators of the River Cam, entered into negotiations with the Council seeking to ensure that 'Mid-summer Common bridge' should have a clear span of 77 feet and a height clearance of 10 foot 9 inches for river traffic. The Bill was allowed to proceed through Parliament unopposed by the Conservators on the basis that a proposed foot bridge was omitted. As a result the Victoria Bridge, linking the Town with Chesterton across Midsummer Common, was completed in 1890.

A further link with the academic world had been forged when Christ's College first appeared in the practice bill books as a client in 1889. One early matter attended to for this College concerned the appointment of the Master of the College Rev. Dr. John Peile as a trustee to receive proceeds of the enfranchisement of copyhold land at Cottenham in September 1890. By June the following year Dr. Peile gave instructions for the preparation of his will, shortly before his installation as University Vice-Chancellor. With the establishment of these contacts it would hardly have been coincidental that Dr. Peile's son Frank Kitchener Peile, then a first year undergraduate at Christ's College, was to join the practice as an articled clerk following his graduation in 1893, being admitted as a solicitor in 1897.

The Spinning House Crisis

The last and one of the most serious confrontations between the Town and the University was to erupt in February 1891 and was only resolved three years later with the loss of the Vice-Chancellor's powers to imprison women of doubtful virtue in the place of confinement called the Spinning House. This source of rivalry and friction between the respective authorities had been the subject of advice given to the University in 1885 when legislation had been under consideration to end the anomaly. The power to arrest and punish suspected prostitutes had first been given to the University under the Charter of 1561. In the general settlement of outstanding issues between Town and University, embodied in the Cambridge Award Act of 1856, this power had been left untouched. Originally introduced to protect the morals of an all-male undergraduate population the summary powers of arrest had by the mid-nineteenth century come to be seen more as a potential threat to the liberties of the subject, "a survival from a bygone and despotic age" (Winstanley). In 1860 court proceedings had been brought in the case of Kemp v. Neville alleging wrongful arrest by the University Proctor following the summary arrest and commitment of five suspects including Emma Kemp. In the years following that case the University Authorities had acted with extreme circumspection but notwithstanding this, on 15th February 1891 (a Sunday),

"Attending the Junior Proctor on his calling and informing us that a girl named Kate Elsden* had escaped from Spinning House on Thursday afternoon last while undergoing a sentence of three weeks passed upon her that morning but she had been recaptured at Dullingham under warrant and on him giving us instructions to appear for the prosecution before the bench tomorrow and conferring on the case when he desired us to see the Vice-Chancellor upon it but agreed with us as to the advisability of getting it set for trial at the Assizes the following day if it could be arranged."

The following day the case was heard by magistrates who committed the prisoner for trial at the Assizes the next day on a charge of breaking prison.

"It having been suggested incidentally from the bench that it might be desirable to prove at the trial the reason for this arrest attending the Junior Proctor thereon and expressing an opinion adverse to such suggestion made to us that we obtain from him such particulars as he had got to give..."

Defence counsel delivered an impassioned speech calculated to raise all the sympathies and prejudices of the jury. This had no effect on the outcome, the Vice-Chancellor had clearly not exceeded his legal powers under the Charter, but the speech was nevertheless greeted with loud applause. While the jury returned a verdict of guilty they also added a rider (which the Judge refused to accept on the grounds that it had no reference to the prisoner) "that the Vice-Chancellor's Court, as now constituted, needs revision". Nevertheless this rider found its way into the press and added further fuel to the flames.

A certain amount of confusion seems to have resulted from the sentence of three weeks without labour passed on

*In the bill book, as in the Spinning House Committal Book, her name is given as Kate, but in all other records as Jane Elsden.

179

the prisoner. Apparently,

> "... the Judge did not actually state that the two sentences his own and
> the Vice-Chancellor's would run concurrently but he used expres-
> sions indicating he held such an opinion..."

Newspaper comment on the case both local and national
ranged from the severely criticial to the downright vitriolic
and when a question was raised in the House of Commons
on 26th February 1891 the Home Secretary announced that
he intended to issue an immediate order for the release of
the prisoner.

It was clearly time to introduce more enlightened procedures into the Vice-Chancellor's Court if only to avert
further deterioration in relations between the University
the Borough and Parliament.

Accordingly the Vice-Chancellor gave instructions for
Counsel's opinion to be obtained as to the right of the Vice-
Chancellor

(1)   To make the Court an open Court
(2)   To receive evidence on oath
(3)   To allow accused the benefit of legal assistance.

The preparation of the case to Counsel appears to have
been a lengthy procedure conducted against an anxious
and thoroughly distracting backdrop of meetings debates
proposals and counter proposals both within and between
the University and Borough authorities, essentially on the
issue of whether to retain or abolish the Vice-Chancellor's
Court. Numerous consultations with University representatives are recorded, along with additional perusal of the
Elizabethan Charter in translation, reference to the Oxford
University Solicitor Mr. Morrell for a comparison of Oxford
procedure, and some uncertainty as to which Counsel

should be approached. Eventually the Vice-Chancellor decided that the opinion of the Attorney General should be taken, his fee of £15 15s was apparently considered satisfactory and a conference with the Attorney eventually took place on 6th May.

By the following November, with Dr. Peile now installed as Vice-Chancellor, further advice was sought with regard to an additional area of procedural uncertainty, whether the Vice-Chancellor had power to adjourn a hearing before his court and if so whether he also had power to remand or to grant bail. In the absence of specific powers, either under statute or the Charter, a case was prepared for the joint opinion of Mr. Wright and Mr. Scott of Counsel, and while that opinion in the matter was received and communicated to the Vice-Chancellor on 22nd January, 1892, other events were already moving so fast that the finer points of procedure to be followed in his court were rapidly losing all relevance. The case of Daisy Hopkin, following only nine months after Kate Elsden's, already had the makings of a further bitter controversy between town and gown.

According to the practice bill books, on 3rd December 1891 a letter had been received from the Vice-Chancellor stating that a woman named Daisy Hopkin had been arrested by a proctor the previous night and asking for advice as to the procedure to be followed. Pursuing the newly adopted and more enlightened procedure the case was heard at the Spinning House in public, witnesses were sworn and the prisoner was defended by a local solicitor Mr. A. Jasper Lyon. The case was found proved on the evidence and Daisy Hopkin was sentenced to fourteen days imprisonment.

There was further loud and adverse press comment as a result of this trial and calls for the abolition of the Vice-Chancellor's Court were made. The day after the trial Mr. Lyon called to announce his intention to apply for a writ of

Habeas Corpus. This prompted a flurry of activity on the University side, the Attorney General was retained to defend for the University along with Mr. Finlay and Mr. Rawlinson. Two conferences with Counsel were held on 9th and 10th December. At the earlier conference it was suggested that evidence of the real character of Daisy Hopkin be collected, though at the second conference on the day of the hearing the Attorney General took the view that evidence as to character was not required. The case was heard in the High Court on 10th and 11th December when Lord Coleridge and Mr. Justice Smith both agreed that Daisy Hopkin's application should succeed, and ordered her release

"... but both giving strong judgement in favour of the Vice-Chancellor in his exercise of this case".

The judgement of the Court was based on a technical imperfection in the charge against the prisoner which should have (but had not) used the words "suspected of evil" contained in the Charter, and not on account of any more serious miscarriage of justice.

Nevertheless a swift reaction followed from the prisoner's side. Mr. Lyon intimated that he had been instructed to take proceedings against Mr. Wallis the Proctor for damages for false imprisonment, Daisy Hopkin's legal expenses by then being met by public subscription. The University decided on 1st January 1892 to defend the action and not make any offer in settlement. When the writ was served on 8th January the claim was for damages for assault and false imprisonment and for malicious prosecution and was accompanied by an intimation that the plaintiff would be prepared to accept in satisfaction the sum of £130 which the writ of Habeas Corpus had cost.

Public opinion in Cambridge, whether led or echoed by

the press, appeared to have reached an unprecedented level of outrage at Daisy Hopkin's treatment and seemed set to go higher yet. An attempt was therefore made to remove these proceedings from Cambridge to London. This application was disallowed by the High Court Master and heard on appeal by Baron Pollock "... when without calling on the other side he dismissed the appeal but marked it urgent for the Divisional Court". Apparently Baron Pollock had suggested changing the venue of the hearing to Ipswich by way of compromise, as an alternative to the appeal to the Divisional Court. Mr. Wallis expressed himself more in favour of accepting the compromise venue "... as he suspects Norwich as a place for trial". Agreement was reached with the Plaintiff's Solicitor Mr. Lyon the following day when he expressed

> "... his readiness to agree to Ipswich as the place for the trial if we would agree to the substitution of the word "illegal" for the word "false" in the first paragraph of the statement of claim..."

Meanwhile some embarrassing enquiries were having to be made in the darker corners of the town to find witnesses who could give evidence of Daisy Hopkin's character and reputation. Some invididuals were less willing than others to testify—

> "Attending Mr. A. R. Harding on his calling but he said he could not be certain that the girl who accosted him several times was the plaintiff but that from Coleby's description of her he had come to that conclusion. He said the night was very dark and he was in addition near-sighted".

> "Attendance on Mr. Lambert as to the evidence he thought he could obtain but though the party was able to speak he declined to come forward".

"Attending Miss Elsden the Parish Mission woman when she informed us that Mrs. Briggs in Gold Street was afraid to say anything on account of the annoyance she feared she and her family would be subjected to".

Eventually eight witnesses were found willing to give evidence, their statements were taken down and they were instructed to attend the court hearing at Ipswich on 24th and 25th March 1892 before Mr. Justice Matthew and a special jury.

"Attending hearing of case before Mr. Justice Matthew which began on Thursday afternoon and ended about 4.00 on Friday with a verdict for defendant with costs".

The University may have been vindicated but they must too have been gravely disconcerted by the general furore and public demonstrations of hostility. A conference had already taken place between the Borough and the University Senate in March 1891 at which little difference had emerged between the University Members of the Borough Council and the members of the Council of the Senate except on the question of proctorial power. The University did not wish to surrender the proctors' power of arrest unless it could be satisfied that the civil power was willing and able to provide equivalent protection for undergraduate morals. A committee of the University and Borough representatives met for the first time on 14th February 1893 charged with finding a solution to this problem. Eventually agreement was reached to promote a Bill in Parliament which reached the statute book the following year as the Cambridge University and Corporation Act 1894. This provided for proctors and the town police to act concurrently in arresting loose women. Any trials would, however, take place before the Borough Magistrates and the Vice-

Chancellor's jurisdiction over them was abolished. Winstanley expressed the view that the controversy had been dragged on by both sides longer than had been really necessary.

The title of the Statute (1894) 57 and 58 Vic.C.ix. was

An Act to amend the Law relating to the jurisdiction of the Chancellor Vice-Chancellor and other authorities of the University of Cambridge over persons not members of the University etc. [3rd July 1894].

The Act contained the following recitals

Whereas by a Charter dated or purporting to be dated 26th April in the third year of her reign Her Majesty Queen Elizabeth granted (among other things) "That the Chancellor Masters and Scholars of the University of Cambridge by themselves or their deputies officers servants and ministers from time to time as well by day as by night at their pleasure might make scrutiny search and inquisition in the town and suburbs and in Barnwell and Sturbridge for all common women, bawds, vagabonds and other suspected persons coming or resorting to the town or suburbs or the said fairs and punish all whom on such scrutiny search and inquisition they should find guilty or suspected of evil by imprisonment of their bodies banishment or otherwise as the Chancellor or his Vice-Gerent should deem fit and the Mayor Bailiffs and other officers and ministers of the town and all other persons whatsoever were commanded not to impede such scrutiny search and inquisition but on request of the Chancellor or his Vice-Gerent aid and assist therein under pain of contempt and incurring the indignation of the Queen her heirs and successors.

And whereas by Section 3 of an Act 6 Geo IV (1825) entitled "An Act for the better preservation of the peace and good order in the Universities of England" it was enacted "the every common prostitute and night walker found wandering in any public walk street or highway within the precincts of the said University of Oxford and not giving a satisfactory account of herself shall be deemed an idle and disorderly person within the true intent and meaning of the Act 5 Geo. IV (1824) C. 83 entitled "An Act for the punishment of idle and disorderly persons and rogues and vagabonds in that part of Great Britain called England and shall and may be apprehended and dealt with accordingly".

And whereas it is expedient to repeal the recited portion of the Charter and so much of the first recited Act or any other Act as conforms or preserves the same and to extend to the University of Cambridge the recited Section 3 of the said Act 6 Geo. IV C.97 and confer further powers on the proctors and pro-proctors of the University of Cambridge for the maintenance of discipline among its members.

Section 7 of the Act provided as follows

"For the maintenance of discipline among the members of the University of Cambridge the proctors and pro-proctors of the University shall by virtue of their respective offices have the powers vested in constables duly appointed and sworn under or by virtue of Section 1 of the said Act 6 Geo. IV C.97 and shall for the same purpose have powers with or without any constables appointed under the same Act to enter any premises licensed for the sale of intoxicating liquors or any premises kept or used for public entertainment of any kind during the performance of such entertainment for so long as any of the public are assembled there".

Deprivation of Degrees
If the University was, during the period 1891–94 deeply immersed in the issue of legal jurisdiction over non-University members, circumstances arose in 1894 which raised the question whether continuing jurisdiction existed in respect of members of the University who had long since graduated and gone down from Cambridge. The examination of this issue resulted from a conviction and prison sentence passed on a medical graduate Dr. Francis Charles Scott Saunders B.A. B.Med. as a result of gross professional misconduct. As

a result of this embarrassing episode the University Authorities requested the practice in November 1894 to submit a case to the University Counsel Mr. A. Cohen Q.C. to advise as to the power of the University to deprive of their degrees graduates "who had been convicted of grave crimes". Counsel's opinion, dated 9th January 1895, advised that any corporation had inherent power to expel any member who had been convicted of a grave crime rendering him unfit for membership. However, he considered that the University Statutes of 1882 were framed in a manner which left great doubt whether they were intended to extend the discipline of the University to members after they had "left the precincts or local boundaries of the University". His conclusion was that a person committing a crime had not committed an offence against the statutes and ordinances of the University as then framed and that therefore no disciplinary jurisdiction existed in such cases.

He recommended that the University should apply to the Privy Council for an amending statute, an application for this purpose was submitted by the practice on 22nd April 1895 and confirmed by the Privy Council on 9th May. As a result the Vice-Chancellor and the Sex Viri or four at least of their number, of whom the Vice-Chancellor should be one... were

> "empowered to deprive of his degrees any person sentenced to penal servitude or imprisonment for a crime which rendered him unfit to be a graduate".

Specific retribution for Dr. Scott Saunders followed on 15th October 1896 when pursuant to the 1895 Amending Statute he was deprived of his degrees "and of all privileges enjoyed by him as a graduate of the University".

It was inevitable in the circumstances then prevailing that the Amending Statute and the decision of the Sex Viri referred exclusively to persons of the male gender, although signs of changing times were already emerging. Women undergraduates in Cambridge had been attending Girton College since 1873 and Newnham since 1875. Both colleges had been recognised by the University in 1881 and from then on their members were admitted to the tripos examinations (though not to full membership of the University and its degrees until 1947). On 11th December 1896, according to the practice bill books,

> "Attending the Vice-Chancellor on his handing to us case prepared by Professor Maitland for the Opinion of Counsel as to whether if it was desired to grant women titular degrees it could be done by Ordinance or whether it would require a Statute and the case was to be laid before Mr. Cohen Q.C. and a Junior to be selected by us".

The case was duly laid before Mr. Cohen and Mr. Wallace and following a conference with Counsel in London the joint Opinion was duly received and passed to the Vice-Chancellor on 19th December. Evidently this was no more than a prelude to the notorious "Women's War" which lasted for many weeks during 1897, culminating in the rejection by the Senate of a proposal that women should be admitted to degrees by 1707 votes to 661. In spite of another attempt to achieve the same reform in 1921, women graduates for the next fifty years had to be content with the "title" to a degree.

The Bank Amalgamation

In April 1896 the practice was first brought into the long and involved negotiations which resulted in the amalgamation of John Mortlock & Co. Ltd with Barclay Gurney & Co. and nineteen other provincial banking businesses to form Barclay & Co. Limited, a company which was to change its name to Barclays Bank Limited on 17th February 1917.

The first record of this development was on 24th April 1896,

"Attending Mr. Parker at the Bank on his giving us instructions with regard to a proposed amalgamation with Messrs. Barclay Gurney & Co., the particulars being included in the correspondence handed to us".

This was the start of fourteen months activity on behalf of John Mortlock & Co. Ltd. which was eventually concluded in early June 1897. The initial stages involved negotiations between Mortlock's Bank represented by the practice and the formation committee for the New Bank represented by Messrs. Markbys in the City of London. Mr. R. J. Parker of Counsel (Edmund Parker's brother) was instructed to peruse, amend and settle the draft amalgamation agreement which was then subjected to further negotiations between the two firms of solicitors. The agreement as presented for approval at a meeting of Mortlock's shareholders on 4th June 1896 provided for a transfer of the business and assets of Mortlock's Bank to Barclay & Co. Ltd. as soon as incorporation had taken place. Shares in the new company were allocated to the Mortlock's shareholders by way of payment and Mr. Edmund Parker was to be appointed liquidator of Mortlock's Bank, to whom the shareholders would deliver their existing share certificates. The arrangements being approved by the shareholders were followed immediately by an exchange of agreements between Edmund Parker representing Mortlock's Bank and Mr. Johnson representing the formation committee.

Valuation of the Mortlock premises in Cambridge and the branch in Ely was undertaken jointly by Mr. Nockolds representing the Bank and Messrs. Lofts and Warner of London representing the formation committee.

Further formalities were required from the Mortlock

shareholders to implement the agreement, the necessary resolutions being passed at a special meeting of the Company held on 30th June 1896.

Advice was obtained from Mr. R. J. Parker as to the mode of transferring the assets of the Bank and their several securities to the new company and as to the duty of the liquidator. Some anxiety seems to have been felt on the grounds that the new company might not be registered within the twenty-eight day period allowed by the shareholders' special resolutions but registration was complete by 28th July, the applications for shares in the new company were prepared and signed by the shareholders, the amalgamation agreement was sealed by the directors and Notices of Special Resolution were published in the London Gazette and filed at the Companies Registry.

The notification of these events in the London Gazette of 17th August 1896 ran as follows

*IN THE MATTER OF THE COMPANIES ACT 1862–1890
AND OF THE BANKING COMPANY CALLED OR KNOWN AS
JOHN MORTLOCK & CO. LIMITED, HAVING OFFICES AT 16A
BENE'T STREET, CAMBRIDGE*

AT an Extraordinary General Meeting of the Company duly convened and held at the Chambers of Mr. R. J. Parker at No. 9 Stone Buildings, Lincoln's Inn, London W.C. on Friday the 30th day of June 1896, the following Special Resolutions were passed by the unanimous vote of all members present in person or by proxy, and the same resolutions were confirmed as Special Resolutions at an Extraordinary General Meeting of the Company duly convened and held at the same place on Tuesday the 28th July 1896 by the unanimous vote of all members present in person or by proxy:—

1. "That the Company be wound up voluntarily under the provisions of the Companies Acts 1862 to 1890, and that Edmund Henry Parker, the Managing Director of the Company, be and he is hereby appointed Liquidator for the purposes of such winding up.

   2. "That the remuneration of the Liquidator for his services in the
       winding up be fixed at the sum of £105 per annum for a period
       of three years".

Cambridge 5th August 1896—
EDMUND HENRY PARKER Chairman of both Meetings.

Ten more months of activity followed involving the transfer of all securities and properties of Mortlock's Bank to the
new company and a charge was given by the former directors E. J. Mortlock and E. H. Parker over bank securities remaining in their names. The amalgamation had required
the same formalities as many larger transactions but the
whole affair was much simplified by the fact that there were
only fifteen shareholders in John Mortlock & Co. Ltd., from
whom the necessary consents and signatures had to be
obtained.*

For a number of years after the amalgamation had taken
place the practice bill books contained entries for "Barclay
& Co.", in respect of new business received from their Cambridge branch and "Mortlock & Co." or "the Bank" for
business continuing in the name of the old bank or for the
liquidator Edmund Parker, including the filing of his reports and half-yearly accounts until these were finally closed
in 1902.

The Case of the Disappearing Solicitor
One unexpected result of the bank amalgamation and
the attendant checking and cross checking of outstanding
loans and securities was the discovery of substantial fraud
being practised by a well established Cambridge solicitor,

*Of 5m. Barclay & Co shares issued 6,000 were issued to Mortlock Shareholders,
representing 0.12 per cent. As principal Mortlock shareholder, Edmund
Mortlock was allocated 2,135 shares (0.0427 per cent) and Edmund Henry Parker
1,000 shares (0.02 per cent).

William Peed. This led in quick succession to his disappearance, the sale by auction of his mortgaged properties and a declaration of bankruptcy.

The closing years of the nineteenth century were marked by a steady increase in the number of defaulting solicitors and although the Law Society was well aware of the problem, debate as to the remedies and severe shortage of parliamentary time meant that the necessary reforms would not be introduced for another thirty years or more. At that time few solicitors understood the principles of book-keeping, the examination in book-keeping and trust accounts introduced in 1862 having been abandoned in 1877. No requirement existed for annual auditing of solicitors' accounts nor for clients' money to be kept in a separate bank account. Worse still, the fraudulent conversion of funds entrusted to an agent did not constitute a criminal offence until the Larceny Act 1901 was promoted by the Law Society to close this loophole. Misappropriation of clients' funds originated more often from ineptitude or folly than from criminal intent but the result was the same if temptation or desperation led to the robbing of one client's funds to replace another's.

In 1896 William Peed was a solicitor with an established practice in Cambridge and an office at 62 Sidney Street. Neither William Peed nor the inhabitants of Cambridge at large were entirely unfamiliar with the financial defaults or difficulties of local solicitors. In 1876 Peed's practice had assisted Mr. John Crane during his period of financial difficulty. In 1888, as a result of "the defalcations of the absconding solicitor Ephraim Wayman of 2 Silver Street... following his sudden departure from the Town" William Peed had been appointed Wayman's trustee in bankruptcy.

Seen with hindsight, the first entries in the practice bill books relevant to Wiliam Peed's impending downfall occur in 1894.

Jan 9th. Attending Mr. Parker on his informing us it had been arranged that Major de Freville should give further security for his indebtedness to the Bank... and we were to hear from Mr. Peed on the subject.

March 13th. Mr. Peed having consented to postpone his mortgage to that of the Bank, writing him suggesting that this should be endorsed on his notice.

November 1st. Having received reply from Mr. Peed requesting notice should not be given to the trustees writing you for instructions but suggesting that the names and addresses of the trustees should be obtained.

November 5th. Attending Mr. Parker on his calling in reply to our letter and consenting to forego notice to trustees on an undertaking from Major de Freville to give information of any second charge... in order that the Notice of Charge to the Bank might take due priority.

1895 March 14th. Writing Mr. Peed for a reply to our letter of November last.

April 17th. Writing Mr. Peed that unless we received the information required by the end of the month the bank would withdraw their consent to dispense with notices to the trustees.

1896 July 21st. Attending Mr. Parker on his giving us instructions for further security upon Major de Freville's life interest... to secure an advance of £1,000.

July 22nd. Preparing draft deed accordingly. Attending Mr. Parker therewith when he stated it was not necessary to submit it to Mr. Peed.

July 23rd. Attending Mr. Parker therewith for him to hand to Major de Freville.

1897 June 11th. Attending Mr. Parker at the Bank on his instructing us to give notice to the trustees of Major de Freville's execution of the Charge in favour of the Bank. Writing to Mr. Peed informing him of our intention.

Attending Mr. Peed's Clerk on his calling to deprecate the notice being given and on his suggestion you should instead obtain power on the India Stock.

Attending Mr. Parker thereon when Mr. Parker informed us he had seen Mr. Peed himself who was to furnish the exact name and description of the trustees for the purpose of the power being obtained.

June 12th. Attending at the Bank with names and addresses of the trustees which had been sent to us by Mr. Peed in 1895 but the Bank thought they had changed and we were to get them checked.

Attending Mr. Peed accordingly when he said they were the correct names and addresses.

(Four months silence was followed by an unexpected visit from Major de Freville).

October 2nd. Attending you on your giving us instructions to act for you on the disappearance of Mr. Peed and explaining to us that there was the sum of £6,000 due to you from him... and giving us further particulars of your property to enable us to obtain the deeds from Mr. Peed's office.

This disturbing news was followed by an official announcement in The London Gazette on 19th October 1897 that the first meeting in respect of the debtor William Peed of Histon, Cambridgeshire, lately practising at 62 Sidney Street in the Borough of Cambridge, solicitor would be held at 12 noon on 27th October 1897 at the Lion Hotel, Petty Cury, Cambridge and that the Public Examination of the debtor was fixed for 11 a.m. on 17th November 1897 at the Guildhall, Cambridge.

Notwithstanding the appointment of a trustee in William

Peed's bankruptcy the Bank was able to proceed with the realisation of its security,

> 6th November. Attending at Sidney Street with Mr. Parker and taking instructions from him and Mr. Witt the Trustee of William Peed's estate for the sale of 9 out of the 13 different properties of which deeds were held by the Bank as security for an advance of just under £10,000.

> 8th November. Attending at the Bank for instructions as to an Auctioneer to be employed...

> 23rd November. Attending the Trustee at his office discussing the date for sale when he agreed with us our sale should be subsequent to that of the London and Counties Bank and he thought it should under the circumstances be after Christmas.

On Friday 7th January 1898 the Cambridge Independent Press contained the following advertisement

> By Order of the Mortgagees, with the concurrence of Tansley Witt Esquire the trustee under the bankruptcy of W. Peed. Messrs. Catling and Son are favoured with instructions to sell [14 properties] by Auction at the Lion Hotel, Cambridge on Wednesday Feb. 2nd. 1898 at 4 o'clock in the afternoon precisely. Solicitors—Messrs. Francis, Francis and Collin, Emmanuel Street, Messrs. Whitehead, Todd and King, Petty Cury.*

This was followed by an announcement in the Independent Press on Friday Feb. 4th 1898

> *SALE OF WILLIAM PEED'S PROPERTY*
> More of Peed's property was disposed of by Messrs. Catling and Son

---

*Messrs. Whitehead, Todd and King had been instructed to act in the sale of Peed's office premises at 62 Sidney Street by the mortgagees, the London and Counties Bank. These premises formed Lot 1 at the auction.

at the Lion Hotel, Cambridge on Wednesday. There was a good
company, brisk bidding, and highly satisfactory results, the total
fetched being £12,440.

[Freehold offices and residence at 62 Sidney Street, Cambridge
£5,000; remainder in and about Histon £7,440 including The Gables,
Histon £650]

If any reassurance is needed by the reader in the light of
these untoward events it should be added that the Larceny
Act 1901 was followed by the Solicitors Act 1933 which
required the Law Society to make rules as to the keeping of
separate accounts for clients moneys and for ensuring that
such rules were complied with. These requirements were
embodied in the Solicitors Accounts Rules 1935, while the
Solicitors Act 1941 required that with every application for
an annual practising certificate, the Solicitor must make a
declaration of compliance with the Accounts Rules and
produce an Accountant's Certificate that proper books
have been kept and clients moneys kept in a separate bank
account. This amounted in effect to a requirement for
annual auditing. The 1941 Act also provided for the establishment of a compensation fund to which every practising
solicitor must make an annual contribution. This development forty four years later was sadly of no help to William
Peed's principal victim Major de Freville. His former client
was left in serious financial difficulties which prolonged negotiations and litigation between himself and his Saville
Row tailors and moneylenders failed to resolve.* His intended appeal in these proceedings to the House of Lords
was abandoned only on his death in October 1901.

✳   ✳   ✳   ✳

*The proceedings before the Court of Appeal are reported in The Law Reports
[1900] 2 Q.B.72.

Mrs. Sarah Francis, widow of Clement Francis died at Quy Hall on 2nd February 1897 and was buried in Quy church-yard on 5th February. Ownership of the Quy Hall Estate and of the Emmanuel Street Lease passed to her eldest surviving son, Musgrave Francis who soon afterwards moved his residence from 17 Emmanuel Street to Quy Hall, remaining there for the rest of his life.

* * * *

Modern trends and modern methods continued to make their appearance in end-of-century Cambridge. One of these involved the preparation of what must now be regarded by every charity and academic institution as an essential part of their fund-raising equipment—the specimen form of bequest. On 28th February 1898,

> "Attending Mr. Parker on his calling by direction of the Vice-Chancellor to instruct us to prepare and have printed form of bequest to the University for the use of intending testators.
>
> Instructions to Mr. Hadley to settle such form.
>
> March 23rd. Attending the Vice-Chancellor with form and for order to get them printed at the Pitt Press.
>
> April 26th. Having received from the Vice-Chancellor letter desiring 50 forms to be sent him, attending Pitt Press accordingly and ordering 25 for ourselves and type to be broken up".

Edmund Parker's involvement with the Vice-Chancellor in these arrangements was indicative of the invaluable part he played over the years in strengthening the finances and widening the activities of the University. According to his obituary published in the Cambridge Chronicle on 18th July 1928,

"The foundation on his initiative of the University Association has
been of the greatest assistance to the University from a financial point
of view, the value of which was recognised and attested when the
degree of Doctor of Laws was conferred upon him".

Another milestone in the march of progress was the
connection of the Emmanuel Street office to the telephone
service in 1901, the first telephone call being made on client
business on 4th April 1901. As already mentioned, telephones had first come to Cambridge twelve years previously, but the service provided by the National Telephone
Company in 1901 was still in its infancy and opportunities to
make telephone calls were at first limited to a small number
of other subscribers. Nevertheless, telephone calls eventually overtook telegrams as a means of rapid communication.
This small step forward in the year 1901 symbolized the start
of steadily increasing involvement in technological progress as the years went by.

Chapter 17

EDWARDIAN TIMES AND
THEIR AFTERMATH

O choose 1st January 1901 as the opening day of the twentieth century displays little in the way of pedantry and in any case this date comes conveniently close to the end of the Victorian era with the death of the Queen on 23rd January 1901. The Duke of York himself had already written "Goodbye 19th Century" in his diary for 31st December 1900. Both these significant January dates fell on a Tuesday and were normal working days at the Emmanuel Street office. So too was Friday 1st February 1901 the day of the Queen's funeral, actually occupied by Musgrave Francis in a "journey to London, attending Mr. Mortlock in his executing Conveyance and making Declaration".

The absence of any more compelling Bill Book entries around this time gives the opportunity to take brief stock of the practice as it stood in the opening days of the twentieth century. Of the three partners in Francis, Francis and Collin, Musgrave Francis was then aged fifty, Walter Hamond Francis aged forty two and John Collin aged thirty three. In addition their assistant solicitor, Frank Kitchener Peile who had been admitted in 1897 and was to become a Partner in 1905 was aged twenty eight. Musgrave Francis was at this time Clerk to the Conservators of the River Cam, the

Trustees of the County Lunatic Asylum and Storey's
Charity. The main institutional clients comprised "The
Bank" (Barclay & Co., Mortlock's Branch) the University
and, among the Colleges, Corpus Christi, Clare, Gonville
and Caius, Downing,Emmanuel, Jesus, Magdalene,
Pembroke, St. John's, Sidney Sussex, Peterhouse, Trinity
and Trinity Hall. Cambridgeshire families included
Ambrose, Allix, Bendyshe, Chaplin, Cust, Hailstone,
Jenyns, Martin, Mortlock, Newman, Swann and Thorneley.

On 1st January 1905 Frank Kitchener Peile was admitted
to the partnership which practised for the next two years as
Francis, Francis, Collin and Peile. As already mentioned,
Frank Peile was a son of the Master of Christ's College, Rev.
Dr. John Peile. He had been born on 14th September 1871
and after attending school at Repton he had entered
Christ's College, obtaining his B.A. degree in 1893 and
proceeding M.A. in 1897.

While reference in the firm name to all partners had been
an accepted custom for the previous fifty years or so the
name "Francis, Francis, Collin and Peile" was perhaps a little
too much for such everyday use as the signing of letters and
cheques and filing of court documents. At all events, the
decision was taken with effect from 1st January 1907 to
shorten the firm name to "Francis & Co." and this name was
retained regardless of changes in the identity of individual
partners until the next change of name took place eighty
years later on 1st June 1987.

Life at Quy Hall

Musgrave Francis being owner of Quy Hall was also Lord
of the Manor and leading land owner in the village of Quy.
His residence there appears to have been benign and
paternalistic, perhaps outmoded to modern eyes, but
evidently sufficient for fond memories to survive in the
village even fifty or more years after his death. His younger

sister Sophia actively filled the role of leading lady for her bachelor brother. The following random excerpts from "*Stow-cum-Quy Through Two Twenty-five Year Reigns*" by Peggy Watts (1977) seem appropriate to recall these times.

"In the days of carriages and horses, the Avenue was the normal approach to Quy Hall... At the Lodge Gate at the top of the Avenue, Mrs. Polly Bilton was ready to open the large iron gates for Musgrave Francis whenever he passed to or fro on his way to and from Cambridge where he worked as a Solicitor. Sometimes he would be driven in a Carriage by Bynge, resplendent in his top hat, sometimes he would be on a bicycle".

"Up to the First World War, the widows and widowers were invited to have dinner in the workshop at Quy Hall on Boxing Day. This would be followed by games or having a book read to them by Musgrave Francis. Dinner was sent to those unable to come. In 1913 so many wanted dinner sent to them that it was decided to send them all out. The children also went to the Hall on Boxing Day and were given two buns and an orange".

"On Empire Day (24th May) the Squire used to visit the school to hear the children sing patriotic songs. But in 1912 the 45 schoolchildren went in a procession with flags to the Hall instead. After the songs they were given tea at the workshop while the teachers had tea in the morning room".

"One Sunday in the Summer all the villagers were invited to the Hall to see the gardens and partake of tea. The men were given one ounce of tobacco, the children a round piece of chocolate. Later there was no tea but many of them would go on the one Sunday afternoon when the Hall Gardens were open to look round the beautifully kept lawns and flowerbeds..."

"In 1910 more than two-thirds of the houses in Quy were owned by Musgrave Francis".

"Great excitement would be caused by a motor car going through the

village at the time of King George's Coronation. The first car in Quy
was an open yellow tourer owned by Colonel Francis* and used by
Musgrave Francis".

Coronation of King George Vth—22nd June 1911

"Celebrations began with a service at noon in Quy Church. At 2 pm.
the villagers assembled at Quy Hall for a programme of sports... An
archway over the avenue between the Hall and the iron bridge was lit
up in the evening and flags decorated the yew hedge, beech hedge
and iron bridge, and St. George's flag flew from a flagstaff in the
middle of the lawn...

Mr. Musgrave Francis gave every cottager a coronation cup and
saucer and also two ounces of tobacco to each man and packets of
sweets to the women and children"

The late John Kitchener Peile (nephew of Frank Kitchener Peile) spent his school holidays in Cambridge with his
uncle during the years 1914–18, his parents being then
resident in Australia. He recalled cycling out to Quy along
the Newmarket Road with his school-friend Walter
Maclaren Francis for lunch of pease pudding and nectar-
ines with Walter's Uncle Musgrave.

Transport in and around Cambridge was to be
transformed during the first two decades of the twentieth
century by the introduction of the internal combustion
engine. Cars and lorries appeared on the streets of
Cambridge, first to compete with and then to displace horse
drawn carriages, omnibuses, trams and carts. Horsedrawn
trams had been in service in Cambridge since 1880,
followed in 1896 by horsedrawn omnibuses. Horsedrawn
public conveyances then faced further competition from
motor bus services introduced by two pioneering

*i.e. Musgrave Francis's nephew J. C. W. Francis

companies in 1905. Owing to a series of unfortunate accidents both companies had their licences withdrawn in 1906 but in August 1907 the Ortona Motor Co. Ltd. commenced operations and succeeded where the other two had failed.* Such was its success that horsedrawn trams were withdrawn from Cambridge streets in February 1914.

Notwithstanding the reference to the open yellow tourer being used by Musgrave Francis, the late Mr. William Plumb, robe cutter with Messrs. Almonds of Sidney Street, recalled Musgrave Francis' pony and trap often standing all day outside the Peas Hill office during the period of the First World War and into the nineteen twenties.

The Birth of Storey's Way

Familiar to all Cambridge residents as a pleasantly superior residential road in West Cambridge, Storey's Way has for the last eighty years connected Huntingdon Road with Madingley Road, being remarkable as much for the alternate right-angle bends which punctuate its three-quarter mile length as for the respectable and in some cases distinguished houses from the nineteen twenties and thirties which line it on either side. The Storey's Way estate was developed from thirty five acres of land forming part of Mount Pleasant Farm belonging to the Foundation of Edward Storey. This ancient Cambridge charity founded in 1693 had received the farmland and other Cambridge properties as part of its foundation endowment. The original objects of the Charity were the provision of benefits for widows and maidens of the parishes of Holy Trinity and St. Giles in Cambridge and of clergy widows generally. By the eighteen nineties the Charity was finding it increasingly difficult to provide adequately for these objects from

*The Ortona company (later taken over by the Eastern Counties Company) established its bus garage at 112 Hills Road on the site occupied by the practice in Francis House from August 1989.

existing income, and the proposal to develop the Storey's Way estate was seen as a means to realise latent capital values and to enhance income return. In 1891 the Charity had been granted a new and modernised scheme by the Charity Commission and the following year Musgrave Francis had been appointed as clerk to the Charity. Evidently at the suggestion of Mr. Jonas, the Charity's surveyor, the practice received instructions from the trustees to make exploratory aproaches to neighbouring landowners whose involvement would be required in order to establish "a New Road". This resulted in the following Bill Book entries in January and February 1897,

Jan 27.
Having been instructed by the trustees at their meeting yesterday to approach the Darwin family and St. John's College with a view to getting a new road from the Huntingdon Road to the Madingley Road across the three properties. Writing Mr. H. Darwin thereon.

28th
Attending him on his calling in reply to our letter indicating to him a suggested line on the Ordnance Map when he promised to communicate with his brother Professor Darwin who he said was more concerned.

Attending the Bursar of St. John's at his rooms indicating the same line to him when he promised to bring the matter before a College Meeting tomorrow.

29th
Attending Mr. Matthew on his calling on behalf of the Darwin family repeating to him what we had said to Mr. H. Darwin and suggesting his clients should agree to appoint Mr. Jonas to advise the three properties he being already concerned with the Charity and the College.

Feb. 19th

Writing Bursar of Trinity Hall as instructed at the last meeting giving him an outline of the views of the Trustees as to the construction of the new road and asking him whether the College would join in the scheme so far as their land lying on the west of The Grove was concerned.

Attending the Bursar on his calling in reply and admitted the development of this land had been for some time in view and he agreed to the appointment of Mr. H. Jonas as surveyor to the proposed scheme for consideration of the three parties interested.

20th

Writing Messrs. Jonas and Sons with full instructions as to the scheme for consideration of the Trustees, St. John's College and Trinity Hall.

23rd

Writing Professor Darwin the proposal was considered abandoned as far as The Grove Estate was concerned.

From then on the practice records fall silent for a period of thirteen years. As the Charity was now subject to the superintendence of the Charity Commission and its properties vested in the Official Custodian for Charity Lands, it seems more than likely, as suggested in *"The Foundation of Edward Storey—A Short History 1693–1980"* (Larke and Shield) that negotiations with the Charity Commission would have taken place during this period aimed at gaining their acceptance to the development scheme.

Eventually,

"In 1909 it was agreed to develop as building land 35 acres of Mount Pleasant Farm, to build a road from Huntingdon Road to Madingley Road, and to ask the Commissioners to allow the value of the land to be written up as £20,000 in lieu of the existing £7,000".

For the sake of strict uniformity throughout the Estate an imposing printed document was drawn up by the practice in co-operation with Messrs. H. Jonas and Son combining the particulars of sale with handsome plans, specimen form of conveyance and form of Sale Memorandum for each plot. Sales proceeded satisfactorily during the year 1912, although formalities were not accelerated by the Charity Commission requirement that the selling price agreed for each plot had to be submitted to them for approval and the issue of a sale order. Fifteen plots were sold during the course of 1912 out of a possible total of sixty-one. Larke and Shield refers to increasing resistance from intending purchasers "… who beat down prices and demanded rights…" There was certainly some evidence of documentation being returned by purchasers' solicitors when it was discovered that the vendors would not covenant to make up the road. After an almost total standstill during the war sales picked up again during the nineteen twenties and were complete by 1930. Pevsner (*The Buildings of Cambridgeshire* 1954) thought it worth including reference in his book to Nos. 29, 30, 48, 54 and 56 Storey's Way, all houses designed by Baillie Scott, "one of the best British architects of the Voysey tradition". The eminent philosopher Ludwig Wittgenstein died at No. 76 (by Moberly) in 1950.

Walter H. Francis—Mayor of Cambridge

After residing at 3 Grange Road for five years Walter Francis stood for the Borough Council in the Fitzwilliam Ward and was elected councillor in 1902. Evidently diligent in his attendance at council meetings (ten out of a possible thirteen in 1909) and in his service on council committees (Market, Pensions and Plans Committees) Walter Francis was eventually elected to serve as Mayor of the Borough for the year 1912–13. During his year in office Walter Francis attracted some public attention on account of his inclination to express unexpected opinions, or points of view inappropriate to the occasion. No better example of this tendency has been recorded than the Mayor's speech at the opening of the new Higher Grade Council Schools in Melbourne Place, Cambridge (the present day Parkside Comunity College) in March 1913. Much expense had been incurred to make the schools (boys and girls being educated separately on the same site) as up to date and well equipped as possible. In the presence of numerous civic dignitaries, the University Vice-Chancellor and several heads of colleges

"... the Mayor in the course of his remarks said they would find they were very magnificent schools, they would no doubt be a great blessing to the town but they did not have his unqualified approval. He thought that for the most part they were very unnecessary. There had been an immense amount of money spent upon them. This had been unnecessary because they would remember that they were built on the theoretical foundations of two other schools which he did not at all approve of".

After suggesting that much expense was being incurred for a probably small result and mentioning a county scholar who was now working as a porter in a college kitchen he concluded by saying that

"until we get a concensus of opinion on the subject, our educational system would continue to be the failure which he was afraid at the present time it undoubtedly was".

The Mayor was followed by the Chairman of the Education Committee who was clearly disconcerted by these unexpected remarks and attempted to brush them aside, observing that it was a little embarrassing to follow the Mayor. He had seen the Mayor under many aspects, but he had never before recognised him as a humorist... He then proceeded to deliver a far more conventional address expressing the satisfaction which all present must have felt at the provision of such a successful building for education in Cambridge.

Having completed his term of office as mayor, Walter Francis was elected an alderman of the borough in 1914 and continued to sit on the Council in this capacity until 1925.

✳ ✳ ✳ ✳

Number Ten Peas Hill

The move of office from 18 Emmanuel Street to 10 Peas Hill had been planned for a number of years before it actually took place, on or about 1st January 1914. No doubt made aware of the plans of his landlords Emmanuel College for the demolition of the Emmanuel Street offices, Musgrave Francis had by a conveyance dated 8th August 1901 purchased from Edmund John Mortlock the freehold property described as

> "All That messuage or tenement and shop situate and being Number 10 Peas Hill in the Parish of St. Edward in the Town of Cambridge... together with the yard garden passage cellars and outbuildings thereto belonging".

Edmund Mortlock's signature on the deed was witnessed by

> "Thomas H. J. Porter, Clerk to Messrs. Francis Francis and Collin Solicitors Cambridge".

The property was at the time also subject to a lease in favour of William Bradford and Mary his wife for a term of two years from 24th June 1901 and thereafter from quarter to quarter at a rent of £135 per annum. The lease contained a covenant that

"... the tenants would not use or permit to be used the said dwelling-house and the appurtenances thereto otherwise than as a private residence or a University lodging house nor the shop for any trade business or manufacture of any noisy noisome or obnoxious nature".

Much clearly had to be done to the building before it could be occupied for use as solicitors' offices. However, before dealing with this part of the story it is first necessary to consider the nature and origins of the building, its previous uses owners and occupiers.

The description contained in RCHM p. 327 reads as follows:

"Peas Hill—South End:—

House, No. 10, five yards east of [Barclays Bank], is of three storeys with cellars and attics. The walls are of gault brick with stone dressings; the low mansard roof is slated. It was built in *c*.1830. Additions were made in the second decade of the twentieth century; probably at the same time the present north wall of the ground floor was substituted for a shop front to form a rusticated classical basement to the colossal Doric order above. This last has fluted pilasters without taper or entasis dividing the front into three unequal bays, the middle bay projecting slightly, and supporting a full doric entablature with low blocking course. In each bay and on each floor is a sash hung window with flat brick arch. In the roof are three squat flat roofed dormer windows; that in the middle is blind. Inside are two fireplace surrounds, of white and grey marble and a door, all of revived character, and several other doors, perhaps reused, with filled-in panels. In the additions are re-used balusters of 1700".

The date 1830 is clearly incorrect. The house appears to have been built by Edward Gillam, banker of Cambridge shortly after the site was leased to him on 14th April 1807 by the Mayor and Bailiffs and Burgesses of the Town of Cambridge. In Holden's Triennial Directory 1805–7, under the heading "Bankers in Cambridge", Thomas Fisher, Edward

Gillam, John Mortlock and Sons, had been listed. Edward Gillam was shown as resident in Pease Market Hill.

A surviving document from the year 1810 refers to Edward Gillam being of "the Cambridge Bank". By establishing his Cambridge Bank only a few yards away from Mortlock's Bank in Bene't Street and choosing such a conspicuous architectural style Edward Gillam clearly intended to challenge his longer established rival. If such was his aim Edward Gillam did not live to see his aim realised.

In the Chronicle for 30th April 1813 appeared an advertisement

> *"To be Let*
> A large dwellinghouse adjoining The Bank of
> Edward Gillam on Peas Hill with yard etc.
> Enquiries of Edward Gillam".

On 13th January 1815—

> "Edward Gillam Banker died very suddenly, Was a gentleman highly respected for his integrity and was about 77 years of age".

On 20th January 1815—

> "Notice to debtors and creditors of Edward Gillam late of the Town of Cambridge Banker and Oil Merchant, apply to his executors Hollick Burley and Finch at his late dwellinghouse on Peas Hill"
>
> By order
>
> John Finch Solicitor"

On 3rd March 1815—

For Sale by Auction
"... Cambridge—a capital house situate in the Peas Market Hill with
handsome entrance hall two good parlours one lately used as the
Bank, light convenient kitchen, spacious modern drawing room and
nine sleeping rooms, large back kitchen... pantry to cellars pleasant
garden etc. etc. The principal part of the house has been built within
the last seven years in which time convenience was materially aimed
at and very happily obtained—no expence was spared to make the
frontage suitable for the very respectable line of business so many
years carried on in these premises. The advantage of the garden and
private entrance renders it peculiarly adapted for the residence of a
genteel family, for an eminent profession and united with the
excellence of the situation makes it equally eligible for the more
enlarged description of trade".

The auction took place at the Rose Inn Cambridge on
Friday 31st March 1815, the successful bid of £1,680 being
made by Frederick Cheetham Mortlock. This was the ill-
starred fourth son of John Mortlock, to become sole surviving partner of Mortlock's Bank when his father died on 7th
May 1816. No equal to his father or elder brother Thomas
in business or banking ability Frederick Cheetham
Mortlock was soon in financial difficulty and eventually
assigned his interest in the business with responsibility for
his debts to his brother Thomas. By 1820 he had retired to
lead the life of a country gentleman in Leicestershire and
died in 1838 aged 52. It was the failure of his son John
Frederick Mortlock to accept that his father had been left
with only modest resources as a result of his arrangement
with Thomas Mortlock that led to the long running feud
with his uncles described in earlier pages.

Frederick Mortlock's successful bid for the property was
clearly a defensive move, aimed at giving himself control
over its use and occupation for the future.

In January 1818 Frederick Mortlock sold the Peas Hill
Bank to Esther Dornford. The property subsequently
passed into the hands of George Fisher (banker), then after
his death into the hands of his family trustees. On 4th March
1872 the trustees sold the property to Edmund John
Mortlock for £2,500.

10 Peas Hill does not appear to have been used as a bank
at any time after the sale by Edward Gillam's Executors in
1815. For a long period during the nineteenth century the
house was occupied by Messrs. Toft's cabinet makers and
upholsterers business and by 1900 the ground floor was
occupied by Messrs. Hill & Co. provision dealers.

Musgrave Francis' preparations for the move to 10 Peas
Hill were already in progress in October 1912. As reported
in the Cambridge Independent Press and Chronicle for
11th October 1912 the building work then in progress
produced unexpected results

"GRIM DISCOVERY
Human remains were dug up in the course of excavation at Peas Hill
(Cambridge) on Wednesday. A number of workmen in the employ
of Messrs. Clark & Son, were engaged in digging a trench at the rear
of the shop where business has been carried on by Messrs. Mason &
Co (Mrs. Bradford keeping a University Lodging House at the rear of
the premises), when they came across a couple of skeletons. Offices
are being erected for Messrs. Francis, Solicitors of Emmanuel Street,
and it is stated that at the back of the buildings which are being
demolished the site used to stand of an old monastery. The skeletons
were found by workmen named Richard Saunders and John Howe,
who were digging under the old kitchen for the purpose of the
sinking of new cellars. The two figures, possibly those of a man and
woman, were discovered about eight feet down and parallel, being
about three yards apart, the heads, which as well as other bones,
suggest that the bodies were buried some hundreds of years ago, are
fairly well preserved. The teeth are in wonderfully good condition..."

Apart from the demolition of older buildings at the rear and construction of a new two-storey office extension in their place, the lockers formerly in Mr. Francis' room at Emmanuel Street were dismantled and re-erected in the first floor front room, to be occupied as Musgrave Francis' office until 1931.

With a new brass plate beside the front door, practice for Francis & Co commenced in January 1914 and was to continue at 10 Peas Hill until close of business on Friday 3rd May 1986, 72 years later.

* * * *

Francis & Co. was already settled and established in its new address by the time of the outbreak of the First World War on 4th August 1914. All four partners were clearly over age for active military service (T. M. Francis sixty four, W. H. Francis fifty six, J. Collin forty seven and F. K. Peile forty three). Captain W. H. Francis had, however, retained his commission in the 4th Battalion Suffolk Regiment as a part-time volunteer, and became involved in service of the kind undertaken during the Second World War by the Home Guard.

Captain Walter Francis' military duties appear to have been performed mainly in the Ipswich area under leave of absence from his partners. This was not too far away for an occasional return visit, for example on the death of Rev. Dr. Atkinson. On 1st March 1915 a telegram was sent to Captain Francis at Ipswich informing him of the funeral arrangements and his journey from Ipswich to attend the funeral the following day was recorded in the bill book.

By June 1916 it was realised that a distinction would have to be made between the younger and more active members of the volunteer forces and those of more advanced years. An announcement appeared in The Times for Thursday

29th June 1916 under the following heading

Royal Defence Corps.
National Reserve in a New Form

A supplement to the London Gazette last night contained a large number of appointments to the Royal Defence Corps. Most of the appointments are to "protection companies" and the rest to "observer companies".

The corps was formed in March but its object was not explained at the time. It was understood, however, that the creation of the new corps was a preliminary to the use of the Volunteer Corps and placing them on a proper basis, which, as had been previously announced, were to be given a definite military status under the Volunteer Act.

The main object which the military authorities had in view in recognising the Volunteer Corps and placing them on a proper basis, was to use those of their members who were willing to devote their spare time to patrol and guard duties at railway bridges, waterworks and other vulnerable points. These duties have hitherto been entrusted to supernumerary companies of the Territorial Units, comprised of old soldiers who belonged to the National Reserve and who had offered themselves for service on the outbreak of the war. The volunteers are now to take the place of these supernumerary companies and the object of the Royal Defence Corps is to organise the supernumerary companies, which number several hundred and are distributed over the whole of Great Britain, into a new body, and to use them in other branches of home defence work.

From the London Gazette—28th June 1916
Royal Defence Corps—Officers Gazetted—
Protection Companies.
The following Officers from the Territorial Force Reserve General List to be transferred as follows with date and precedence as in the Territorial Force Reserve General List
To be Captains (inter alia)
Captain W. H. Francis (Late Captain and Hon. Major 4th Bn. Suffolk Regiment).

In this less demanding role Walter Francis served in the

Royal Defence Corps until it was disbanded shortly after the cessation of hostilities in November 1918. By this time he had been promoted to the rank of Major.

At least one client is known to have received a letter in his absence from the office stating that

> "Mr. W. H. Francis is at present away on active service but will attend to your business on his return".

Frank Peile had held the post of secretary to the Cambridgeshire and District Law Society since 1908 and in this role he co-ordinated the society's involvement in the Tobacco Fund. Through this scheme packages of cigarettes and tobacco were sent out to "our soldiers at the front". Postcard acknowledgements were thoughtfully provided in these packages for recipients wishing to send back messages of thanks. A collection of cards from men of the 1st Battalion Cambridgeshire Regiment has survived from the spring and summer of 1915, all addressed to "Cambs. Law Society per Frank K. Peile Esq., 10 Peas Hill, Cambridge." At this time the Regiment was first involved in the early operations for defence of the Ypres Salient near Hill 60, later moving further south to the Givenchy/Festubert/Ferme de Bois sectors.

The impact of war time conditions on client business, as reflected in bill book entries, was noticeable but not overwhelmingly so. The following selection of entries appropriately reflect the times:

1914 — Oct. 14
Having received a letter from the Registrary informing us that the Censor of non-collegiate students had made application to enter an alien enemy and enquiring whether he had the legal power to do so. Writing him carefully in reply...

Nov. 4.

Attending Mr. Rottenberg (Red Cross Society) on his handing us correspondence with the Surgical Manufacturing Co. with reference to an order for 12 stretchers which were not satisfactory and giving an outline of the correspondence...

Nov. 11.

Attending the Bursar and Dr. Bond on their giving us instructions for an amendment within the College Statutes reducing the number of Fellows from 13 to 11.

Nov. 19th.

Attending the Master on his calling as to the construction of Statute XV as Mr. Knox Shaw was appointed Lecturer in June and was now at the front and they wished him to retain the lectureship on which depended his fellowship...

Dec. 7th

Attending the Master and Bursar on their calling and giving us instructions to prove the Will of Lieutenant J. G. M. D.—who was killed in action on the 25th August leaving a Will under which he had appointed the College executors...

1915 — Feb. 17.

Journey to Norwich to attend conference of representatives of the asylums in the Eastern Counties with a view to the appropriation of the Norfolk County Asylum for the accommodation of wounded soldiers and the distribution of the patients therein amongst the other asylums, when it was intimated by the Board of Control, Dr. Cook, who was present, that the Board would allow asylums to overcrowd to the extent of twenty per cent and it was intimated by Dr. Thompson that the Visitors under these circumstances would be prepared to receive one hundred additional patients, fifty of each sex...

July 7th

Attending you on your calling giving us instructions to prepare Power of Attorney in favour of your brother on your going abroad on active service...

Sept. 21st.
Attending Mr. C.—on his bringing Will of Captain R. M. S.— of St. Neots who was killed in the Dardanelles, the Will being executed on the way out and unattested and we were to advise upon it...

Sept. 24th
Attending you on your calling consulting us with reference to an idea for promoting the sale of your proprietary brands of cigarettes and cigars but it involved the loan of £600 or £700 or the formation of a Company and we advised that in view of the increased duty and the times generally it could not be undertaken with any chance of success...

1916 — June 12th
Attending the Bursar on his referring to the conviction of Mr. Bertrand Russell under the Defence of the Realm Act and to the fact that last year he was appointed Lecturer for the term of five years contrary to the usual practice which was during the pleasure of the Council in accordance with the Statute and he enquired the position of the College and whether he could be removed...

1917 — 24th Oct.
Sugar Rations
Attending Mr. Brindley the steward on his informing us that it had been arranged with the Food Committee that the College should be considered an Institution and rationed accordingly except with regard to the non-resident fellows who would be treated on hotel basis and cadets would have 8 ounces a week but that the Committee had now changed its mind and decided that everyone in College including U.Gs must be considered householders with cards and that they must hand over to the kitchen a proportion of the sugar used for common meals. On referring to the instructions issued by the Food Controller we advised that the Local Committee had a discretion under which the College could be treated as an Institution and that we thought the best plan was for the steward to decide what was really desired and then approach the committee again if necessary the Food Controller himself...

From 1917 onwards warlike thoughts of the "Hang the Kaiser" variety became gradually to be shared in the public mind with considerations of reconstruction and social amelioration. Mr. Asquith's appointment as Minister of Reconstruction marked the start of these changing attitudes and echoes of the new thinking penetrated to local level. With the appointment of Dr. P. C. Varrier-Jones, an exceedingly active County Tuberculosis Officer for Cambridgeshire, the scourge of T.B. was addressed vigorously at county level. Musgrave Francis was appointed chairman of the Cambridgeshire Tuberculosis Committee in 1917 and the practice was involved in the formation under this name of a company limited by guarantee for the purpose of acquiring the Papworth Hall Estate as a County T.B. sanatorium. An industrial settlement for patients and their families was also to be provided. The purchase was completed on 17th December 1917. Papworth Hospital and Papworth Village Settlement have since become household names, the former for transplant surgery and the latter for the goods of all kinds made in the settlement workshops. Musgrave Francis remained chairman of the committee until 1931.

Major electoral reform was achieved by Parliament when the Representation of the People Act received the Royal Assent on 6th February 1918. Outstanding contributions to the war effort by women had earned for them the parliamentary vote (initially for those over thirty) which the suffragette movement had failed to win. However, the bill did not pass through Parliament without causing anxious debate and active lobbying in Cambridge. The practice was first brought into the discussions when the Vice-Chancellor called with a print of the Parliamentary Bill on 4th December 1917. The main cause of University anxiety was that the Cambridge University constituency consisted solely of voters with Cambridge degrees. The bill itself was intended to give the vote to women yet at this time Cambridge women students were only given "titular" degrees and would not become graduates of the University for another thirty years. Meetings with the Vice-Chancellor, the Master of St. John's, the Registrary and the two University Members followed in rapid succession during December 1917 and January 1918. Contact in the House of Lords was established with Lord Peel and with Edmund Parker's brother, now Lord Parker of Waddington and in the Commons with Sir Arthur Thring. By mid-January letters were received both from Lord Parker and Sir Arthur as to the extent of the amendments being sought by the University and "deprecating our pressing for anything further". Once the bill received the Royal Assent on 5th February a case was prepared for the joint opinion of Mr. J. A. Fook K.C. and Mr. Whittaker as to the implementation of the relevant sections of the Act to the Cambridge University constituency. Following receipt of the opinion on 22nd February the Council of the Senate issued a statement on 25th February. This commenced by quoting the relevant sections of the Act,

Section 2
"A man shall be entitled to be registered as a parliamentary elector for a university constituency if he is of full age and not subject to any legal incapacity and has received a degree (other than an honorary degree) at any University forming, or forming part of, the constituency..."
Section 4(2)
"A woman shall be entitled to be registered as a parliamentary elector for a university constituency if she has attained the age of thirty years and... has been admitted to and passed the final examination and kept under the conditions required of women by the university the period of residence necessary for a man to obtain a degree..."

S.4(2) was in effect tailor-made for the Oxford and Cambridge constituencies without actually saying so. When Oxford allowed women to graduate in 1921 this section became of exclusive application to Cambridge.

The Council then made a number of recommendations for implementing the new legislation including

> "(2) the Council think it desirable that in order to meet the expense of preparing and maintaining the parliamentary register a registration fee of £1 shall be charged to persons taking their first degree after the passing of the Act..."

> "(5) It will be observed that since the University does not admit women to degrees, the Senate is not empowered by S.19 (relating to the keeping of Parliamentary registers in the University constituencies) to require women to make a claim in order to be registered, or to charge any fee for registration to women. The Council think it desirable to ask for the assistance of the authorities of Girton and Newnham Colleges in the preparation of the register... by giving such information as they possess with regard to qualified women and in particular by supplying certificates of age and of residence kept".

As a result of this skirmish between the forces of reform and reaction, Cambridge women for the next thirty years enjoyed a privilege which was to become unique in any of the university constituencies, having a second parliamentary vote without being graduates of their university.

Relief from this paradox was vouchsafed by separate and quite unco-ordinated reforms. Cambridge women were admitted to degrees in 1947 and the university constituencies were abolished by Parliament in 1948.

The Haldane Episode
Moral attitudes were showing signs of change in the aftermath of the First World War. Among many remarkable figures in Cambridge in the nineteen twenties none was more arresting nor more outrageous than J. B. S. Haldane (1892–1964). After distinguished service in the Black Watch in the First World War, being described by Haig as

"the bravest and dirtiest officer in my army", Haldane was in 1922 appointed reader in biochemistry at Cambridge. The author still recalls his commanding presence and voice when 30 years later Professor Haldane held the chair of biometry in the University of London. In 1924 he formed a strong and very public attachment with an unhappily married journalist, Charlotte Burghes. To obtain grounds for divorce from her husband, Haldane and Charlotte determined to provide the necessary evidence of adultery. Never given to secrecy in his personal life, Haldane informed his professor and the University Vice-Chancellor, Prof. A. C. Seward, of his intentions well in advance.

Evidence of adultery having been produced and accepted in court and the divorce decree pronounced, Haldane was then placed in confrontation with those six senior members of the University who together comprised the Sex Viri or University Court. With the Vice-Chancellor they were charged with the guardianship of morals and discipline within the University. The members of this body evidently felt that there was reason to deprive Haldane of his readership on the grounds of gross immorality within the meaning of the University statutes. After a preliminary meeting with the Sex Viri, the Vice-Chancellor warned Haldane that his case was to be considered, and gave him the opportunity to resign. This Haldane ignored and appeared before the Sex Viri on 6th November 1925 to defend his actions on the ground that the divorce had been in the best interests of Charlotte and her child. On 12th December the Sex Viri met again and passed a motion depriving Haldane of his readership. This decision appeared in the University Reporter on 22nd December 1925 as follows:

Communcation from the Sex Viri
22nd December 1925
WHEREAS in proceedings in the probate divorce and admiralty

division of the High Court of Justice, Mr. J. B. S. Haldane, reader in biochemistry in the University, had been pronounced by a verdict of a jury to have been guilty of adultery with the wife of Mr. John McLeod Burghes

AND WHEREAS Mr. J. B. S. Haldane, on appearing before us on the 6th December 1925, admitted having committed adultery

NOW THEREFORE We the Vice-Chancellor of the University of Cambridge and the six persons elected and acting in accordance with Chapter VII of Statute A of the University do hereby in pursuance of the powers conferred upon us by Statute B Chapter IX Section 7 of the said University unanimously adjudge

(1) That Mr. J. B. S. Haldane has been guilty of gross immorality within the meaning of the said Statute 8 Chapter IX Section 7
(2) That Mr. J. B. S. Haldane be therefore and is hereby deprived of his said office of reader in biochemistry.

Signatures:

A. C. SEWARD Vice-Chancellor.
E. C. PEARCE (Master of Corpus Christi).
CHALMERS (Master of Peterhouse).
(Professor) H. D. HAZLETINE (Master of Trinity Hall).
(Professsor) W. W. BUCKLAND.
(Professor) COURTNEY S. KENNEY.
HENRY BOND.

A right of appeal existed from this decision and entirely true to form Haldane decided to exercise it. Being rarely invoked, the appeal procedure caused considerable anxiety on the university side. Having instructed Musgrave Francis to engage counsel to appear for the University at the hearing Seward, according to Howarth p.55, revealed

"...signs of haste, if not panic, accentuated by the fact that he had no great confidence in the University's solicitors, 'whose senior partner is not always up to date; he declined to have a bathroom in his house for some time, and I do not know that he has one even now'. Meanwhile, the Council of the Senate had to nominate five Judges Delegate of whom two were required to have legal experience. Five distinguished names were chosen and the Judges Delegate met at the High Court in London on 17th March 1926 under the chairmanship of Mr. Justice Avory, "the celebrated hanging judge".

The technical difficulty facing the University was that they would have to prove to the tribunal not only that immorality had taken place, but that it was gross immorality. After hearing counsel for both parties, and retiring for fifty minutes, the tribunal issued their verdict

"that the majority of the court is of the opinion that in view of all the circumstances of this particular case, which have been more fully before us than they were before the Sex Viri, the appeal should be allowed; but this decision is not to be taken as any expression of opinion that adultery may not be gross immorality within the meaning of the Statute".

Professor Kenney, a distinguished lawyer, commented that the decision surprised him greatly while Seward, after visiting Musgrave Francis, wrote

"I saw Francis today in his kitchen-midden; he did not tell me anything fresh, but said that in his opinion, Avory, Bragg and Fletcher were the majority" (quoted in Howarth p. 57).

As a result Haldane returned to his readership and started married life with Charlotte in Old Chesterton in 1926, the marriage enduring until divorce proceedings again intervened in 1945.

The account delivered to the University by the practice four months later ran as follows:

July 1926

The Chancellor Masters and Scholars
of the University of Cambridge
1926, March.
Costs of and incidental to the
appeal by Mr. J. B. S. Haldane to the
Judges Delegate against the
decision of the Sex Viri,
depriving him of his readership in
Biochemistry; preparing brief for
Sir Malcolm Macnaughten KC to
appear for the University at the
hearing—copy minutes of the
meeting of the Sex Viri and
correspondence. Journey to London
attending hearing when the appeal
was allowed—including the cost of
London Agents and correspondence
throughout   £31.10s.0.
Paid Counsel's fees.   £60.16s . 0d.
Paid shorthand transcript.   £14. 3s. 7d.
Paid Court Fees.   £2. 0s. 0d.
Paid Travelling Expenses.   £0. 16s. 3d.
Paid copy documents.   £0. 14s.10d.
Paid Telephones, Telegrams and
Miscellaneous disbursements.   £1. 1s. 0d.   £79.11s.8d

TOTAL   £111.1s.8d

In defence of Musgrave Francis, it has to be said that he
was as little practised in the conduct of appeals from decisions of the Sex Viri as Seward himself was in convening
them. If Seward thought the seventy-six year old Francis old
fashioned, Musgrave Francis seated in his open yellow
tourer might have thought the same of Seward. Only the
previous year the Vice-Chancellor had told the Senate that

"the motor habit, when it becomes an obsession, induces a state of
mind out of harmony with the best traditions of Cambridge",

and shortly afterwards, undergraduates were forbidden to have cars.

As a rather odd semantic epilogue, it may be mentioned that on 2nd February 1937 a new University statute was approved by the King in Council substituting the title "The Septem Viri" for "The Vice-Chancellor and the Sex Viri" as the name of the University Court.

Even if not preoccupied with the conduct of an appeal from the Sex Viri, every practising solicitor in England and Wales was, with effect from 1st January 1926, faced with momentous and far reaching changes in the law of property brought about by the property legislation of 1925, the collective name for the Law of Property Act, the Settled Land Act, the Administration of Estates Act, the Trustee Act, the Land Registration Act and the Universities and College Estates Act. The nature of land tenures of all kinds was effectively transformed and overnight the new order displaced the old. Professional practices observed for generations had to be forgotten or re-learned. Especially was this so in the case of Francis & Co. The abolition of manorial courts and copyhold land tenure meant that their venerable managing clerk Thomas Porter (1857–1936) would no longer proceed in his pony and trap to the farther corners of the county and beyond, to convene the manorial courts.

Conscious of their responsibility to members, the committee of the Cambridgeshire and District Law Society had already held a meeting at 10 Peas Hill on 19th May 1925 and resolved

"to recommend that a series of six lectures on the Law of Property Acts be arranged for the months of October, November and December, the fees to be paid by the Society".

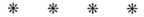

In 1927 the practice suffered the loss of its youngest partner, and the local Law Society its secretary, as announced in the Times on Thursday, 29th September 1927.

"Deaths
PEILE On September 27th 1927 at the Bishop's Hostel, Lichfield Frank Kitchener Peile MA of 29 Lyndewoode Road, Cambridge son of John Peile Litt.D. formerly Master of Christ's College, aged 56. Funeral at Lichfield tomorrow (Friday) 2.30.

Obituary
Mr. Frank Kitchener Peile, solicitor of Cambridge who died at Lichfield on Tuesday at the age of 56 was the son of the late Dr. John Peile, Master of Christ's College, Cambridge and brother of Mrs. Kempthorne, wife of the Bishop of Lichfield. Mr. Peile had been in ill health for the past three months and recently spent a fortnight with the Bishop and Mrs. Kempthorne in the Lake District. He returned with his sister to Bishop's Hostel, Lichfield, where he suddenly became worse on Saturday. The funeral will be in Lichfield Cathedral Close tomorrow at 2.30."

Frank Peile lies buried in the Cathedral Close at Lichfield.

Public Life of Musgrave Francis
It was only from the commencement of the 20th century that Musgrave Francis was to acquire a series of public appointments appropriate in more general terms to his standing in the Borough and the County, as distinct from those appointments either of a legal character or appropriate to a qualified Solicitor which he had received until then. He was appointed a magistrate in 1907 and this led in turn to his appointment in 1918 to the Standing Joint Committee of the County with its supervisory role over the County Constabulary. He also became a visitor to prisons and institutions under the Mental Deficiency Act. After serving as Vice-Chairman of quarter sessions under

Professor Kenney he was appointed chairman in June 1922 and held the chairmanship of the Licensing Committee of the County for one year.

In the health field Musgrave Francis first joined the general committee of Addenbrookes Hospital in 1903 and during his first three years on the committee became vice-chairman in 1906. He was re-elected to the committee in 1918 and became chairman in 1923, continuing to hold this position until he died. According to Musgrave Francis's obituary in the Cambridge Chronicle (11th March 1931)

> "He had been Chairman of the Finance Committee of Addenbrookes Hospital for a number of years. All through his connection with the Hospital he has been Honorary Solicitor. In 1921 he was Chairman of the House Committee. The fund raised for the purchase of radium was organised by him. He has had considerable responsibility in connection with the planning of the new buildings and the changes of policy and matters which have been discussed for 2 years. A ward has been named after him".

Musgrave Francis's service as Chairman of the Papworth Hospital Committee from 1918 to 1931 has already been mentioned.

In the local government field Musgrave Francis served as a member of the Chesterton Rural District Council, becoming Chairman of the General Purposes and Sanitary Committees. His position in public life also led to his election as a governor or manager of the Old Schools of Cambridge, Park Street School and St. Phillips School, continuing as chairman of the managers of Park Street School until his death.

✳   ✳   ✳   ✳

Business undertaken by the practice in the early nineteen twenties continued to reflect the changing times. In 1922 instructions were received from Jesus College for the grant of a lease to Messrs. Marshall and Rayner in respect of premises in Jesus Lane for use as a garage from 25th March 1922. Marshall's filling station and motor showroom continues to operate from this site to this day.

On 29th January 1923 the Union Society enquired whether a proposal to install a wireless set at the Union would render the Society liable to entertainment tax. The answer obtained from the Inland Revenue was that it would not.

In the same year an unusual request was received from Professor Alexander Pearce Higgins, (grandfather of A. T. Pearce Higgins the present partner). Dr. Pearce Higgins announced that he had exchanged his residence at 3 Salisbury Villas, Station Road with the occupier of number 5 Salisbury Villas next door. He asked for all necessary formalities to be carried out to regularise this transaction.

Death of Musgrave Francis

At the conclusion of a long career from which he had not yet retired, Musgrave Francis died on 6th March 1931, prompting the following report in the Cambridge Chronicle for Wednesday March 11th:

MUSGRAVE FRANCIS
CAMBRIDGESHIRE MOURNS LOSS OF GREAT GENTLEMAN
MARKS OF HIS CAREER

Within a few weeks of his eighty-first birthday Mr. Thomas Musgrave Francis of Quy Hall, Cambridgeshire died on Friday morning last. The end came unexpectedly and was due to a blood clot. He had been operated upon in the Evelyn Nursing Home and was making satisfactory progress towards recovery when the complication arose.

He died, probably as he had hoped to die, "in his tracks" and he worked practically until the end. He kept on public and private work knowing that his day was nearly done and it was always cheery to hear him say of a project reaching fulfilment in two or three years time, "I shall not live to see it, but...". He looked at life calmly and dispassionately, almost as it seemed in advanced years from a detached position. Everybody thought of him as a great gentleman. He had charm of manner which was not superficial but was the product of character and had the strength of growth. There was an air about him reminiscent of courtlier days but he could be stern when the occasion arose. As a Magistrate and as a district councillor the detachment of his personality persisted. He regarded affairs with a cultivated mind and the rough and tumble of controversy always appeared to startle him. He was firm of his opinion and independent in thought even if he did not always resist strongly contrary views.

He came into local public life comparatively late and the greater part of his career was as a solicitor. Since the death of his father Mr. Clement Francis he had been Senior Partner in the Firm of Francis and Co., Solicitors for the University of Cambridge and to most of the Colleges.

THE SQUIRE

The people of Quy will think of Mr. Francis as the Squire. He entered upon possession of Quy Hall when his Mother died in 1895. He was the second son of a family of 13 children.

The encouragement that he always gave to younger men was characteristic of Mr. Francis's public work...

Throughout his long life he had abundant physical energy and in the last years he made light of the attacks of pain and weakness maintaining his habits as far as possible. It was only a month ago that he last walked from his office to the railway station as was his custom and he did so in the cold weather without an overcoat. He was always reluctant to order his car...

THE FUNERAL

SERVICE AT QUY CHURCH

The funeral took place at Quy Parish Church on Monday afternoon. The service was conducted by the Vicar (Rev. L. Hansen Bay) assisted by the Vicar of Bottisham (Rev. W. A. Uthwatt). The Hymns sung were "Now the Labourer's Task Is Over" and "Abide with Me"

and the Nunc Dimittis was chanted. Miss Watts was the organist and she played Handel's Largo and "Oh Rest in The Lord" (Mendelssohn)
(Among the mourners were Staff of Quy Hall, and the Members of the Staff of Messrs. Francis & Co. including Messrs. T. J. H. Porter, S. J. Dunn, F. Hale, S. E. Woods, R. D. Charter, H. Martin, W. J. Collins, P. G. Wheeler, and Miss Jupps).

REPRESENTATIVE CONGREGATION AT ST. ANDREWS CHURCH

At the hour of the funeral there was a memorial service at the Church of St. Andrew's Cambridge. In the large congregation were the heads of local government in Town and County and representatives of the University, Addenbrookes Hospital, and other organisations and interests, with which Mr. Francis was specially connected.

PUBLIC TRIBUTES

At the special meeting of the Cambs County Council on Saturday, the Chairman (Alderman W. C. Jackson) said that one of the most prominent men in the County had died in Mr. T. Musgrave Francis. In connection with the County Council Mr. Francis had been a member of the Standing Joint Committee since 1918 he was also a co-optive member of the Committee for the care of the Mentally Defective and the Public Assistance Committee. But besides these things, Mr. Francis had done an enormous amount of public work to the great benefit of the County for a great number of years. "The County has lost what I might term a very great gentleman and I am sure we will all very greatly regret his passing and agree that the County will be very much indeed the poorer for his loss".

Presiding at the Cambridge Divisional Court on Saturday his Honour Judge Farrant said "I should like to express on your behalf what I am sure we must all feel our deep regret of the death of our friend Mr. Musgrave Francis. His public career must be well known to all of you and it is therefore unnecessary for me to enlarge upon it beyond saying that probably no one ever undertook more voluntary work than he did or performed it more conscientiously. His loss is a great one not only to the Borough and County but also to his many friends of whom I was privileged to be one. I beg to move that we place on record our deep regret of his death and our great appreciation of his services in many capacities and our sympathy with his relatives in the great loss which they have sustained".

The Mayor of Cambridge (Councillor E. Jackson), the (Clerk Mr. S. J. Miller) the Chief Constable (W. Varney Webb) and Mr. W. Copleston associated themselves with the tribute.

In an editorial comment in the same issue of the Chronicle,

"Mr. T. Musgrave Francis was approaching his eighty-first birthday but he was an old man of such vigour that he seemed to have another ten years of life and his unexpected death has grieved the whole community in which he lived himself. There have been few men held in such complete affection during the last 25 years by the County and Borough of Cambridge. He was a power in the community and he drew from all trust and confidence. It was not what he did or what he said but personality. He gave himself freely in serving the community during the last quarter of a century of his life at Addenbrokes Hospital at Papworth in the Police Court and on the Bench and at the County Court of Session".

An obituary had already appeared in the Times for 7th March 1931 in the following terms:—

MR. MUSGRAVE FRANCIS

Mr. Thomas Musgrave Francis of Quy Hall Cambridge who died suddenly yesterday after an operation in his eighty-first year was a much respected figure in Cambridge.

He went to Eton in 1862 the first year of Dr. Balston's Headmastership, was in the Rev. F. Vidal's dame's house and "Ionica" Johnson was his tutor. He went up to Trinity College Cambridge and after taking his degree joined his father Mr. Clement Francis in business as a Solicitor. The firm had been appointed Solicitors to the University in the early 60's and with the exception of a brief interval after the death of Mr. Clement Francis this connection has continued up to the present time, Musgrave Francis having held the position for more than 40 years. The firm also acted for about a dozen Colleges.

Mr. Francis had been a Clerk to the County Mental Hospitals since

1880 and was Clerk to the Conservators of the Cam, and to various endowed charities. He also took an active interest in the public life of the County and the Borough. He served as a County Magistrate from 1907, was a Deputy Lieutenant and was Chairman of Quarter Sessions from 1922 to 1929. He was further Chairman of the Governors of Addenbrooke's Hospital and Chairman of the Committee of Management of Papworth Tuberculosis Colony from its foundation in 1917 until 1928.

Having succeeded his father in the ownership of Quy Hall near Cambridge Mr. Francis as a resident land owner was deeply concerned for the welfare of the village and its inhabitants. He was a man of extensive reading and a keen observer of social life, taking special interest in the biography and the reminiscences of public men. His knowledge of art was considerable and he made a fine collection of Cambridge prints. He retained his activity in a wonderful way and his spare and upright figure was a familiar sight in the streets of Cambridge as well as in the immediate neighbourhood of his home. He seldom desired to break away from his habitual routine and he used to say that he took his last holiday away from home in 1915. He was a man of sensitive and scrupulous honour and was in all his relationships characterised by the punctilious courtesy of a gentleman of the old School. He was unmarried".

On Musgrave Francis's death the ownership of Quy Hall passed to his nephew Lt. Col. John Clement Wolstan Francis. From that time onwards legal practice and landowning were divided between separate branches of the Francis family. Quy Hall was to become in turn the residence of J. C. W. Francis (1888–1978) and of his son Major J. C. G. Francis (b. 1919) the present owner.

[It is necessary to record with regret that Major John Francis died on 19th October 1989, after the text of this book had been prepared.]

Chapter 18

CHANGING SCENES—1931–45

 HE story of the practice recorded in this chapter, a period running from the middle of the depression until the conclusion of the Second World War, was inevitably to be played out against a backdrop of crisis, gathering clouds and world conflict.

On 1st January 1931 a new partner, Walter Maclaren Francis, was admitted to the firm, barely two months before the death of Musgrave Francis.

As already mentioned, Walter Maclaren Francis (1900–1970) was the only son of Walter Hamond Francis. After attending school at St. Faith's Cambridge and Repton he had entered Trinity Hall in 1919, obtaining his B.A. Degree in 1921 and proceeding M.A. in 1925. Departing from previous practice, Walter Francis had been articled in 1922 outside the family, to Mr. M. F. Tweedy of 5 Lincoln's Inn Fields WC2 for three years and had been admitted as a solicitor in 1925. He had then worked as an assistant solicitor with the practice until his admission to the partnership.

Musgrave Francis was succeeded as senior partner by his brother Walter Hamond Francis. The three partners of the firm were then W. H. Francis (seventy three) John Collin (sixty four) and W. M. Francis (thirty one).

By this time the institutional clients listed at the start of the last chapter had increased by the addition of Addenbrooke's Hospital, the Evelyn Nursing Home, Girton College, Newnham College and the Ely Diocesan Board of Finance.

Also working for the firm at this time as an assistant solicitor, later to join the partnership, was John Collin's son Hugh Collin.

Hugh Garret Collin had obtained a B.A. degree at Trinity Hall in 1926, proceeding M.A. in 1931. He had been articled for three years from 1st October 1926 to John Collin and had been admitted as a solicitor in 1930. He was to become a partner on 1st January 1934.

Even a four man partnership was inadequate to handle the increasing volume of business if two of them were by now well over sixty. However, assistance was sought and found in 1935 when Dudley Durell was invited to join Francis & Co. as an assistant solicitor.

Dudley Vavasour Durell, already known both to the Francis and the Collin families, had strong Cambridge connections. As mentioned in an earlier chapter, his grandfather Rev. J. V. Durell had held two livings in Fulbourn and his father Col. A. J. V. Durell had served for part of his career as Bursar of the Leys School Cambridge. Educated at Oundle and Clare College (B.A. 1931 M.A. 1936) Dudley Durell spent two years in an advertising agency and two more on the staff of the newly formed University College at Hull before commencing articles in 1931 first at Messrs. Torr & Co. in Bedford Row and then with Messrs. Altree Johnson and Ward in Gray's Inn, being admitted as a solicitor in 1935.

Excerpts from Dudley Durell's reminiscences of this period, kindly supplied to the author, are reproduced below,

"I knew both the Collin and Francis families and when they learnt that I was on the market they offered me a job specifically to deal with College and University work. I was asked to join the firm in May 1935 as Hugh Collin was getting married in June.

At that time there were four Partners, John Collin, very much the senior partner, but suffering from emphysema (he had a distinguished career as an oarsman at St. John's) and in consequence spending half the year in Devonshire; Walter Hamond Francis, a dim figure who sat through the year in front of his gas fire in a room hermetically sealed, refusing to answer the telephone and insisting on press copying such letters as he wrote; Walter Maclaren Francis (W. H. F's son) and Hugh Collin (J. C's son). The Collins and Francises were not on good terms and I found myself as something of an intermediary. The Francises did no College or University work.

(In 1937 Durell received an invitation to return to his former firm in London)

"By that time I had decided that I preferred provincial life. Francis and Co. offered me a partnership so I stayed, as a salaried Partner—my salary raised from £150 to £200 a year.

"It is interesting to consider what sort of a town Cambridge then was and what its legal profession consisted of.

"Cambridge was then essentially a market town with a total population of some 60,000. The only substantial business firm was Chivers at Histon—still a family firm as were Marshalls, Pye and the Cambridge Scientific Instrument Company (started by the Darwin family). The University were the main employers of labour. The total rateable value of all the residential houses was around £700,000. There was still a thriving Cattle Market and Corn Exchange. Solicitors closed on Thursday afternoons and were open all day Saturday to catch the farmers who came in for the markets (the younger generation, after bitter opposition achieved Saturday afternoon closing before the War).

There were less than 40 qualified Solicitors and some 16 firms. Francis and Co. were the largest with five Partners—few others had more than two.

The Court work was almost completely in the hands of two

solicitors—Wild (Roy Hewitson had not yet arrived) and Kester a former Managing Clerk who was effectively taking over Few & Co. (formerly Few & Wild). Wild had set up on his own taking with him some of Few's best clients.

The University closed down throughout the whole long vacation—though a new generations of bursars was beginning to infiltrate from the outside world.

Hansom cabs and trams—which I remember as a child—had disappeared but in the vacation their memory lingered on.

When I arrived at Francis & Co. apart from the partners there was one middle-aged (or at least thirty-ish) woman typist and clerk who looked after John Collin, Fred Hale who had been W. H. F's batman in the First World War (known as the sergeant) who did Storey's Charity, tax commissioners and the Internal Fen Drainage Boards, Henry Martin who dealt with other appointments and some conveyancing, Jim Collins who looked after the elder Francis and W. M. F. Charter the probate clerk (who suffered from recurrent nervous breakdowns and finally had to leave—it took me months of midnight oil and a good deal of tact to clear up his uncompleted matters), Wheeler a managing clerk who dealt with Hugh Collin's and my work, plus an office boy. In due course, a number of junior typists graduated from the front office to secretarial status and by 1937 I had two girls working for me. Apart from the rooms at the back of the office, and W. H. F's room, all rooms had open fires. One woman laid and cleaned these every day and returned at 4 o'clock to make cups of tea. She and her husband cleaned the office in the evenings.

Our practice was generally regarded in the town (and by us) as elitist. We did no common law (and had recently lost Downing because John Collin would not look after an errant under-graduate). Our private practice was small—the Francises had the County families but private clients were nearly all dons—we were suspect as acting primarily for College landlords. We held a number of exceedingly remunerative offices.

From the outset I was determined to build up private practice—although very heavily engaged in the University and College work. I took on any common law work that I could—County Court, Magistrates Court and a certain amount of divorce, though it was never my forte. Professional negligence insurance was virtually unknown and was met by considerable opposition from the senior partners when I insisted on taking it out.

There was very little co-operation between firms, for example John Few was not on speaking terms with John Collin and would only communicate with the firm through me.

When I first arrived, Hugh Collin went off for a month's honeymoon and I was left (having only been admitted for about four months) to deal with all the University and College work unsupervised—except that my letters were signed by W. M. F. Thereafter Hugh and I shared the work. Completions tended to be fairly leisurely affairs on which we always both went, often taking our wives with us, and not infrequently staying the night. In those days many—perhaps the majority of firms were run entirely by managing clerks, the partners being little more than figureheads. I remember one completion at Melton Mowbray when we were greeted by the senior partner in hunting pink—given a drink at the local hotel and handed over to the managing clerk. In the season he hunted at least three days a week and throughout the summer played county cricket.

When I started, we had an old engrossing clerk, almost blind so known as "Moley". He wrote a real law stationery hand. All College registers were hand written by us and deeds of presentation, important wills and conveyances—even leases still had to be engrossed on parchment. Peppercorns could still be purchased in Chancery Lane".

As Dudley Durell mentions, the issue of Saturday afternoon closing was one of some contention between different members of the legal profession in Cambridge between the wars. The matter was raised at a special general meeting of the Cambridgeshire and District Law Society on 2nd October 1928 but it had then been agreed that early closing should not be transferred from Thursday to Saturday.

At the Annual General Meeting of the Society held on 29th May 1935 a report on the subject was submitted to the members. At first Walter H. Francis (seconded by Walter M.

Francis) had proposed "that there be no further discussion". However, by an amendment to this resolution the Society agreed to meet other professional bodies in Cambridge to discuss the issue.

At the next committee meeting of the Society held at 10 Peas Hill on 1st July 1935 it was noted that Few & Co. were opening for business on Thursday afternoons. It was felt undesirable that individual members should depart from the practice adopted by the Cambridge members of the Society as a whole. The Hon. Secretary was asked to write to Few & Co. expressing the committee's views.

The committee next met representatives of the Chartered Surveyors, Auctioneers and Estate Agents, Chartered Accountants, insurance companies and Incorporated Auctioneers at 10 Peas Hill on 14th October 1935. All present expressed themselves in favour of Saturday afternoon closing, "if this practice was adopted by all else concerned".

The issue was again raised at the 65th Annual General Meeting of the Society held on Saturday 23rd May 1936 and as a result a meeting of solicitors practising in Cambridge was held on Saturday 20th June. At this meeting Walter H. Francis proposed (seconded by Mr. C. W. Ellison) a motion which was carried by the meeting "that the report of the committee be received and Thursday closing be maintained".

Very shortly after his retirement from employment with the firm, the death occurred in 1936 of Francis & Co's longest serving managing clerk Thomas Porter at the age of 79. He had become associated with the conduct of manorial courts over a wide area for many years until their abolition in 1925. His memorial tablet in Trumpington Church commemorates his outstanding record in appropriate terms

In Memoriam
Thomas Humphrey John Porter
1857–1936
For Sixteen Years Churchwarden of this Parish
For Sixty Five Years Servant of One Firm

Seest Thou a Man Diligent in his Business,
He Shall Stand Before Kings,
He Shall Not Stand Before Mean Men*

A further involvement with Grove Lodge occurred in June 1938. The house had been conveyed by Peterhouse to the University in 1915 and on 10th June 1938 the practice completed on behalf of the University an agreement with the Luxicab Owner Drivers Association permitting them to attach and fix a telephone to the railings of the premises known as Grove Lodge, Trumpington Street, Cambridge. The agreement was signed by George Henry Baker, University Treasurer, in the presence of H. G. Collin, Solicitor, Cambridge. The reference to railings, where nowadays the front wall is surmounted by close boarded fencing, suggests that the railings were removed barely two years later as scrap metal for the war effort, perhaps only to be dumped in Spithead with the rest of such patriotically gathered but essentially useless material.

The outbreak of the Second World War on Sunday 3rd September 1939 served to overshadow a happier event the following day.

From The Times Tuesday 5th September 1939

Marriages—Mr. W. Maclaren Francis and Miss M. B. Brunker.
The marriage between Mr. W. Maclaren Francis and Miss M. B. Brunker took place quietly at Holy Trinity Church Cambridge on September 4th.

*Proverbs 22 : 29

Dudley Durell continues:

"When the War came Hugh Collin and his clerk disappeared instantly into the Army and were not seen again. I was deferred and W. M. F. was over age. John Collin retired to Devonshire".

The Times 21st September 1939—Cambridge University in War Time

Under this heading a series of photographs showed the sandbagged entrance to the Divinity School in St. John's Street "which now houses a recruiting office", a sandbagged doorway at Queen's College, "among the many special war time activities at the Universities is that of sandbagging vital points of the buildings from the possible effects of exploding bombs", and protecting the window at King's College Chapel "the glass has been removed and the spaces covered in by wood".

Death of Walter Hamond Francis

Walter Hamond Francis died on 5th September 1940 and his death was reported in the Cambridge Independent Press the following day,

"A familiar figure in Cambridge of which he was Mayor before the Great War, Mr. Walter H. Francis passed away on Thursday at the age of eighty two. His home was at 3 Grange Road and he had been in failing health for some time. Since the death of his brother (Mr. Musgrave Francis) Mr. Francis had been senior partner in the firm of Francis & Co Solicitors of Peas Hill. He was a brother of Major Wolstan Francis of Quy. Mr. W. H. Francis was a member of the Town Council for twenty three years. He was first elected in June 1902 and was made an Alderman in 1914. He did not seek re-election in 1925. He was Mayor of Cambridge in 1912–1913 and his year of office was made memorable by his outspokenness and his independent attitude at various functions it was his duty to attend as Mayor. At a sale of work he once expressed his disagreement at such a method of raising money. On another occasion—the opening of the

Melbourne Place School—he criticised the scheme. Politically he was a conservative and he was a church warden of St. Andrew's the Great for a great many years, relinquishing the office two years ago".

This event effectively left only two partners in control of the practice, Walter Maclaren Francis and Dudley Durell. Dudley Durell continues:

"WMF and I were in the Observer Corps and we all fire watched at the office in turn—Beryl* on her own when I was on duty at night. I had then to take on all the University and College work single-handed. The University and Colleges were running on skeleton staff—the University run almost entirely by the Treasurer—Knox Shaw—later Master of Sidney—and together we dealt with a vast variety of University affairs. After Dunkirk, having had a duodenal ulcer, the army would not touch me and as I was getting virtually no sleep I switched to the Home Guard where I became the Intelligence officer of the Intelligence Section of the Fifth Battalion. We then acquired a conscientious objector called Stanley Prothero (son of one of the "Big Five" at Scotland Yard) who was a protegé of Charles Rowan, the Master of Christ's and a crusading pacifist. Prothero was deferred on the understanding that he worked full time for us and took over all the fire watching—a great relief. He later became the Registrar at Westminster County Court. In 1940 I took over the Deputy Coronership—though for sixteen years this was in effect a sinecure".

Dudley Durell served as deputy to the Cambridge Borough Coroner Walter Wallis until 1956.

A further depletion in the partnership occurred in August 1944 with the death of John Collin at the age of seventy-seven, as reported in the Times.

COLLIN—On August 20th 1944 at Saunton North Devon, John Collin MA dear husband of Kate Collin (Kit) of Trumpington Cambridge. Funeral Private. No flowers.

*(his wife)

It was not surprising that an obituary in one of the Cambridge newspapers chose to emphasise his rowing prowess.

"It is with profound regret that Cambridge oarsmen will have heard of the passing of Mr John Collin during this week.

He was connected with rowing both in University and town circles. When an undergraduate he rowed for Lady Margaret and became a member of the Rob Roy Boat Club about the same time.

John Collin had a brilliant record with Lady Margaret Boat Club. Possibly his best year was 1888 when he was their stroke and won the Thames Cup as well as the Ladies Plate at Henley.

It was only natural after this that Rob Roy should seek the benefit of Mr. Collin's experience and advice and ask him to coach them. This he did for several seasons and in this way was cemented an association which continued for nearly sixty years, during which time he became their President and later their Patron.

Mr John Collin was proud of his long membership of the Rob Roy Boat Club and the members were equally proud of him. In 1935 when he had been a member for fifty years the Rob's gave him a complimentary dinner at the Dorothy and presented him with a silver salver. We recall him saying that evening "those who go on from year to year, as I do going to the same old office and seeing the same old people, do not count the years as they are slipping by. When one comes to reckon time in cycles of fifty years, one begins to think one has lived quite a number of years".

This was typical of John Collin. He was as "A.P.H." the club's historian, wrote of him on the occasion of the Rob's Jubilee, five years earlier "unassuming, but always candid when his advice is sought... Those of us who have ten or twelve years membership to our credit— short as it may seem compared with the forty odd of Mr. Collin—can to some extent realise the great value his services have been to the club over this long length of time".

The Cambs Rowing Association knew him too. He was President from 1895 until 1901. For a number of years he acted as an umpire at the bumping races a dignified figure wearing his Leander cap. In 1927 he presented the Association with the John Collin Cup for junior sculls.

Mr Collin will be sadly missed by Cambridge oarsmen. The Rob Roy's, especially, have lost a very dear friend. The severance of so long an association leaves a wide gap".

Little more than a year later, the strength of the partnership was further reduced. According to Dudley Durell

"When the War ended Hugh Collin's marriage broke up and his wife divorced him. Strange though it may seem it was accepted without question that it would be impossible for him to return to Francis & Co. So WMF and I bought him out. By that time I had acquired a full equity partnership."

Hugh Collin's departure from Cambridge also represented something of a loss to Cambridge rowing. He had acted as a coach to the rival 99 Club crews in pre-war years. Being only in mid-career at the date of his retirement from Francis & Co., Hugh Collin moved to Liverpool and eventually gained another partnership in the firm of Gair Roberts Hirst and Walker. His retirement from this Liverpool practice was followed by a move to Somerset where he died on 18th December 1982.

As the year 1945 drew to a close, Francis & Co. with only two continuing partners, Walter M. Francis and Dudley Durell, was at its lowest partner strength since the Francis brothers, Musgrave and Walter, had invited John Collin to join them in partnership forty-seven years previously.

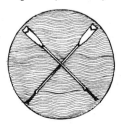

Chapter 19

TRANSITION AND
TRANSFORMATION 1946–1989

NOTE:
The period covered by this chapter is inevitably one of recent and living memories. While it is a matter for debate whether the events of this period qualify as true history, the story is nevertheless continued through to the bicentenary of the practice for the sake of completeness. Considerations of professional confidence must, however, prevent the examination or discussion of client business in all save the most general or indirect terms. Therefore while the fascination of some earlier chapters may be missing, the duty to preserve professional confidences is one which the author is bound to observe. It is nevertheless his hope that at some major future anniversary the history of this period may be more adequately told.

 AMBRIDGE may have emerged from the war with far fewer signs of war damage than elsewhere but nevertheless the aftermath of wartime would be slow to clear. Public air-raid shelters had to be removed from streets, open spaces and school playgrounds. Airfields and army camps had to be cleared from the countryside and the land restored to agriculture. The woefully inadequate housing stock had to be repaired, refurbished, and in some cases released from requisition. Food rationing and general austerity lingered on far longer than expected and seemed to get worse before it improved. Victory celebrations in Cambridge had been more muted than elsewhere owing to the longer wait for victory over Japan and the return of many servicemen in the East Anglian Division from Far East prisoner of war camps. Here they had been held since the fall of Singapore in February 1942. The economy faltered and nearly came to a standstill with the severe coal and power shortages during the winter of 1947. Against this background the legislative programme of Mr. Attlee's Labour Government resulted in the nationalisation of the railways and the coal mines and the introduction of the National Health Service. Of more immediate concern to the practice were measures such as the Agricultural Holdings Act 1948, introducing elaborate and stringent protection for agricultural tenants, the Town and Country Planning Act 1947, which placed control over development in the hands of Local Planning Authorities, the series of Rent Restriction Acts, culminating in the Landlord & Tenant (Rent Control) Act 1949, which introduced strict protection for residential tenants and the Legal Aid and Advice Act 1949. The introduction of legal aid is said to have fallen short of the Government's original intention to introduce a National Legal Service equivalent to the National Health Service. The Law Society owed its ability to negotiate more favourable terms for solicitors to a much higher percentage membership of the solicitors' profession than the British Medical Association could claim as representative of the doctors.

For the first ten of the postwar years there was hardly any increase in the ownership or use of private cars. Virtually all new car production was destined for export, permits to purchase new cars being issued only to individuals in authorised occupations or claiming exceptional circumstances. Petrol too was rationed and was available in short supply only from grey painted Pool petrol pumps. Not surprisingly the demand for public transport remained correspondingly high, motor traffic not yet causing any threat to the numerous railway branch lines and country bus routes.

Against this background the practice entered the postwar years with a clientele substantially undiminished from

before the war and beginning to emerge from the
suspended animation of wartime. The new legislation
provided difficulties and challenges for landlords and
landowners generally and new legal problems for the
practice. It soon became clear that the two continuing
partners Walter Francis and Dudley Durell, with more than
enough non-contentious work to handle, must be joined by
a partner to specialise in common law work. Hitherto
Dudley Durell had handled work in this field and had been
responsible for the practice moving away from the more
traditional reliance on London Agents,

> "One principle I adopted (which made me rather unpopular with
> London Agents) was dealing with all High Court litigation, planning
> enquiries and matters relating to College Statutes and so on myself
> direct. It proved a great saving in time and money".

In 1948 a third partner, Kenneth Welfare, joined the
partnership specifically to undertake the common law
work.

Kenneth William Welfare was a graduate of Emmanuel
College (B.A. 1934, M.A. 1942). He had been articled for
three years from 5th September 1934 to F. L. Hutton in
London and had been admitted as a solicitor in February
1938. He served as a partner in the practice from 1948 until
1951 when he left to become County Court registrar, first in
Cambridge and later in Ipswich.

The need for a common law specialist being no less
pressing, the place vacated by Kenneth Welfare was filled
the same year by the appointment of an assistant solicitor
already two years qualified, Bernard William Cox. After two
years service as an assistant Cox was admitted to the
partnership in 1953.

Bernard William ("Bob") Cox (1918–1982) was a

graduate of Pembroke College, Cambridge, (B.A. 1940, M.A. 1944). His was the generation of emergency or wartime degrees; he was called up for active service with the Army in 1940 and served with the Royal Artillery in France, North Africa and Italy. On demobilisation he was articled from 7th October 1947 for a two-year term (again an emergency concession) to Edward G. Raynes of Messrs. Eaden Spearing and Raynes of Cambridge, being admitted as a solicitor in November 1949. He then served as an assistant solicitor with Messrs. Turner Martin and Symes of Ipswich until he moved back to Cambridge in 1951.

Economic conditions slowly began to improve during the nineteen fifties resulting in relaxation of rationing, austerity and building controls. New housing estates began to appear on the outskirts of Cambridge, in the "necklace villages" and beyond, providing relief from the severe housing shortage. For the University too, new buildings began to appear to provide for older departments long since outgrown or inadequately housed — (Bio-Chemistry on the Downing Site, Chemical Laboratories in Lensfield Road, extended Engineering Laboratories in Scroope Terrace and Arts Faculty buildings in West Road); buildings for entirely new subjects — (Veterinary School, Madingley Road, Radio-therapeutics at the New Hospital site, Radio-astronomy near Lords Bridge and Chemical Engineering on the New Museum Site); — new colleges — (among them Fitzwilliam, Darwin, New Hall, Clare Hall, Hughes Hall). All this new development came under planning authority control since the Town and Country Planning Act 1947 and had to comply with a development plan. In a planning area as sensitive and important as Cambridge, the specially commissioned Planning Proposals by William Holford and H. Myles Wright (1950), resulted in a prolonged and controversial public enquiry at which substantial representation was provided by the practice for a wide range of college and university interests. Many of the resultant academic developments involved the practice in the disposal or acquisition of the relevant sites and in the formation of various new foundations.

Two further partners were to join the practice during the nineteen fifties Derek Hanton and Peter Hall.

Derek Gibson Hanton had graduated from Magdalene College Cambridge (B.A. 1950; M.A. 1955). He had then been articled for a term of three years from 13th October 1950 to Mr. A. W. Brown of 30 John Street, London W.C.1 being admitted in November 1953. His short-lived entry into the partnership occurred in 1957 but he left the same year.

Peter Edwin Burr Hall had graduated from St. Catharine's College (B.A. 1948, M.A. 1951, LLB. 1952). He was articled for a term of two years from 3rd October 1949 to Ernest Vinter of 6 St. Andrew's Street, Cambridge, being admitted as a solicitor in March 1952. Peter Hall joined the partnership in 1957 and remained a partner until 1970 when he chose early retirement and took up residence in Switzerland.

The Landlord and Tenant Act 1954 established statutory protection for business tenants of all kinds, but no restraint was imposed on rent levels. This factor, coupled with the emergence of rent review clauses during the later nineteen fifties resulted in far more active and commercially attractive letting activity in the commercial sphere, and many College clients were able to take advantage of the new conditions both in the more static rack rent leasing of retail shops and office accommodation and in more imaginative development schemes, notable among them being the Felixstowe Dock Scheme and the adjoining Trimley Industrial Estate from the mid-nineteen sixties onwards. Given the degree of property activity being undertaken by the University and Cambridge colleges during the nineteen sixties and thanks to effective representations from the University and other interested bodies, a major relaxation in the restraints on property transactions by the University and Colleges was permitted by the Universities and College Estates Act 1964.

In response to the much heightened property activity of institutional clients during the 1960's, further recruitment resulted in the engagement of Hugh Thirlway as an assistant with the practice in 1964 and he was admitted to the partnership in 1965.

Hugh Wilfred Augustine Thirlway had graduated from St. John's College, Cambridge, (B.A. 1958, LL.B. 1959, M.A. 1962). He was articled for a period of three years from 8th October 1958 to Mr. H. W. Owen of Windsor being admitted as a solicitor in March 1962. He was a partner in Francis & Co. from 1965 to 1968 when he left to take up an appointment at the International Court of Justice at The Hague. During his time as a partner Hugh Thirlway took study leave to acquire a doctorate in law (Dr-en-Droit) at the University of Nancy.

At the date of Hugh Thirlway's admission to the partnership in September 1965 the partners of Francis & Co., were W. M. Francis, D. V. Durell, B. W. Cox, P. E. B. Hall and H. W. A. Thirlway.

Already serving his Articles of Clerkship with the practice at this time was the last individual to be articled to a member of the Francis family, Alexander Timothy (Tim) Pearce Higgins.

Tim Pearce Higgins (b. 1938) had graduated from Christ's College Cambridge (B.A. 1962, M.A. 1966). He was articled in 1962 to Walter Maclaren Francis for a term of three years and was admitted as a solicitor in June 1965. He then served as an assistant solicitor in the practice until he joined the partnership on 6th September 1968, one of several changes in the partnership to take place that year.

Having reached the age of 68, Walter Maclaren Francis retired from the partnership on 5th September 1968 and was succeeded as senior partner by Dudley Durell who held this position for the next four years. Walter Francis was the first retired partner to be re-engaged as consultant to the practice, involving the payment to him of a salary and relief from all partnership responsibilities. In effect, this reflected a considerable change from the attitudes of the previous generation of partners. No formal provision had been made in partnership terms for the retirement of Musgrave Francis, Walter H. Francis or John Collin, all three had been full time partners of the firm, at least in theory, at the time of their deaths notwithstanding their advanced years. Walter Maclaren Francis' retirement to consultancy in 1968 reflected the changed concept of a partnership "ladder" by which shares in the partnership profits were linked to seniority as partner. Francis & Co. was by this time no exception to the generally emerging trend in solicitor's practices to define terms for entry, shares of profit and retirement applicable to all partners whether descendants of the original founder or (increasingly) strangers in blood.

Another partnership event to occur in September 1968 was the departure of Hugh Thirlway, as already mentioned, to take up his appointment at the International Court. It being deemed necessary to fill this gap in the newly emerging ladder structure the decision was taken to appoint Christopher Jackson (the author of this history) as an assistant solicitor "with a view to partnership" with effect from October 1968.

Christopher Eric Hallinan Jackson (b. 1934) had graduated from University College London (Ll.B. 1956). He had been articled for a term of three years from August 1956 to Christopher Stewart Buckle of Rawlison and Butler of Horsham, Sussex, being admitted as a solicitor in

October 1959. He served for seven years as an assistant solicitor with Farrer and Co. in Lincoln's Inn Fields before moving to Cambridge and was admitted to the partnership on 6th April 1969.

The author's first impression of the office at 10 Peas Hill, apart from its attractive period exterior, was that internal refurbishment was long overdue, especially in the reception area. Within two years, renovation of the reception area had taken place under the direction of an architect and interior decorator, Sarah Platt. While the result produced much favourable comment it inevitably set off a chain reaction of further improvement and renovation. From 1970 to 1986 it seemed that builders and decorators were never long absent from 10 Peas Hill whether attempting to improve the internal appearance or the available office space.

The adoption by British Railways in 1965 of the Beeching Plan for the closure of uneconomic branch railway lines resulted in line closures in Cambridgeshire and the practice was often brought in to re-acquire the disused track for adjoining landowners. More often than not these were the same owners from whom the lines had been acquired a century or more previously. At the same time the exploitation of the North Sea Gas fields and the establishment of a gas pipeline network throughout the country meant that easements in favour of British Gas were granted by College landowners in most parts of Eastern England. It is said that the conversion of the City of Cambridge from town gas to natural gas was a high priority of the programme in order to remove an all too frequent cause for under-graduate suicides.

The dwindling railway network was matched by an increase in motorway and by-pass construction during the nineteen seventies and consequential land disposals for these purposes from the holdings of Colleges and County landowners. Planning advice and representation was also called for in respect of the controversial routing of the M11 Cambridge Western By-pass and the A45 Cambridge Northern By-pass.

On 5th September 1970 Peter Hall retired from the partnership, the continuing partners then being D. V. Durell, B. W. Cox, C. E. H. Jackson and A. T. P. Higgins. Soon afterwards, on 24th September 1970, the death occurred of Walter Maclaren Francis at the age of 70. Not only was this a sad loss to all his friends at the firm and in the profession generally but it marked the end of the Francis family involvement in the practice after a continuous period of 120 years.

The event was reported in the Cambridge Evening News for 1st October 1970 as follows:

"A MAN WHO SERVED COMMUNITY
The late Mr. Walter Maclaren Francis.
Walter Francis who died on September 24th represented the third generation of a family which has been associated with the Law in Cambridge for upwards of 130 years.

It was early in the 19th century that Clement Francis joined a long established legal firm in Cambridge in which he became a partner in the year 1838. He was in due course joined by his sons Musgrave and Walter Hamond, both of whom played a prominent part in the life of the City. Musgrave was the Chairman of Addenbrookes Hospital Board, (his portrait hangs in the Board Room) and Walter was Mayor of Cambridge in 1912.

Walter Maclaren Francis the son of Walter Hamond Francis was born on August 2nd 1900 and educated at St. Faith's School, Repton and Trinity Hall. After being articled in London he joined the family firm of Francis & Co., in which he became a partner in 1933 and of which he was senior partner on his retirement in 1968. He remained with the firm as a Consultant.

He always threw himself wholeheartedly into the service of the community. In the law he served as a member of the Law Society's Constitution Committee, was a Past President of the Solicitors

Benevolent Association, served as Secretary of the Cambridge and District Law Society of which he was a Past President and had been Secretary of the East Anglian Law Society.

He was always active in church affairs; for 18 years he was a Church Warden of Holy Trinity and was, at the time of his death, Registrar to the Archdeaconry of Ely. He was formerly a member of the Cambridgeshire and Isle of Ely Executive Committee of the National Health Service.

Walter Francis had an outstanding gift for friendship—once made, his friends were friends for life and their children after them. His many friends will always remember him for his unfailing kindness, sympathy and good humour. His passing will leave a gap in many circles and homes where he will always be affectionately remembered. In 1939 he married Maud Brabazon Brunker who survives him. His funeral took place at Madingley Parish Church on Monday but a memorial service will shortly be held in Cambridge."

During the nineteen seventies Cambridge began to emerge as a centre for research and development of electronics, computer software and biotechnology. For the first time the highly regarded scientific research work of the University was finding technical applications and commercial outlets. Before long the Cambridge Science Park, originally based on American prototypes but soon to acquire its own name and world reputation, was to draw the practice into long and deep involvement in the letting arrangements for tenants.

On 5th September 1972 Dudley Durell retired from the partnership and was re-engaged as a consultant in the practice for a period of ten years. He was succeeded as senior partner by Bob Cox who held this position until his retirement nine years later.

Upon Dudley Durell's retirement Clive Sutton who had served in the practice as an assistant solicitor since October 1970 was invited to join the partnership but left in March 1973 to take up an appointment as a Resident Magistrate in the Seychelle Islands.

B. W. Cox, C. E. H. Jackson and A. T. P. Higgins then continued in partnership until September 1976 when David Anthony (Tony) Cowper and Desmond Hutchinson were admitted to the partnership.

David Anthony Cowper (b. 1948) had served four years of his five years Articles of Clerkship in Liverpool, first with his father John Cowper until his death in 1967 and then with his father's successor practice Messrs. Rutherfords. He completed his service under articles with Francis & Co. and was admitted as a solicitor in February 1972.

Desmond Charles Fitzgerald Hutchinson (b. 1946) had commenced a five year period of articles with Bernard William Cox at Francis & Co., in May 1970, having previously served as a regular officer in the Royal Artillery. He was admitted as a solicitor in May 1975. Desmond Hutchinson ceased to be a partner on 31st May 1989 but continued as a consultant to the practice.

The pace and the character of legal problems to be contended with during the late nineteen sixties and throughout the nineteen seventies was largely set by the partly reforming and partly interventionist legislation of the Wilson and Callaghan administrations. The Leasehold Reform Act 1967 gave many College tenants in Cambridge the opportunity to enfranchise their leases. The Redundancy Payments Act 1965, the Contracts of Employment Act 1972, The Health and Safety at Work etc. Act 1974 and the Employment Protection Act 1975 gave new protection to employees and consequential problems for employers especially where hearings before industrial tribunals were required. The introduction of Development Land Tax administered by the Land Commission provided problems for landowners in the disposal of land deemed to have development value taxable for the public benefit. Problems associated with inflation prompted the introduction of counter-inflation legislation (including the Counter Inflation (Business Rents) Order 1972) and the establishment of the Price Commission with its supervisory powers over wage and price increases including solicitors' costs. The inflationary trend had not been particularly assisted by the introduction of decimal currency on 15th February 1971, this too gave all solicitors' practices the challenge and problems associated with changes in their accounting systems. Further complications arose two years later with the introduction of value added tax. As an introductory note to staff said at the time

"On 1st April 1973 Francis & Co., will become, in common with one and a half million other businesses, unpaid collectors of value added tax for H. M. Customs and Excise".

Other reforms were in the air as well. The Consumer Credit Act 1974 required Francis & Co., and all other solicitors practices to register in respect of relevant client transactions but this was only part of an advancing trend towards greater consumer protection. Many more members of society were coming into contact with the legal profession for the first time, partly due to a greater use of the legal aid and partly owing to the rapid increase in home ownership. Perplexity that legal costs did not appear to bear much relationship to the price structuring of the retail trade had already led to the abolition of conveyancing scale fees with effect from 1st January 1973. In response to mounting pressure on behalf of the consumer both within and outside Parliament the Royal Comission on Legal Services sat during 1975 and 1976 under the Chairmanship of Sir Edward Benson. While not seriously critical or damaging in its report on the structure of the legal profession and the provision of its services the report did not provide lasting reassurance or satisfaction to the more vocal critics of the legal profession, especially on the subject of conveyancing fees for house buyers. The issue was to emerge in Parliament more actively seven years later when the House Buyers Bill of 1983 was withdrawn against a government pledge which resulted in the establishment of licensed conveyancers, authorised to compete with solicitors in the provision of conveyancing services.

Meanwhile, no doubt wishing to retain reforms and improvements in the solicitors' profession under its own control, the Law Society began, in 1978, to undertake a close study of entry standards, training, and service under articles, and submissions were made from the practice both to the Law Society Working Party on Articles in 1978 and in response to a further Law Society invitation on the subject of monitoring articles in 1980. A radical and on the whole beneficial reform of the training of articled clerks was to be introduced with effect from 1980. However, it has to be said that the practice viewed the new training regulations with some dismay, especially the requirements for an economic rate of pay and for a rotation of the articled clerk through a minimum of three distinct types of legal work. As a result, no-one was invited to enter into articles with the practice for the next six years.

In September 1979 Duncan MacGregor Ogilvy joined the partnership having served a four year period of articles with Tim Pearce Higgins from October 1972, being admitted as a solicitor in November 1976.

Bob Cox was an able and largely single handed administrator of the practice even before he assumed the position of senior partner but by 1979, with advancing ill-health, he was ready to relinquish this role to his younger partners and made this announcement in a circular to staff on 15th November 1979. It is perhaps a compliment to his ability that none of his partners felt able or willing to take over more than a share of the tasks which he had hitherto carried alone.

The division between the twin themes of this chapter, transition and transformation, coincides conveniently with the close of the nineteen seventies. The existence of Francis & Co., as a small and long-established provincial practice, albeit of a somewhat specialised character and with an enviable clientele in University as well as City had been one of constant adaptation. Changing times, external factors and legislative challenges of all kinds had required appropriate reaction and response. By 1980 it began to be plain for all to see that Cambridge was becoming something else apart from an ancient university town and centre of academic excellence. If the commercial exploitation of scientific research was playing its part, so too was the prospect of vastly improved communications. After centuries as a quiet backwater Cambridge seemed to bid fair to become a major regional centre for East Anglia. Bob Cox was due to retire on 5th September 1981 and with the prospect of some relief from the hectic pace of legislation in the previous fifteen years the partners recognised the need, and took the opportunity, to consider the future direction of the firm at a weekend conference held at Southwold in July 1981.

By no means the first solicitors' practice to engage in this kind of activity this was nevertheless for Francis & Co. a major departure in its long history. The benefit of a weekend partners' meeting detached from the pressures and distractions of office life was clearly apparent and ensured that this first conference was certainly not the last. The arrangements and planning of all four Francis & Co. partners' conferences between 1981 and 1986 were undertaken by Desmond Hutchinson.

Having retired from the partnership on 5th September 1981 Bob Cox died exactly six months later on 5th March 1982. His death was recorded in the Cambridge Evening

News for Monday 22nd March as follows:

"Ex-Deputy City Coroner dies just after retiring.
Mr. Bob Cox a former Deputy Coroner for Cambridge has died aged
63. His death, a few months after his retirement as Senior Partner of
solicitors, Francis & Co. in Cambridge came after a long period of ill-
health.
   Mr. Cox, who lived at 183 Huntingdon Road, Cambridge, was the
Past-President of the East Anglian Coroners Society. Mr. Cox leaves
a widow and two children."

If the decisions taken at the first partners' conference
were, seen in retrospect, unexceptionable, they were in
themselves major departures from past practice. Instead of
allowing individual partners to handle most types of
business for any given client, the merit of specialisation was
recognised and the firm's work was for the first time divided
between four departments, Conveyancing, Leasehold,
Probate and Litigation. Accepting that domestic
conveyancing by now represented a considerable share of
the firm's business and yet was coming under increased
competitive pressure, junior clerks were to be engaged for
the more economical performance of routine
conveyancing procedures. Further, in an attempt to
improve profitability against increasing overheads, the
decision was taken to introduce a system of computer-based
daily time recording for fee earners. The implementation
of these decisions in the succeeding months was to prove
two simple propositions. The first was that computer
equipment then available on the market fell considerably
short of "user expectations" and of salesmen's assurances.
The second was that space in the firm's offices at 10 Peas
Hill, after allowing additional adaptation for junior clerical
staff and all statutory requirements and regulations, was
now effectively used up. This fact was confirmed to the
partners by the report of a Cambridge chartered surveyor,

Mr. Maurice Pleasance in March 1983. This in turn resulted in a major and radical departure in firm policy. For the previous ten years at least, it had been accepted that the practice would have to contain its level of activity within the accommodation available at 10 Peas Hill. Modern times and modern methods were between them generating greater activity, demanding more fee earner and supporting staff and a much loved and admired building was increasingly becoming a strait-jacket. As a first step towards the solution of this problem a decision was made in July 1983 to take additional office space on the second and third floors of No. 17 Market Street, some two hundred yards distant from 10 Peas Hill. Fitting out work started in December 1983 and was finished by February 1984 at which point the Litigation Department under Desmond Hutchinson and the Leasehold Department under Tony Cowper both moved to the Market Street annexe.

Meanwhile, Peter Hallinan had been admitted to the partnership in September 1983.

Peter Anthony Joseph Hallinan (b. 1956) had been articled to Christopher Jackson (his second cousin) for a two year term from February 1979. Peter Hallinan was admitted as a solicitor in April 1981 and had then served as an assistant with the practice until his admission to the partnership.

Birth of a Commercial Department
Other pressures were at work during 1983. It became apparent that if the practice was to attempt some diversification into the fields of company and commercial law for which clear demand was apparent among existing and potential clients, a specialist in these fields would have to be engaged, charged with the responsibility for a specialized department within the practice. This resulted in the appointment of Michael Barley as an assistant solicitor

in March 1984.

Michael Desmond Tennyson Barley (b. 1944) had graduated from Keble College, Oxford (B.A. 1971). He had been articled from 1973 to 1975 to Mr. J. W. Scott of Clifford-Turner & Co., of the City of London. After serving as an assistant solicitor there and in the Persian Gulf, Michael Barley had then served as an assistant solicitor with Messrs. Hedleys before moving to join the practice in 1984. He was admitted to the partnership in October 1984.

In May 1984 the second partners' weekend conference was held at Thornham, Norfolk. It being clear that an expanding practice could no longer afford the division of administrative functions between individual partners, decisions were taken to strengthen and centralise the administration of the practice. To meet a pressing need to provide additional resources for the heavy volume of commercial conveyancing being undertaken by the firm, two of the departments established in September 1981, Conveyancing and Leasehold, were re-organised into Commercial Conveyancing under Christopher Jackson and Tony Cowper and Residential Conveyancing under Duncan Ogilvy.

The picture was further changed twelve months later. In May 1985 the third partners weekend conference was held at Long Melford, Suffolk, addressing itself almost exclusively to the question of premises. The partners had before them a specially commissioned report from Coopers & Lybrand's Professional Services Division. This contained a careful assessment of accommodation needs for the practice and compared the relative merits of city centre or peripheral locations in or around Cambridge. The main recommendation to emerge from this report was that client needs and staff needs would be better served by retaining a location in Cambridge city centre, preferably in the main axis running southwards from St. Andrew's Street through

Regent Street and Hills Road as far as Station Road.* The decision then made to expand to new premises did not at first imply abandonment of 10 Peas Hill. The association with the Peas Hill office which the practice had acquired over the previous seventy years was considered sufficiently valuable to be retained for the foreseeable future, possibly an issue to be addressed as a second stage later on. Office premises in course of construction at 63 Regent Street were considered appropriate for a phased move with interim two site occupation. Constructional delays during the autumn and winter of 1985 and a consequential postponement of the completion date gave the partners an unexpected pause for reflection. By now they had two years experience of running the practice on separate sites and the prospect of attempting the same thing even further apart in Peas Hill and Regent Street grew progressively less appealing. Two further possible sites became available a little further to the south, one at 24 and the other at 37 Hills Road. Both were larger developments however and carried the implication of a complete move away from 10 Peas Hill. By the time the 24 Hills Road premises became available at the beginning of February 1986, the partners were ready to act decisively. The lease of 24 Hills Road was completed on 19th February 1986, fitting out commenced immediately and was ready for the move by 3rd May. Taking advantage of a Bank Holiday weekend, the entire operation of the practice was moved from 10 Peas Hill and 17 Market Street and opened for business at 24 Hills Road (then christened "Francis House") on 6th May 1986. The partners in Francis & Co. at this date were Christopher Jackson, Tim Pearce Higgins, Tony Cowper, Desmond Hutchinson, Michael Barley, Duncan Ogilvy and Peter Hallinan.

When the fourth partners' weekend conference took

*"The Spine" as Holford and Wright had described it thirty-five years previously.

place in September 1986 the venue chosen, not without some pride, was the Conference Room at Francis House.

Not surprisingly, the main theme of the fourth weekend conference was a Blueprint for Expansion. The adoption of a higher profile in terms of a modern office building also had to be matched in terms of improving the firm's market share in the provision of legal services. Carefully weighing ambition against resources, the agreed programme estimated an increase in partner strength over the following five years from seven to twelve and of staff from sixty to one hundred. It was fully appreciated by all concerned that this objective would only be achieved if much care was taken in the application of resources and in the engagement of suitably qualified staff. There were of course other possible routes to achieve this clearly ambitious objective. The report on the conference circulated to the staff members contained a significant final paragraph,

"The Partners see expansion particularly in the commercial sphere as necessary for the continuing health of the firm. They do not discount the possibility of merger or practice acquisition and will therefore not be blind to opportunities of that nature as and when they arise, but irrespective of that the main concentration will be on improving this firm as it currently exists in the form indicated above."

The events which followed took place too recently to be seen in a proper historical context. It cannot yet be claimed that there was a degree of inevitability about them. It can, however, be said that Mills & Reeve, a leading Norwich practice founded by Henry Jacob Mills in 1880, had for some time been planning to open a branch office in Cambridge, primarily with a view to providing in the Cambridge region more specialized legal services for private clients and commercial interests than then seemed available from existing practices. This ambition was at length realised in November 1986 with the opening of Mills & Reeve's Cambridge branch office at 6, Clifton Court, Cherry Hinton Road.

If the Francis & Co. partners did not hesitate over the merger opportunity which was soon to present itself, this can be explained in the main by their appreciation that it would give rapid realisation to their declared objectives. Without assisting the reader in any way as to identity, it has also to be said that this was to be the fourth merger possibility considered by the partners in the previous forty years and on the whole the partners felt that this time they knew what to do. To trace the sequence of events in no more than the briefest outline, it is enough to say that a chance encounter between Michael Barley and Robin Carver (responsible for opening Mills & Reeve's Cambridge branch) at a Christmas party led to a lunchtime meeting in Francis House on 16th December, a confidential encounter between the senior partners on 7th January 1987 and the appointment of negotiating teams from both practices, given the task of concluding, by 1st April 1987, agreed terms for a merger. The signature and exchange of Heads of Terms on 22nd March meant that a carefully planned programme of announcements and publicity could be put into effect. An announcement to staff on a confidential basis was followed by a programme of visits by partners to major clients in Cambridge and the preparation and signature of three thousand letters to clients, involving considerable late night and early morning working by those staff involved. The purpose of this preparatory activity was to avoid any client being left with the feeling of having first heard the news in the papers. Press releases to the local, national and legal press were placed under embargo until Friday 27th March 1987 when the news was first made public.

The merger of the two practices under the name "Mills &

Reeve Francis" was fixed to take place on Monday 1st June 1987. The spirit in which the merger was achieved is perhaps best recalled in the following message to Francis & Co. staff dated 29th May 1987.

"Today is our last day working together as Francis & Co. On Monday 1st June 1987 our new existence starts as Mills & Reeve Francis. This is certainly not an occasion for regret, rather an opportunity to look back at our past and forward to our future. Even in the six years or so since I took office as Senior Partner the changes we have seen have been rapid and in some cases quite dramatic. Nearly everyone to whom this letter is addressed has contributed in one way or another towards these achievements and I am proud of what you have done. On Monday we join for the first time with our new friends in Cambridge and Norwich and start together the process of building an organisation of which we can all be truly proud. It is worth mentioning that every contact that we have had with our colleagues in Norwich in the last three months or so has produced nothing but genuine friendship and willing co-operation. I offer my warmest thanks to those among us who have helped to bring the two firms together into one and to all of you I offer my warmest good wishes as we join in this exciting new enterprise in which we all have a part to play.

In one way it seems that our success has been too great and too rapid. Most of us will remember the relief we felt twelve months ago on moving into Francis House, all under one roof again. Now the expansion in Cambridge resulting from this merger has been such that once more we will be separated. While the Litigation Department finds its feet for a time in Clifton Court, much effort and planning will be undertaken to bring us all back together in one office as soon as ever possible.

Our merger is an occasion well worth celebrating and I am very much looking forward to the party on 5th June when we can "celebrate the Wedding". A special word of thanks must go to the ... secretaries for all their efforts in making what I am sure will be a most successful and enjoyable occasion...
Yours sincerely, CHRISTOPHER JACKSON.

Among the many benefits of the merger, one in particular was to be enjoyed even before the official merger date. Mills & Reeve's membership of the M5 Group of provincial solicitors allowed a party of partners and fee earning staff from Cambridge to join the M5 Training Conference at New College, Oxford, on 10th/11th April 1987, the first of many training events arranged by the M5 group which Cambridge partners and staff have attended and something which Francis & Co. as a small provincial practice could never hope to offer. Combined training publicity and recruitment programmes have all had a beneficial effect on the practice in its extended form and these benefits become increasingly apparent both to clients and staff as time goes by. With M5 member firms now located in Birmingham, Bristol, Cambridge, Exeter, Leeds, Manchester, Norwich and Plymouth the Cambridge partners of the practice enjoy an increasing degree of contact both on a professional and social level with upwards of one hundred and forty other partners in these provincial centres.

An event without precedent in the history of the practice took place on 1st June 1987, the date of the merger. Michelle Gail Cookson was admitted to the partnership on this date, the first woman partner in the Cambridge practice. This news, given at the staff meeting ten weeks previously, was greeted with spontaneous applause. This response was undoubtedly intended in part as a compliment to the individual concerned and in part to demonstrate approval of an historic step forward.

A mounting volume of client business resulting from the merger led to increased staffing and further pressure on office space. By the spring of 1988 additional space had to be taken on a temporary basis in a third office at 16 Union Road in addition to the offices by then fully occupied at 24 Hills Road and 6 Clifton Court.

As the story of a two hundred year old legal practice in Cambridge draws to a close the promise given to Cambridge staff in 1987 has already been fulfilled. The bicentenary year has seen the move to newly completed office premises located at FRANCIS HOUSE 112 Hills Road and again all Cambridge partners and staff are working together under one roof, at the conclusion of the firm's second century in Cambridge, and on the threshold of its third. The aims of the 1986 Blueprint for Expansion had been exceeded in less than three years.

Chapter 20

PROFESSIONAL INVOLVEMENTS
II (TWENTIETH CENTURY)

S a sequel to Chapter 12 dealing with nineteenth century professional involvements, this chapter reveals a remarkable continuity of commitment by later partners, whether in serving their professional bodies or undertaking public service appropriate to a qualified solicitor.

The Cambridgeshire and District Law Society
Participation in the activities of a local law society often leads to further involvement in the Law Society itself. Especially is this true of service in a presidential or secretarial role at local level where the establishment of contacts in Chancery Lane tends to result in an identification of individuals willing to take part in the activities of the Law Society. Several of the partners in the practice were to demonstrate the validity of this tendency, others were content to remain involved at local level only.

Frank Peile's involvement in the local law society has already been referred to in connection with the Tobacco Fund during the First World War. He served as secretary to the Society for a period of 19 years from 1908 until his death in 1927. His place was filled for a short time (1927–31) by

Walter Maclaren Francis who also served for a further period as secretary from 1938 to 1948.

Musgrave Francis had already served as president of the local law society in 1889 and he was again elected to office, then aged 74, in 1924. He was followed as president by John Collin in 1935, Walter Maclaren Francis (date unknown) and Dudley Durell in 1960.

The Law Society

Following in his father's footsteps, Musgrave Francis was elected to the Council of the Law Society in 1918 and continued in office until 1931. If Musgrave Francis' nephew Walter had an ambition to serve as the third generation of the Francis family on the Council of the Law Society this was never to be realised. Deeply involved in Law Society affairs nationally and locally for close on forty years, Walter Francis nevertheless felt obliged to refrain from seeking election as a Council member for his local constituency when the opportunity arose in the nineteen fifties, recognising that the resulting uneven distribution of the workload in a three partner firm would have been unfair alike on the other two partners and on clients. Walter Francis nevertheless served as a member of the Law Society's Constitution Committee in 1948 and for thirty eight years as a Director of the Solicitors' Benevolent Association, becoming Vice-Chairman in 1942 and Chairman in 1943.

After eight years service as a committee member of the local law society, having some involvement during that time in the revision of the society's rules and the formulation of local "Conveyancing Practice Guidelines", Christopher Jackson was appointed to serve on the Law Society's Bye-laws Revision Committee in 1984 and took part in a three year examination and updating of the Society's internal workings, principally with regard to representation of members, management of general meetings, organisation of constituencies and duration of council members' terms in office.

Recognition of a more active role for younger solicitors in the affairs of their profession led to the formation from the middle nineteen sixties onwards of young solicitors' groups throughout England and Wales. Younger partners and assistant solicitors in the practice were fully involved in the formation and subsequent running of the Cambridge Young Solicitors' Group. Increasing numbers and influence led to the formation of a Young Solicitors' National Committee with seats allocated to chairmen or other representatives of the local groups. Duncan Ogilvy's chairmanship of the Cambridge Young Solicitors' Group led him to active participation in the affairs of the Young Solicitors' National Committee and his election to serve as chairman for the year 1986–87. He was involved in a very full programme of activities during this year, attending international law conferences in Los Angeles and Bermuda and leading delegations to a number of European countries and hosting return visits of delegations of young lawyers from abroad.

Dudley Durell—Cambridge City Coroner

Of all the offices held by the partners in the practice that of coroner, dating from about 1194, is the most ancient. Dudley Durell was the only partner to hold the office of coroner for Cambridge during the two hundred year period covered by this history and he was the last City coroner.

He was first appointed to act as deputy coroner by his predecessor Mr. Walter Wallis in 1940 and served in this role until Wallis' death in 1956. He was appointed Coroner for the City of Cambridge in 1958 and served until 1978, appointing Bob Cox as his deputy. For twenty years 10 Peas Hill became a focal point for all those involved, however indirectly, with sudden or unexplained deaths occurring within the Coroner's jurisdiction, which included the University. The day to day administrative duties of the office — dealing with the police, undertakers, bereaved relatives and the press, taking witness statements and attending post mortems, were handled by an officer of the Cambridge C.I.D. seconded to the coroner on a full time basis. Inquests were generally held in the Board Room at old Addenbrooke's Hospital (beneath a portrait of Musgrave Francis) or in the Magistrates Court at Cambridge Guildhall. On rare occasions they were even held at 10 Peas Hill. Once Addenbrooke's Hospital became fully operational at its new site, however, inquests were almost invariably held there.

Dudley Durell's appointment came to an end with his retirement on 31st December 1978 as a result of the introduction of a statutory superannuation scheme for coroners linked to a compulsory retiring age of seventy. By 1978 Dudley Durell had already reached the age of seventy two.

Although Bob Cox had served as deputy coroner he had no desire to take the post of coroner nor did any of the other partners in the practice. Dudley Durell was succeeded on 1st January 1979 by the first County Coroner for Cambridge, the late Mr. Robert Sterndale Burrows.

Hospitals and Health Services
The outstanding service of Musgrave Francis as chairman of Addenbrooke's Hospital and of Papworth Hospital has already been mentioned. Soon after his uncle's death Walter Maclaren Francis was appointed as a Borough Member of the Addenbrooke's Hospital General Committee and served in this role from 1933 until the re-organisation of hospitals under the National Health Service Act in 1946. From this time he served as a member of the National Health Service Executive Committee for Cambridgeshire and the Isle of Ely until 1969.

When Walter Francis retired from this appointment his place on the Executive Committee was taken by Tim Pearce Higgins who still serves on the Family Practitioner Committee, successor body to the Executive Committee, and has held the position of Chairman of the Service Committees since 1974.

Tim Pearce Higgins also served as a member of the Cambridge District Health Authority from its formation in 1974 until his retirement from the Authority in 1988, serving his last two years as vice-chairman.

Service in City and County

To conclude this survey of professional involvements in the twentieth century, brief reference may be made to Walter Francis's service twice as Under Sheriff of Cambridgeshire, once for his cousin Roger Parker and once for Gordon Frost, at the time Chairman of the County Coucil. He also served as Clerk to the General Commissioners of Taxes for the Town and University from 1950 to 1969.

Dudley Durell served for six years as county councillor for the Market Ward of the City. Increased pressure of legal work and the possibility of recurring conflicts between major clients of the practice and the County Council led to his retirement as a councillor even though close to election as chairman.

When Cambridge Corn Exchange was re-opened in 1986 after major refurbishment two Cambridge citizens who were deemed to have done most for the community were invited to sign the official documents, Dudley Durell being the senior of the two. This can be seen as fitting recognition not only for Dudley Durell himself but for the part played in Cambridge life by all his partners and predecessors over two hundred years.

Appendix I

You are receiver general for the county of Cambridge? — Yes, I am; and
have been for fifteen years.

How many circuits do you make in the year for the purpose of collecting
the money? — Two circuits only; I receive half yearly.

Do you receive almost the whole of the money on the circuit, or between
that and the quarter-day? — The whole, except from £1,000 to £2,000, is
paid on the circuit.

On the receipt of the money, what do you do with it? — I bring it to my
bankers in London, Messrs. Hoares, of Fleet-street; I leave no part of what
is collected upon my receipt with my country banker.

You go the circuit at the usual time after the expiration of the twenty one
days? — Yes, I do. I understand it to be the wish of the board of taxes that
I should collect quarterly, therefore I always send notices to the clerks of
the commissioners of the day I shall attend, quarterly, if the collectors are
ready to pay me any thing; and I have always received information from
the different clerks, that my attendance to receive the quarters taxes due
in July and January would be useless. The quarters that I do receive any
thing are the July and January quarters.

When do you pay this money into the exchequer? — The money I receive
for the Lady-day half year I pay in the first week in July and the Michaelmas
half-year the first week in January.

A day or two before the quarter? — Yes.

And that applies to the other receipt also? — Yes.

Do you make any profit of the money between the time of the collection
and the period of paying it over? — I do, occasionally, not always, by
investing the money in exchequer bills.

Do you make any profit on the permanent balance you are entitled to
retain? — Yes, I do; by investing the same in the public funds or exchequer
bills, and in no other manner.

Can you state to the Committee what is the amount of the poundage and
interest upon the permanent balance, and the advantages arising from

the use of the current balance, putting on the other side the expenses? — Yes; the amount of the collection is about £88,000 for the whole county; that is my annual receipt. I have to state to the Committee, that with respect to the profits of the money in my hands, that I retain the floating balance about six weeks, not quite; this money I bring to my bankers, Messrs. Hoares, as soon as each receipt is finished, and generally have desired them to lay out the money in exchequer bills till it was wanted for government. Since exchequer bills have paid only three percent, the profit from the investment is much reduced, and I have sometimes doubted whether it would answer.

What is the amount of the floating balance? — About £40,000 in general; from £40,000 to £42,000. Exchequer bills are always at a higher premium when the money can be invested, than when it is wanted for government. In 1819 I did not think I should gain any profit by the investment of the floating balance, therefore no part of it was laid out that year, it remained at Messrs. Hoare's till paid to government, without any advantage to me, for if I had invested it I thought I should have been rather a loser than a gainer.

Then you made no profit that year of the floating balance? — None during the year 1819.

The other years you have made a profit? — Yes.

Have you ever employed it in any other way excepting by investing it in exchequer bills? — No, never.

What might that source of profit produce to you? — Since exchequer bills have fallen to three per cent it has made a considerable difference; I now doubt whether I shall lay out any part of the floating balance in exchequer bills again; when they paid three pence and three pence halfpenny, there was a considerable advantage arising from the investment.

To what amount do you suppose? — I have made as much as £300 a year. When they paid five per cent? — Yes.

Do you mean one year with another, or any one favourable year? — Generally I think the advantage has been from £200 to £250. The poundage for the year 1819 was £590, and the interest on the permanent balance, taken at four per cent is £240. The profit on exchequer bills is small except, when they pay five per cent as stated before. I have only made £45 advantage by the floating balance of the taxes for the year 1820.

What is the whole profit? — £830 is all that I made in the year 1819, having derived no advantage by the floating balance, from which sum the expenses are to be deducted.

Where do you live? — At Cambridge.

Will you state the expenses? — The auditor's fees are £49; the fees and stamps for the bond are £70; there is a Mr. Salmon, whom I employ to take the tallies from the exchequer, the fees for which, with what I give him for his trouble, amount to £6. 10s; I reckon the expenses of the two receipts at £52, which is the least they can be taken at.

What is the length of your circuit? — It lasts ten days, and I go as far as Wisbeach. I find it necessary to have two clerks with me during part of the receipt; then there is coming up to town with the money, which occupies three days after each receipt.

What do you take the whole of your expenses to be? — I have reckoned them at £273. It is impossible to carry on this office without having a clerk.

What is the amount of your security? — £48,000.

Who are your sureties? — A Mr. Eaton of Stetchworth, near Newmarket in Cambridgeshire.

What is he? — He is a gentleman of large landed property; he is in no profession.

Who else? — The reverend Mr. Jenyns, who lives at Bottisham near Cambridge.

Any other? — Mr. Thomas Mellish, the brother of Mr. William Mellish the late member for Middlesex.

Where does he live? — In London, in Bishopsgate street, with his brother.

Is Mr. Jenyns a gentleman of landed property? — Yes, of considerable landed property.

To what amount are they security? — £48,000.

Do you see any objection to pay over that amount of your receipts into the exchequer, instead of allowing it to lay so long at Messrs. Hoare's? — I see no objection to it, except that I should not be able to avail myself of any profit that might arise from the floating balance; and as Messrs. Hoare are not my private bankers, they would probably expect some remuneration for their trouble, if no part of the money was invested or left in their hands; they derive an emolument from the purchase and re-sale of the exchequer bills.

Then you keep the money at Messrs. Hoare's, in case it cannot be profitably employed? — I do.

Did you give any general instructions to them to employ it for you? — Never; without giving them particular instructions, no part of the money is invested: this appears from none of the floating balance being laid out in the year 1819.

Will you have the goodness to state the days and the months you go the two circuits? , I generally begin as near as I can the first Monday after twenty-one days from the quarter-day the tax is due. Supposing the taxes to be due on January the 5th, I never go till twenty-one days after that day. I generally begin upon a Monday.

It appears by the return that in the quarter, July 1820, you paid in £44,529; on what days did you collect that money? — It must have been collected the beginning of May. Nearly the whole of the money is received on my circuit, except as before stated.

Does not the act of parliament require you actually to go ten miles within every collector quarterly? — It does.

But in point of fact, you have been in the habit of going only twice a year? — Only twice; for the reason I have already stated.

Did you ever receive any complaint for not going more frequently? — No; but I believe I should have great complaints from the persons who pay the taxes if I went oftener.

Have the tax-office never remarked to you the small payments made in the April and October quarters? — Never; because in these quarters I make a return to them, showing what is in arrear: this return explains the reason. They require me, although I do not go the receipt at the end of the quarters alluded to, to make a return to them of the amount of the taxes in arrear, that they may inquire whether that is the fact.

As far as your experience goes, do you apprehend that there would be any inconvenience in abolishing the July and January circuits? — I cannot conceive there would be any. With respect to the country, (I mean those who pay taxes), I am satisfied that they will pay their taxes with greater satisfaction half-yearly than quarterly.

Supposing the present practice to continue, do you think there would be any inconvenience from relieving the receivers general from two of the circuits? — I am not aware of any. I should be very sorry to have to go four. You now only go two, though the law says you ought to go four; do you apprehend any inconvenience would arise if you were legally relieved from the necessity of going four? — No.

In what manner is the money received? — It has been the rule with me not to take any money for taxes in notes of the bank of England. There is one exception, when I go to Wisbeach, which is the most distant place;

there I take the country bank notes of that neighbourhood, and for them I take Gurneys and Peckover's draft payable in London, at three days; that is the only exception, Gurneys and Peckover are bankers at Wisbeach, and I take this draft before I quit the town.

Do you ever receive any country gentleman's draft on London in payment for taxes? — I sometimes receive about £200 in the course of the receipt in that way, but not more than that.

Have you any account with a country banker? — None for the taxes.

How are the sums which are to be paid by you paid? — I receive almost the whole of the money when I am on the receipt, which I bring up to town myself, and whatever sums are paid afterwards, say from £1,000 to £2,000, that comes into my general account, and just before the quarter day I pay it through my banker at Cambridge to Messrs. Hoares, who have orders to pay it to government with the rest of the money collected upon my circuit.

How are the small sums required to be paid by the receiver general of the county paid? — If I have cash in the house, I pay them in cash, if not, I draw upon my country banker.

Will you tell the Committee whether the emoluments of your office belong to yourself exclusively, or whether there has been any understanding, by virtue of which any other person has shared them with you — No, never.

Nor when you received the office, you never gave any thing as a consideration? — No, I was appointed on the resignation of my father, in 1806.

How long had your father been appointed? — For about twenty years.

What was he, a professional man? — No; he was a gentleman, being in no profession.

Appendix II

*A GLIMPSE INTO AN EARLY 19th CENTURY BILL BOOK OF
PEMBERTON FISKE & HAYWARD, 1823-25*

Bill books were maintained at this time and for many years later by all solicitors' practices. Any item of activity relevant to a client's matter was entered up on a daily basis, probably also with a standard charge added, the whole record being carried forward into one of the traditionally long itemised solicitor's bills well known and sometimes parodied by eighteenth and nineteenth century writers. Itemised charging was nevertheless a necessity and not simply a quaint survival from earlier centuries. Since the Statute 1729 2 Geo. 11 c.23 a client could require his attorney or solicitor, in any contentious matter, to submit his bill of costs to the court for taxation. Itemised listing of activity was an essential preliminary to this review procedure.

By 1823 the Eau Brink Commissioners had completed the Eau Brink Cut in its original form. The possibility of a further stage of the scheme had however been left open. According to Section 22 of the Eau Brink Act 1819 provision for drainage from the Parishes of Tilney Clenchwarton and West Lynn, hitherto taken by the final bend of the Great Ouse, was to be left over until the effect of the Eau Brink Cut was seen. Whether an additional "Marshland Drain" was needed was to be determined "in such manner as the Engineers (or an Umpire) shall direct or appoint". The following bill book entries record litigation brought by aggrieved interests in this corner of Marshland, evidently seeking the construction of the Marshland Drain as a remedy for their drainage problems.

In this Bill Book, disbursements out of the solicitors' own pocket are shown in the left hand cash column, items of charging in the right. There was no universal 'rule of the road' about this. Messrs. Gunning and Francis' Bill books were maintained the other way about. These records highlight above all else the distinct handicap suffered at that time by all business and professional activity, namely the lack of any rapid form of communications for messages and of transport for persons. There are numerous instances of appointments or hearing dates not kept, resulting in wasted journeys and time away from the office.

It should also be noted that no civil litigation of any significance was at this time conducted in Cambridge, all actions were brought before the Courts in Westminster and involved the instruction of Counsel. County Courts, at which solicitors could appear without Counsel, were not established in Cambridge and many other localities until the County Courts Act 1846. Even then, actions of the kind illustrated here were beyond the jurisdiction of a County Court and would still have been brought in Westminster.

THE EAU BRINK DRAINAGE COMMISSIONERS

	£	s	d	£	s	d
1823 November 6th An order having been made at the Quarterly Meeting held on the 9th October last that in case a Mandamus (1)* should be applied for to compel the Commissioners to make a New Drain in Marshland the steps necessary on the part of the Commissioners should be conducted by Mr. Pemberton and Mr. Lemmon, under the directions of a Committee, Attending Mr. Bevill one of the Committee thereon, and he gave instructions to retain Mr. Scarlett (8) and Mr. Adam on the part of the Commissioners.					6	8
Writing to Agent to retain them accordingly.					3	6
Retaining Note to Mr. Scarlett.					2	6
Paid fee to him and Clerk.	1	3	6			
Attending him.					6	8
Retaining note to Mr. Adam					2	6
Paid fee to him and Clerk.	1	3	6			
Attending him.					6	8

1824 January 22nd
A Notice having been served upon the Commissioners at the Quarterly Meeting on the 8th instant that in the next term a Mandamus would be moved for the above purpose and an Order being again made for resisting the Motion (3).

*See Explanatory Notes p.294

	£	s	d	£	s	d
Writing to Agent to instruct Mr. Adam, to take Notes of what might pass on the Application for the Mandamus.					3	6
January 23rd Agent attending Mr. Adam accordingly when he promised to take Notes if he should be in Court without receiving any additional fee.					6	8
April 29 The Motion not having been made in the last term and a fresh Notice of Motion for the ensuing term having been given at the Quarterly Meeting held on the 20th instant. Writing again to Agent to instruct Mr. Adam to take Notes.					6	8
Agent attending Mr. Adam accordingly.					6	8
May 30th Mr. Lane the Solicitor to the Applicants having informed us that the Motion for a Rule Nisi (2) for a Mandamus would certainly be made tomorrow. Writing to Agent instructing him to attend the Court on Motion and employ a Shorthand Writer to take notes of what passed.					5	0
31st Agent attending at Westminster accordingly when Motion was made and Rule Nisi granted.					6	8
Paid Shorthand Writer for attendance and transcript.	1	4	4			
Copy of his notes.					20	0
Letter to Mr. Bevill informing him the result of the Motion.					5	0
Attending to bespeak and afterwards to obtain Copy of Rule Nisi and Affidavits in support thereof						
Paid for Office Copy of Rule Nisi		7	6			
Paid for Office Copy of Affidavit of Mr. Lane folio 86						
The like of Mr. Hoseason folio 16	4	4	8			
The like for Mr. Jollife folio 5						

	£	s	d	£	s	d
June 3rd						
Close copy Rule Nisi					2	0
Close copy of affidavit together folio 107				1	15	8
7th						
Making copies of the Affidavits for Mr.						
Bevill 15 Brief Sheets				2	10	0
Letter to him therewith.					5	0
8th						
Mr. Bevill having written to appoint a						
meeting with Mr. Pemberton to consider						
the Affidavits writing to him in reply						
thereto					5	0
10th						
Writing again to Mr. Bevill to appoint the						
13th instant for a conference with him.					5	0
11th						
Making two more copies of the Affidavit to						
be laid before Mr. Scarlett and Mr. Adam						
previous to a consultation on the most						
advisable mode of resisting the motion for						
making the Rule absolute (15 brief sheets						
each).				5	0	0
15th to 19th both inclusive						
Journey to Mr. Pemberton to London to						
attend Mr. Bevill and the consultation with						
Counsel and take the measures necessary						
for opposing the rule being made absolute						
but in consequence of an unexpected						
illness of Mr. Bevill consultation was post-						
poned though Mr. Pemberton went to						
Newington to conference with Mr. Bevill,						
out 5 days.				15	15	0
Paid coachhire and expences to and from						
London	2	0	0			
Paid expences in London	5	5	0			
Paid Coachhire to Newington		5	0			

TRINITY TERM 1824

	£	s	d	£	s	d
Attending to instruct Clerk in Court					6	8
Drawing Mr. Pemberton's Affidavit in opposition to the Motion with statement of finances annexed folio 24				1	4	0
Ingrossing same					12	0
Paid stamp and paper.		2	8			
Attending at Public office to be sworn.					6	8
Paid for Oath and Exhibit		2	0			
Paid filing Affidavit of Mr. Pemberton and also other Affidavits prepared by Mr. Lemmon	1	16	0			
2 copies of Mr. Pemberton's Affidavit for Counsel (3 brief sheets each)				1	0	0
Copy thereof for Mr. Bevill (3 brief sheets)					10	0
2 Copies for Counsel of 5 Affidavits procured by Messrs. Lemmon and Orton to oppose the motion (9 sheets each)				3	0	0
2 copies for Counsel of Brief as prepared by Mr. Bevill (12 sheets each)				4	0	0
Copies of Plan to accompany same.					4	0
Attending to appoint consultation with Mr. Scarlett for 25 instant and afterwards to apprize Mr. Adams thereof.					6	8
Paid consultation fee to Mr. Scarlett and Clerk.	2	9	6			
Attending him.					6	8
Paid fee to M. Scarlett with Brief	15	15	0			
To his Clerk.		5	0			
Attending him.					6	8
Paid consultation fee to Mr. Adam and Clerk.	2	4	6			
Attending him.					6	8
Paid fee to Mr. Adam with Brief.	10	10	0			
To his Clerk.		5	0			
Attending him.					6	8

June 21st to July 1st
Journey of Mr. Pemberton again to London
to attend the Court in Expectation of the
Motion coming on but which was postponed from day to day, Mr. Pemberton
attended the Consultation on the 25th
and was detained in London until 1st July
(out 10 days)   31 10   0

	£	s	d	£	s	d
Paid Coachhire to and from London	2	2	0			
Paid expences in London.	10	10	0			
Paid Coachhire and Porterage in London		18	0			

July 2nd
Agent attending Mr. Scarlett to appoint
time for another Consultation when he
fixed the Evening of the 5th instant and
afterwards attending to apprize Mr. Adam
thereof.   6   8
Consultation fee to Mr. Scarlett and Clerk.   2   9   6
Attending him.   6   8
Fee to Mr. Adam and Clerk.   2   4   6
Attending him.   6   8

5th
Attending Consultation at Mr. Scarletts
Chambers.   13   4

6th
Attending Court the whole day when the
Rule for the Mandamus was made
absolute.   13   4
Paid Court fees.   2   6
Paid Clerk in Court attendance.   6   8
Term fee (4) Clerk in Court and Solicitor.   13   4
Letters etc.   6   0
Paid the Expence of Shorthand Writers
attendance and of a transcript of the
Arguments of Counsel and the decision
of the Court (the other half being paid by
Mr. Lane the Solicitor for the Applicants).   3   4   6

17th
Attending Dean Wood this day when he
gave us some information respecting the
proceedings of the Parties applying for
the Mandamus.   6   8

August 11th
Copy of Mr. Hoseasons Affidavit for
Dean Wood folio 16.   5   4
Writing to him therewith.   3   6

September 18th
Writing to Mr. Holden the Secretary to the

	£	s	d	£	s	d

Exchequer Bill Loan Commissioners (5)
informing him that Mr. Pemberton would
be in London on Thursday next to attend
a Board of the Commissioners for the
purpose of laying before them a Statement
of the finances of the Eau Brink Drainage
Commissioners and ascertaining whether
they would advance a sum of money equal
to the sum required for making the
Marshland Drain. — 5 0

Writing to Sir Edward Banks (9) informing
him that Mr. Pemberton intended to call
upon him at the same time for the purpose
of ascertaining whether in case the Loan
Commissioners refused to advance the
money he (Sir E B) would advance it and
upon what terms. — 5 0

Drawing Statement of annual income to be
laid before the Board Folio 12 — 12 0

Fair copy thereof. — 4 0

Drawing statement showing the presence
of the former loans. — 6 0

Fair copy. — 3 0

Drawing out a calculation showing within
what period a loan of £30,000 with interest
of 4 per cent would be paid off by
instalments. — 10 0

Fair copy thereof. — 3 4

29 & 30
Journey of Mr. Pemberton to London,
when he was examined before the Loan
Commissioners who refused to advance
beyond £30,000 and would not advance
even that sum unless the Engineers would
certify that £30,000 would entirely complete
the whole of the works necessary for
completion the Drainage of all the land
intended to be drained by means of the
New Cut but Sir E. Banks was disposed to
advance the money if he was allowed 5 per
cent interest and also employed to execute
the work. — 6 6 0

Paid Coach hire to and from London.   2 0 0

Paid expences to London.   2 0 0

	£	s	d	£	s	d

October 1st

Writing very long letter to Mr. Holden stating what Mr. Pemberton conceived had passed at the Board of Commissioners in the interview on Thursday last and requesting to be informed whether it was substantially correct in order that Mr. P might accurately report it to the Commissioners at the next Quarterly Meeting.   5   0

Writing also to Sir Edward Banks stating what Mr. Pemberton conceived had passed in the interview between them and requesting for the same reason that he would inform Mr. Pemberton whether it was substantially correct.   5   0

Writing to Mr. Telford (7) informing him what had passed at the Board of the Loan Commissioners and requesting he would state whether he could give the Certificate required.   5   0

Writing similar letter to Mr. Rennie (6)   5   0

Making copies to keep of the above 4 letters (which were very long) in order that the same might be produced and read at the next Quarterly Meeting.   8   0

Making Copy of Correspondence between Mr. Pemberton and Mr. Holden, Sir E. Banks, Mr. Telford, and Mr. Rennie to be sent to Mr. Lemmon and entered upon the Minutes of the last Quarterly Meeting. 6 Brief Sheets.   1   0   0

Writing to Mr. Lemmon therewith.   3   6

20th

The Commissioners having at their Quarterly Meeting on the 14th instant desired that a state of their funds and also of the facts of their case should be laid before Counsel in order that he might advise as to the return to be made to the Mandamus, writing to Agent instructing him to endeavour to obtain a consultation with Mr. Scarlett on the 29th instant.   3   6

	£	s	d	£	s	d

October 21st
Agent attending accordingly at
Mr. Scarletts Chambers but found he would
not be in Town on the 29th. — 6 0

23rd
Agent attending at Mr. Scarletts to appoint
consultation for the 27th and to apprize
Mr. Adam thereof when he learnd
Mr. Adam would not be in Town until the
1st November. — 6 0
Drawing Statement of Facts to be laid
before Counsel to enable them to advise
on return to Mandamus (8 brief sheets) — 2 13 0
2 fair copies thereof for Mr. Scarlett and
Mr. Adam. — 2 13 0

26th
Instructions for Special return to the
Writ of Mandamus — 6 8
Drawing return Folio 40 — 2 0 0
Fee to special Pleader to settle same. 1 1 0
Copy Statement of Facts to accompany
Draft (8 brief sheets). — 1 6 0
Attending Special Pleader with Draft and
several times to give explanations. — 6 8
Copy of Shorthand Writers Notes on the
Motion for the Mandamus for the use of
Mr. Scarlett on settling Draft Return. — 16 8
Copy of Return as settled by Special Pleader
to be laid before Mr. Scarlett (Folio 40) — 13 4
Paid fee to Mr. Scarlett with Draft of return
to Mandamus Statement of facts and other
papers and to his Clerk. 6 11 0
Attending him thereon. — 6 8
Agent attending at Mr. Scarletts when his
Clerk informed him that nothing could be
done towards settling the Draft return
until after a consultation and afterwards
writing to us thereon. — 6 8
Writing to Agent informing him it was
absolutely necessary to have the Draft
Return to produce at an adjourned
Quarterly Meeting of the Commissioners
on the 2nd November and therefore

	£	s	d		£	s	d
requesting he would again see Mr. Scarlett and urge him to settle the Draft previous to that day and that a consultation might be had afterwards previous to filing the Return.						5	0
Agent attending Mr. Scarlett accordingly and several times until he procured the Draft settled with Mr. Scarletts Opinion thereon.						6	8

Nov. 2nd

	£	s	d		£	s	d
Journey of Mr. Pemberton to Ely to attend adjourned Quarterly Meeting and confer with the Commissioners on the Draft return, as settled by Mr. Scarlett.					2	2	0
Paid Chaisehire and Expences.	1	16	6				

10th

	£	s	d		£	s	d
Mr. Wells the Register of the Bedford Level Corporation, having written to inform us that he was ordered by the Board to attend the meeting of the Committee appointed to conduct the Opposition to the Mandamus. Writing to the 4 Members of the Committee aprizing them thereof.						14	0
Writing also to Mr. Wells in reply to his letter.						5	0

MICHAELMAS TERM 1824

	£	s	d		£	s	d
Making fair copy of proposed Return to Mandamus for Mr. Scarlett (5 brief sheets)						16	8
The like for Mr. Adam.						16	8
Making fair copy for Mr. Scarlett of the correspondence between Mr. Pemberton, Mr. Holden, Sir E. Banks, Mr. Telford and Mr. Rennie (6 Brief sheets).					1	0	0
The like for Mr. Adam					1	0	0
Drawing additional Statement of facts to accompany the above papers 2 1/2 Brief sheets						10	8
Fair copy for Mr. Scarlett.						8	4
The like for Mr. Adam.						8	4
The like for use						8	4
Agent attending to instruct Clerk in Court.						6	8

	£	s	d	£	s	d
Agent attending Mr. Scarlett to appoint Consultation for the 18th inst. and afterwards upon Mr. Adam for the same purpose.					6	8
Fee to Mr. Scarlett with papers to peruse previous to Consultation and Clerk.	3	5	6			
Attending him.					6	8
Fee to Mr. Scarlett on Consultation and Clerk.	2	9	6			
Attending him.					6	8
Fee to Mr. Adam with papers to peruse previous to Consultation and Clerk.	4	6	6			
Attending him.					6	8
Fee to Mr. Adam on Consultation and Clerk.	2	4	6			
Attending him.					6	8
Mr. Scarlett having sent to our Agent to say that he could not attend Consultation in the Evening of the 18th but that it might be appointed for 9 o'clock in the Evening of the 19th, Agent attending Mr. Adam thereon, found he was otherwise engaged and that hour and attending again at Mr. Scarletts when it was proposed to have the consultation at Westminster at 2 o'clock on the 19th.					6	8
Agent attending Mr. Adam thereon, when he agreed to the Appointment and attending to acquaint Mr. Scarlett therewith.					6	8

November 16th to 20th

	£	s	d	£	s	d
Journey of Mr. Pemberton to London to attend the Consultation when the return to the Mandamus was finally settled; out 5 days in consequence of the postponement of the Consultation.				15	15	0
Paid Coachhire to and from London.	2	0	0			
Paid expences to London.	5	5	0			

20th

	£	s	d	£	s	d
Ingrossing return to Mandamus.				1	9	6
Paid for Parchment.		4	0			

	£	s	d		£	s	d
Agent attending on Mr. Wells at Grays Inn Coffeehouse and procured his signature to the return as one of the Commissioners.						6	8
Agent attending for same purpose at the Chambers of Mr. Eagle one of the Commissioners upon whom the Mandamus was served and afterwards at his House in Arundel Street and then found he was at Westminster.						6	8
Attending again at Mr. Eagles in Arundel Street but he refused to sign the return.						6	8

22 & 23

In consequence of Mr. Eagle declining to sign the return and it being necessary to have it signed by one of the Commissioners upon whom the Mandamus was served and also to file the return by the 24th in order to prevent an attachment issuing. Journey of Mr. Hayward to March to get same signed by Mr. Orton he being one of the Commissioners upon whom the Mandamus was served the other two residing at a greater distance out 2 days.					4	4	0
Paid Chaisehire, Coachhire and expences (being obliged to travel on Sunday)	3	3	6				
Instructions to Counsel to move to file return to Mandamus.						3	4
Fee to Mr. Campbell therewith.		10	6				
Attending him therewith.						3	4
Attending Court on Motion.						6	8
Paid Clerk in Court.		6	8				
Paid for Rule.		2	0				
Paid for Inrolling the Writ and Return.	1	9	6				
Paid for Transcript sent into the Treasury.	1	9	6				
Paid Clerk of the Crown.		13	4				
Paid for Office Copy of the Writ and Return	2	19	0				
Close copy thereof.					1	9	6
Term fee Clerk in Court and Solicitor.						13	4

Dec. 2

Copy of return to Mandamus for Mr. Orton one of the Commisssioners to sign same, 5 Brief sheets.						16	8

	£	s	d	£	s	d
Writing to him therewith.					3	6
Copy of Return for Mr. Wells the other Commissioner who signed same.					16	8
Writing to him therewith.					3	6
Copy of Return sent to Mr. Lemmon to be deposited with the proceedings of the Commissioners.					16	8
Writing to him therewith.					3	6
Paid Postage of Letters and Carriage of parcels.		2	3	0		

	£117	3	4	141 18	10
				117	3	4

	TOTAL	£259	2	2

1825 January 26th
In consequence of the return to the
Mandamus obtained in Trinity Term 1824
to compel the Commissioners to make the
Marshland Drain not having been yet
argued and Mr. Pemberton being requested
to attend this day a Meeting of the Conflicting Parties with a view to endeavouring
to put an end to the matters in difference,
attending meeting at the Red Lion Inn in
Cambridge.   2   2   0

HILARY TERM 1825

February 4th
Attending at the Crown Office searching
for Rule Nisi to quash the return (filed
last term) to the Mandamus and found
that a Motion had been made for such a
Rule that the Court had refused, but
ordered the case to be set down in the
peremptory paper and also attending to
bespeak Office Copy of the Affidavit filed
in support of the Motion.   6   8
Paid for Office copy of the Affidavit of
Mr. Frederick Lane folio 105   3 10   0
Close copy for the Country.   1 15   0
Perusing and considering same.   6   8

	£	s	d	£	s	d
Paid Clerk in Court accepting and Transmitting Notice of Case being put in the Crown paper for argument.		3	4			
Making two copies of Brief of Mandamus Return for Counsel 7 sheets each.				2	6	8
Paid Clerk in Court for copy of Mandamus for Mr. Justice Holroyd.	2	19	0			
Paid ditto for copy of Objections thereto for ditto		6	8			
Attending to deliver it.					6	8
Paid Judges Clerk.		2	0			
Paid Clerk in Court for Copy of Mandamus etc. for Mr. Justice Littledale.	2	19	0			
Paid ditto for Copy of Objections thereto for ditto		6	8			
Attending to deliver it.					6	8
Paid Judges Clerk.		2	0			
Copy points to be argued for each Counsel.					13	4

FEBRUARY 15th and 16th

	£	s	d	£	s	d
The Court having signified its intention to proceed with the Crown paper on the 15th and 3 following days, and it being fully expected that this Case would be heard, and the Committee of Accounts, having at the Meeting on the 1st instant directed that Mr. Pemberton should attend in Town on the Arguing of the Case, Journey of Mr. Pemberton to London for that purpose but the case was not called on. Out 4 days.				12	12	0
Paid Expenses in London.	4	4	0			
Paid Coachhire to and from London.	2	4	0			
Paid Clerk in Court for attendance.		6	8			
Paid Clerk in Court term fee.		6	8			
Solicitors Term fee, letters etc.					12	8

EASTER TERM 1825

	£	s	d	£	s	d
Agent attending instructing Clerk in Court.					6	8
Paid Clerk in Court Transmitting Notice of Case in paper.		3	4			
Paid carriage of parcels from Messrs. Lemmon and Orton with briefs.		4	8			

	£	s	d	£	s	d

May 7th
Attending Court case in paper but not
called on. — 6 8

May 9th
Attending to appoint a Consultation with
Mr. Scarlett when he fixed the 11th at
Westminster and afterwards attending to
apprize Mr. Adam thereof. — 6 8
Paid fee to Mr. Scarlett with Brief and
Clerk 3 5 6
Attending him. — 6 8
Paid Consultation fee to Mr. Scarlett and
Clerk. 2 9 6
Attending him. — 6 8
Paid fee to Mr. Adam with Brief and Clerk. 3 5 6
Attending him. — 6 8
Paid Consultation fee to Mr. Adam and
Clerk. 2 4 6
Attending him. — 6 8

11th
Attending Court this day, when it being
understood that the Judges did not intend
to proceed on the Crown Paper the
Consultation stood over. — 6 8

17th
On receipt of Notice from Clerk in Court
that the case would come on tomorrow,
attending to instruct Counsel and to get a
Consultation appointed, but found that
neither Mr. Scarlett nor Mr. Adam could
attend, the one being engaged in the Nisi
Prius Court, and the other in Parliament. — 13 4

18th
Attending Court Case not called on. — 6 8

30th
The Cause being peremptorily fixed for
10 o'clock tomorrow morning, Agent
attending to appoint Consultation with
Mr. Scarlett and afterwards to inform
Mr. Adam of the time appointed. — 6 8

	£	s	d	£	s	d

Several attendances at Mr. Adam's
Chambers, to alter time for Consultation
at Mr. Scarletts request, and also attending
at the House of Lords, for the same
purpose, but without effect.   6   8

30 and 31
Journey of Mr. Pemberton to London, to
attend the Consultation and also the
hearing of the Case, but at Mr. Scarletts
wish the arguing of the Case was ordered
to stand over until Trinity Term, as he
stated it was impossible for him at the
present time to attend at the Argument
which he was desirous of doing.   6   6   0
Paid Coachhire to and from London.   2   4   0
Paid expences to London.   2   2   0

June 1st
Agent attending Mr. Adam at his house in
Great Russell Street to communicate the
result of the consultation with Mr. Scarlett
last night.   6   8
Attending Court, Cause called on and
ordered to stand over until Trinity Term
in consequence of Mr. Scarlett not being
able to attend.   13   4
Paid Clerk in Court for attendances during
this term when the Case was in the paper.   10   0

TRINITY TERM 1825

Attending instructing Clerk in Court   6   0
Paid Clerk in Court accepting Notice of
Case in paper.   3   4

June 6th
Attending Mr. Scarlett and Mr. Adams
severally to appoint time for consultation.   6   8

7 & 8
At the hearing of the case being fixed for
the 8th and Mr. Pemberton not being able
to attend, journey of Mr. Hayward to

	£	s	d	£	s	d
London for that purpose but the case was again postponed until the 11th — out 2 days.				4	4	0
Paid Coachhire to and from London.	2	4	0			
Paid expences in London.	2	2	0			

10 and 11

	£	s	d	£	s	d
Journey of Mr. Hayward again to London to attend the hearing of the Case, but it was then again postponed until the 15th — out 2 days.				4	4	0
Paid Coachhire to and from London.	2	4	0			
Paid expences in London.	2	2	0			

14th, 15th & 16th

	£	s	d	£	s	d
Journey of Mr. Hayward again to London to attend the hearing when the case was again put off in consequence of Chief Justices attendance being required in the House of Lords — out 3 days.				6	6	0
Paid Coachhire to and from London.	2	4	0			
Paid expences in London.	3	3	0			
Paid Clerk in Court for attendances during the term.		10	0			
Paid Clerk in Court term fee.		6	8			
Solicitors Term Fee					6	8
Letters etc.					6	0
				£49	1	0
	£49	10	8	49	10	8
				£98	11	8

Here the record ceases abruptly though the ending of the story was a happy one. It is recorded in the Eau Brink minutes for 25th June 1825 that the conflicting parties agreed to compromise their dispute, discontinuing these Court proceedings as well as a concurrent application in Parliament for another Eau Brink Act. This compromise had been anticipated in the entry for 26th January 1825 and involved the Drainage Commisssioners agreeing to "the immediate widening of the new Cut and the closing of the lower dam" and their opponents refraining from "Parliamentary or legal proceedings 'till three years experience has been had of the effect of these measures". The agreed remedies evidently solved the problems to the satisfaction of the two sides and no further proceedings were needed or threatened thereafter.

EXPLANATORY NOTES

(1) *Mandamus*— A Writ issuable out of the Kings Bench in all cases where there was a legal right but no other specific remedy. Then, as now, it was used to compel Public Officers to perform duties imposed upon them by Common Law or by Statute where no other means of compelling such performance exists.

(2) *Rule Nisi* — An Order of the King's Bench which would be made absolute only after a Defendant had been called on to show cause why the rule applied for should not be granted.

(3) *Motion for Mandamus*— an oral application by Counsel to the Court for the issue of a Writ of Mandamus.

(4) *Term fee* — From the 15th century onwards the fee for an attorney conducting a Court case at Westminster became settled at 3s 4d per term, i.e. one mark (13s 4d) per four term year. By the eighteen twenties declining purchasing power had pushed the term fee up to 6s 8d (two marks per annum) but by this time the attorney was entitled to charge additionally for all such other items as are specified in this Bill record.

(5) *Exchequer Bill Loan Commissioners* — Responsible to the Treasury for aproving the issue of the Exchequer Bills for raising temporary loans, occasionally for the purpose of carrying out public works and where involving a body such as the Eau Brink Commissioners, generally in anticipation of taxes from which the loan would be repaid.

(6) *MR. RENNIE*—John Rennie (1794–1874) Scottish Civil Engineer, second son of John Rennie (Old Waterloo Bridge; Plymouth Breakwater), appointed Engineer to the scheme on behalf of the Eau Brink Drainage Commissioners following the death of his father in 1821.

(7) *MR. TELFORD* — Thomas Telford (1757–1834) Scottish Civil Engineer responsible for the Menai Suspension Bridge and St. Katharine's Docks. Appointed to represent the Eau Brink Navigation Commissioners in the scheme.

(8) *MR. SCARLETT*—James Scarlett K.C., of the Inner Temple, M.P. for Peterborough, Attorney General 1827–30, appointed Chief Baron of the Exchequer and created Baron Abinger in 1834.

Appendix III

THE CAMBRIDGE AND OXFORD RAILWAY
(An Extract from Messrs. Gunning & Francis' Bill Book for 1846)

1846

Jan. 2nd.

Drawing and fair copy Schedule of Services by Mr. Looker in form required by Messrs. Bircham and Dalrymple's letter of this morning. The like by Mr. Francis. Visiting Messrs. Bircham and Dalrymple therewith and thereon.

3rd

Attending Revs. Dr. Hodgson the Master of St. Peters College and Mr. Locker the Bursar of the same College who called together to ascertain the intention of the Company with regard to the Terminus on those premises in Lease to Mr. Hazard when we explained to them the position of the Terminus for which Notices had been given and they stated their intention to oppose the Bill in case the Railway was brought either to Mr. Beales or Mr. Hazard's premises.

6th

Writing Messrs. Bircham and Dalrymple thereon for the information of the Board.

7th

Attending at Sessions house posting a Notice of Application. Paid Keeper of Sessions House his fee.
Visiting Messrs. Bircham & Co. with Orig. endorsed.

12th

Attending Mr. Locker Bursar of St. Peters College conferring further on proposed Termini and we gave him at his request the Secretary's name and address in order that he might communicate immediately with the Board.

Attending Mr. Ekin at the request of Messrs. Bircham and Dalrymple informing him of our interview with the Master and Bursar of St. Peter's College and stating our opinion that for this Session at any rate it would be prudent to give up the Station at the head of the River and run at once up to the Eastern Counties Station. The like Mr. Arlett.

16th

Having received Petition to Parliament to bring in the Bill attending severally The Rev. Robt. Phelps Master of Sidney — Rev. John Lamb Master of Corpus, Chas. Finch Foster Esq., Mr. A. G. Brinley, R. M. Fawcett Esq., and Rev. Robert Bristow obtaining their signatures thereto.
Writing Messrs. Nash and Thurrall with Petition and postage.
Writing Messrs. Bircham and Dalrymple acknowledging receipt of Petition and informing them we had sent same to Messrs. Nash and Thurrall.

27th

Messrs. Bircham and Co., having written to inform us that in consequence of the strong opposition of the University to the proposed Terminus at Mr. Beales' as well as that at Mr. Hazards' premises both Termini had been abandoned and Mr. Locker Bursar of St. Peter's College had been informed to that effect and requesting to know if any other parties should be similarly apprized. Writing them to say that Mr. Rance Hon. Sec. of the Cambridge Railways Committee should have a like communication which might be read at the next Committee Meeting.

30th

Drawing and two fair copies List of parishes and names of Clerks with whom plans Sections and books of reference were deposited.
Writing Messrs. Bircham and Dalrymple therewith.

31st

Writing Messrs. Bircham & Co., in reply to their letter of yesterday's date that Mr. E. E. Wrench was a Clerk in our office and would be in readiness on the 4th proxo and requesting particularly to know at what time and for how long the witnesses would be required.
Attending Mr. Ekin at his Counting House who had written to us on the subject of a Petition to ensure the support of the Local Members when

after much discussion it was deemed advisable to have 3 petitions prepared for general signature in the University Town and County respectively the two first of which we were to take in hand and the latter he would see after.

Writing Messrs. Bircham and Dalrymple fully on the subject.

Feb. 3rd.

Mr. Francis and Clerk attending in the parishes of Hauxton Harston and Haslingfield to procure witnesses immediately as directed by Messrs. Bircham and Dalrymple's letter of this morning to prove before the Standing Orders Committee of the House of Commons that the road described in the Book of reference as a public road was in fact a private Drift and with a public Bridle road and footway over the same when after conferring with and examining several persons in these parishes who were acquainted with the locality Mr. Holmes the Tenant of the Land through which the Road ran and Mr. Whitechurch an adjoining Occupier was induced to go to London.

Horse hire etc

Attending at the Office of Clerk of the Peace as requested by Mr. Denton's letter of yesterday's Evening to ascertain if Nos. 15 to 18 in the parish of Eddlesboro' were inserted in plan there deposited where same were so found.

Paid search

The like attendance searching for and bespeaking extract from the award as to Nos. 3 and 4 in the parishes of Harston and Hauxton Railway was described as a Driftway and making tracing from the award Map and paid for extract.

Attending Mr. Arlett and afterwards Mr. Ekin as to the proposed petitions to Parliament when the former thought they had better not be attempted and they therefore agreed to be dropped.

Mr. Francis' journey to and attendance in London as witness before the Standing Orders Committee of the House of Commons engaged 5 days. Paid expenses in Town and Travelling expences.

The like two Clerks as similar Witnesses engaged the like time. Paid the expenses of the other witnesses Messrs. Whitechurch and Holmes in Town and travelling expenses.

17th

Perusing Draft petition sent for our consideration and making alterations therein and several suggestions thereto.

Writing Messrs. Bircham and Co. therewith and thereon.

23rd

Messrs. Bircham and Co. having written us that two petitions were thought desirable the one from the Town and other from the University and that it was now time to interest the three sets of Members in support of the Bill and requesting us to see Mr. Ekin and Mr. Arlett immediately upon both matters. Attending Mr. Ekin at his Countinghouse when we found he had received ingrossed petition for the Town and had sent his Clerk with it to the Mayor and afterwards to a few of the principal inhabitants for their signature and we arranged that on the Clerks return the petitions should be sent to his to place in the hands of a person who would wait on the Inhabitants generally and obtain their signatures. And with respect to the Members we agreed that a copy of the Resolutions at the Town Meeting should be sent to the Members of the Town requesting their support that the County Members should be applied to through Messrs. Nash and Thurall and that we should both make the best arrangements we could for getting the support of the members of the University.

Attending at Mr. Arlett's rooms in Pembroke College to confer with him on the same business and on the University Petition where we found that he had not been in College for the last fortnight and the porter did not know when he was expected.

Mr. Arlett being from home attending again twice at Mr. Ekins Countinghouse when the second time we saw him and agreed the matter must stand over until Mr. Arlett's return.

Visiting Agents with a full account of what had taken place.

Paid Parchment for Petition — 35 skins in all.

24th

Having received petition from Messrs. Bircham & Co., this morning for signature of Members of the University and requesting us to see Mr. Arlett immediately thereon attending that Gentleman accordingly when he was quite of opinion we could not procure it to be generally signed and it

would otherwise be injudicious to set it on foot but said he would make enquiries the next 3 or 4 days and let us know the feeling.
Paid parcel.

25th
Attending Mr. Ficklin an influential friend of Mr. Manners Sutton M.P. begging him to interest that Gentleman in support of the measure in Parliament when he consented to write at once to him on the subject.

Mar. 2nd
Attending Rev. Mr. Arlett at his rooms in Pembroke College discussing the propriety of attempting a petition in favour of the Bill from the Members of the University which he had undertaken to enquire about and consider when he was of opinion that from Trinity College being to a Man adverse to the Measure and St. John's College being a good deal so together with the fact that many members of the smaller colleges were indifferent it would be advisable not to attempt it but that if a Petition were desirable one from the Members of the University and Landowners jointly would be better which we agreed accordingly should be prepared. Writing Messrs. Bircham & Co., to this effect and requesting a Petition for signature.
The like Rev. Mr. Robinson Vicar of Barrington.
The like Mr. Leigh Bursar of Kings College.
The like Mr. Foster of Trumpington and Mr. Howard of Granchester who were severally not at home when we called at their residences.
The like Mr. Salmon who promised to see his colleague Mr. Gotobed.
Attending various persons in Cambridge to get them to consent to the proposed Railway so far as same affected their property engaged whole day.
Attending Mr. Denton the Surveyor in London conferring on the purchase he wished to have made of the Vicarage house and Land at Granchester and taking instructions to negotiate for same.
Attending Messrs. Bircham & Co., in London on the assents required to be procured and various other matters.
Attending Mr. Cooper who called at our office on the Traffic case on which we conferred severally and he promised to see us again on Monday.

4th

Paid parcel with petition in both houses of Parliament for signature by the Members of the University and Land owners.

Attending Mr. Arlett therewith when found he was absent for the day but left petition in his room. The Town petition having been brought to us by Mr. Doughty with 500 signatures attached who required to know if any more were required Clerk attending Mr. Ekin for instructions on the matter and again Mr. Doughty begging him to procure as many more as he could get.

5th

Attending Mr. Arlett conferring on the two petitions we left for him yesterday at his rooms when he was of the opinion that some of the allegations might be objected to by some Members of the University and could be improved and we accordingly made several alterations and finally settled Draft petitions with Mr. Arlett to accord with his wishes.

Ingrossing petition to the Lords as altered.

The like to the Commons.

Parchment.

Ingrossing petition to Lords for signature of University and Land owners.

The like to Commons.

Parchment.

6th

Attending Mr. Arlett upon Mr. Drake's letter on the Clause against Sunday Travelling required to be inserted by the University Solicitor when he stated that both himself and Mr. Ekin were of opinion that the wishes of the Univ. should be acceded to and the Clause inserted for that otherwise the University would oppose the Bill and begged we would convey this opinion to Messrs. Bircham & Co., by this nights post.

Writing Messrs. Bircham & Co., accordingly and on Sir Fitzroy Kelly's Letter of this afternoon promising support to the Bill in Parliament and the state of the 2 petitions.

Attending Mr. Ekin on the Town Petition which he had returned to us enquiring what further was to be done with it when he requested that as many more signatures as possible might be obtained and we conferred also upon the progress that we had respectively made in obtaining support in Parliament to the bill.

Attending afterwards Mr. Doughty giving him the petitions with instructions to obtain signatures.

Copy Resolution of the Railway Committee Meeting in favour of the Cambridge and Oxford Railway and visiting Sir Fitzroy Kelly M.P. therewith and thereon requested his support in Parliament to the intended measure.

The like Honourable Manners Sutton M.P.

10th

Attending several Members of the Senate obtaining their signatures to the University petition to both houses of Parliament in favor of the Bill.

11th

Attending at the post office enquiring of the Post Master the average number of Letters per week dispatched from this Town towards the West including the District of the Railway together with the mode of route by which they are at present conveyed but that person expressed himself unable to give such information as most of the Letters were now conveyed through London and no account was or could be kept.

Writing Messrs. Bircham & Co. with the result of the interview.

Attending Mr. Arlett with the Petition suggesting to him that as the University clauses in restriction of Sunday Travelling were agreed to be inserted it would be desirable to wait on the Heads of Colleges for their signatures.

Mar 16

Having received a letter from Messrs. Bircham & Co., stating that it was supposed a considerable traffic in pigs existed towards the West which might be made available on this line and requesting that every particular relating thereto might be ascertained Attending Mr. Ekin conferring on the subject when he gave us generally such information as occurred to him but said that Robert Goldsmith who kept the George and Dragon in Barnwell where many of the Drovers stopped on their way could give us some if not all of the particulars we required And we agreed to go together which we accordingly did but could not find him.

Attending a second time in search of Goldsmith but he was not at home and we made an apointment for him (with his Wife) to attend us at our Office the next morning.

17th

Attending Mr. Robert Goldsmith conferring with him on the pig traffic from Norfolk and Suffolk through Cambridge to Beds. Bucks and Northamptonshire and taking minutes of the information he gave us respecting it.

Paid him.

Writing fully to Messrs. Bircham & Co. therewith.

Attending Revd. Dr. Webb Master of Clare Hall when he suggested the great advantage which would result from connecting this with the Eastern Coys Line by a continuation through the extremity of the intended Botanic Garden from the proposed Terminus at Coe Fen to the Eastern Counties Railway at the Bridge on the Hills road instead of the Branch Line as now laid out at the same time that in his Opinion the University would be favourable to such a measure provided the Companys would make them a sufficient offer for so much of the Land purchased for the site of the Botanic Garden as might be required for the purpose and we went into the matter at some length promising to bring it before the Notice of the Directors at an early opportunity.

19th

This being the day on which the principal Cattle and Pig Jobbers passed through Cambridge Attending at the George and Dragon Newmarket Road the place of their chief resort examining several of them on the traffic likely to arise from the Conveyance of Stock by this Line and taking Minutes of their evidence.

20th

Attending Mr. Robert Goldsmith obtaining further information from him respecting the Pig Traffic and examining Mr. Hawkes of this Town Jobber who accompanied him to our office taking Minutes of his evidence in the matter.

Writing Messrs. Bircham & Co., fully on the matter.

23rd

Having heard that Mr. Pemberton was procuring signatures in the parishes of Trumpington and Grantchester to a petition against the Line attending Mr. Ekin to suggest the propriety of setting on foot petitions from the several parishes in the County on the Line when he thought such a step highly desirable and directed petitions to be prepared accordingly. Conferring with Mr. Ekin also on Dr. Webb's suggestion of the 17th inst. as to the continuation of the Railway from the Coe Fen Terminuses by the side of the Botanic Garden and begging he would bring the subject before the Notice of the Board on Thursday next which he promised to do.

Drawing petition to the House of Lords from the Owners and Occupiers of Lands in the parishes on the Line.

The like to the House of Commons.

Writing Sir Fitzroy Kelly M.P. acknowledging receipt of his Letter of yesterday's date and thanking him for his prompt offer of support at the same time informing him what progress the Bill had already made.

27th

Attending severally on all the above witnesses with and upon their proofs as prepared and altering and correcting the same when and where necessary.

Having received a Letter from Messrs. Bircham & Co. this morning requesting us to bring up all the witnesses immediately to Town for examination before the Committee on the Bill who were expected to commence sitting at once attending severally Messrs. Foster Beales Eyres Arlett & Dr. Phelps making arrangements for their immediate attendance in Town accordingly.

Instructing Mr. Goldsmith Special Messenger to go at once to St. Ives Market and bring away with him Mr. Rook and Mr. Bicheno who were expected to be in attendance there.

Writing Messrs. Bircham & Co., in reply to their letter.

Apr. 4

Attending Rev. Mr. Robinson Vicar of Barrington in long conference as to the Line passing thro' or by the side of his Garden when he stated as it must under any circumstances come so close he should prefer it being caused through his premises and selling same to the Company and that his price was £4000 — He also stated that the Bursar of Trinity was absent from Cambridge and would not return for a fortnight — that he had conferred with him and was of opinion if his present suggestion was acceded to the opposition of Trinity College would be withdrawn but otherwise he thought it would be continued.

9th

Writing Messrs. Bircham & Co. in reply to their letter of yesterday's date recommending their communication immediately with the Bursar of Trinity College to the effect that they were willing to avoid passing through the Barrington Vicarage House and Grounds provided the College opposition was withdrawn that being the reason alleged in Mr. Martin's letter for its continuance.

Attending twice before and again today at Corpus Christi College to confer with the Bursar or Master on the purchase of the Vicarage House Garden and premises at Grantchester when we now found the Master at home and went into the matter — he did not anticipate any objection to treat provisionally on the part of the College but would summon a meeting as early as possible (it could not be within a fortnight) and inform us the result and if they could the price they would require.

Apr. 9

Writing Messrs. Bircham & Co., the result of the interview.

Attending Mr. Cooper conferring on the Traffic Case to be made out and arranging that we should attend Mr. Beales and the other principal Merchants and induce them to give such information as lay in their power relative to the traffic, that might be expected and to request them also to give evidence before the Committee on the Bill.

21st

Attending Mr. Hazard conferring on the particulars and amount of the various articles of merchandize sent by him thro' the District of the Railway and from which a traffic might be reckoned upon if the railway were made and after giving us what information he could at the time he promised to look into his accounts and let us know further particulars in a day or two.

The like Mr. Beales.

The like Mr. C. F. Foster.

22nd

Attending Mr. C. F. Foster conferring on the Traffic case when he informed us giving the quantity of merchandize he was in the habit of sending per week into the District of the Cambridge & Oxford Railway but stated that his father would probably give evidence before the Committee on the Bill as he would be in London about that time.

Attending Mr. Ekin on the Traffic Case as at present got up.

The like Mr. Cooper.

23rd

Attending Mr. Ebenezer Foster conferring on the traffic case taking down his evidence and after some discussion he agreed to attend before the Committee on the Bill when required as a witness in favour of the Line.

The like Mr. Patrick Beales.

The like Rev. C. Eyres Bursar of Caius College.

The like Rev. H. Arlett Pembroke College.

The like Rev. Dr. Phelps Master of Sidney Coll.

Writing Messrs. Bircham & Co., with names of witnesses and enquiring on what day they would be required to attend in London.

25th

Attending Mr. Benjamin Vials Horse Dealer who offered himself as witness on the Traffic case conferring thereon and taking down his evidence.

24th

Fair copy Draft petition of Owners and Occupiers of Land and residents in the parishes thro' which the Line will pass in the County of Cambridge.

Attending Mr. Ekin with same for his perusal and afterwards for same.

Ingrossing same for Lords.

The like for Commons.

Parchment etc.

27th

Attending Mr. E. M. Smith who called on Mr. Dentons suggestions conferring on Mr. Pemberton's opposition and other matters.

31st

Journey to Shelford Hauxton and Harston attending on various persons affected as Owners or Occupiers by the proposed Line who have returned themselves as dissentient to induce them to alter their return to "consenting" or at any rate "neuter".

Hire and expenses.

Attending on Mr. Cooper by request of Messrs. Bircham & Co., conferring on the Traffic case the evidence already taken by us and the witnesses generally whom it would be desirable to obtain.

Attending Rev. Mr. Bosanquet Vicar of Harston who called at our office for the purpose conferring on the Notice of Dissent which he had sent and begged he would re-consider the matter and return himself as assenting to the Undertaking.

Apr. 30 – May 1st

Journey to and attendance in London these days Bill in Committee and the Cambridge Witnesses in course of examination.

Paid travelling expences and expences in Town.

Attending the several witnesses Messrs. Foster, Eyres, Beales, Bicheno and Goldsmith paying their several expences and settling with them.

Attending Mr. Rook who required £15.15 and we tendered him £3.

16th

Attending several times before and again today on Rev. I Goodwin Bursar of Corpus College conferring on purchase of Vicarage House and Grounds at Grantchester when he requested we would furnish him with a plan of the Estate and the adjacent property.

Writing Mr. Denton for the plan accordingly on the business.

17th

Messrs. Bircham & Co., having written to inform us that the Scripholders Affirmation Meeting was fixed to take place on the 28th instant and begging we would use our utmost endeavours to ensure favourable votes in the Town and Neighbourhood. Writing them for forms of authority to vote to be signed by Scripholders.

18th

Engaged canvassing Scripholders in the University Town and Neighbours obtaining their Scrip and authority to vote in favour of the measure proceeding.

22nd

Writing S. Parlour Esq. with circulars and request to attend meeting.
Writing Messrs. Bircham & Co., informing them of the general success we
had met with.

26th

Drawing and two fair copies Schedule of Scrip received by us.
Writing Mr. Hope with one copy and informing him we should be in
London on the 28th and would bring with us the Scrip of which we advised
him.
Attending persons who were registered as holding Scrip and whom we
had not previously been able to see obtaining their Scrip with authority
to vote in favor of project at Thursdays Meeting. Writing Mr. Watts St. Ives
in reply to his letter of the 25th instant.

28th

Attending Scrip holders Meeting at Radley's Hotel.

June 1st

Drawing and fair Copy of Schedule of Scrip Certificates received for the
affirmation meeting with full particulars thereof. Attending the several
proprietors thereof returning same to them and taking their receipts.
Attending Master of Clare Hall who called at our Office to confer on the
advantage that would be derived from taking the Railway across the New
Botanic Gardens by the side of Mr. Foster's Fence and the feeling of such
a measure in the minds of several influential members of the University
when we informed them that we had brought the subject before the Board
of Directors but it was their opinion nothing at present could be done in
the matter.

10th

Attending Mr. Ekin for his signature to Bill to be produced before
Committee of the House of Lords and which was to be sent back to Messrs.
Bircham & Co., signed by return of post called twice before we could meet
with him.
The like Revd. H. Arlett
Writing Messrs. Bircham & Co. therewith
Having received a Letter from Messrs. Bircham & Co. requiring our Mr.
Francis with Mr. Looker and Mr. Wrench to be at their offices in Old

Palace Yard at 4 o'clock tomorrow (Thursday June 11th) to attend at the House of Lords and be sworn previous to going into Standing Orders Committee on the next day. Writing to say that all parties would attend as requested.

11th

Mr. Francis' Journey to and attendance in London to be examined as a Witness before the Standing Orders Committee in the House of Lords. Absent 11–12–& 13 – 3 days
The like 2 clerks as similar witnesses.

17th

Having received from Messrs. Bircham & Co., a form to be filled up showing the description of Coals used and present price to the Consumer and the place or places where obtained.
Attending Mr. Patrick Beales conferring thereon and requesting him to fill up same which he did
Writing Messrs. Bircham & Co., therewith.

19th

Having received a letter from Mr. Drake this morning stating that he had just heard that the Lord's Committee was appointed for Monday next and requesting we would get our witnesses in readiness to be sumoned as he would inform us tomorrow.
Attending Mr. Patrick Beales at his Countinghouse (called twice and the last time found him at home) when he informed us he was tonight off for Dover but would attend the Committee any day next week except Wednesday and he gave us his address in case we wished to comunicate with him.
Attending Mr. Ebenr. Foster at his residence in Trumpington when he stated that he could not possibly leave Cambridge on Monday, Tuesday and Wednesday but would attend the Committee afterwards if required but his Son Mr. C. F. Foster was going to London tonight and we might be able to arrange with him to attend on Monday or Tuesday.
Attending Mr. C. F. Foster who informed us that he should be at the 4 Swans Inn Bishopsgate from this evening until Tuesday afternoon when he returned to Cambridge And would on Monday and Tuesday attend the Committee as required but could not possibly be absent from Cambridge on Wednesday.

Attending at Clare Hall Lodge to enquire for the Revd. Dr. Webb the Master who we found was at Litlington and would not be in Cambridge until Monday next.

The like at Sidney Lodge when we found that the Revd. Dr. Phelps the Master was in Town but was expected to return this afternoon.

Attending at Pembroke College to enquire for Revd. Mr. Arlett who we found was absent and his address and period of return uncertain.

The like at Caius College for Revd. Mr. Eyres with the like result.

Writing letter to Mr. Drake informing him the whereabouts and engagements of each witness which we sent him by 4 o'clock Train this afternoon in the form of a parcel.

20th

Having received a letter from Mr. Drake this morning stating that the Committee in the Lords met tomorrow (Monday) at 11 o'clock in the forenoon and begging we would attend with all requisite witnesses at that time — Attending Mr. Ekin informing him of the meeting of the Committee and conferring on his attendance in London as a witness which we finally arranged and that he should go to Town by the early train in the morning.

The like attendance on Dr. Phelps Master of Sidney College with the like result.

Journey to Litlington to confer with Dr. Webb Master of Clare Hall who also agreed to go to London.

Writing C. F. Foster 4 Swans Inn Bishopsgate Street apprizing him of the Meeting of the Committee and begging he would attend if possible at 11 o'clock at the House of Lords.

22nd

Attending the several witnesses reading over to them their proofs and correcting same where necessary.

Journey to London this day for the purpose of attending the Committee in the House of Lords which met at 11 o'clock and rose at 5 when some of the Cambridge Witnesses were examined.

23rd

The like attendance this day before the same Committee when the remainder of the Cambridge Witnesses were taken.

24th

Visiting the Rev. d. Dr. Phelps Master of Sidney with Check for £5. 5.0. for attendance as witness in favour of the Bill before the Committee of the Lords on the 22nd inst.

The like Patrick Beales Esqr. with £6.6/- for the like attendance on the 22nd and 23rd inst.

25th

Attending the Master of Clare Hall by his request at the Lodge when he informed us that a Traffic taker employed by the Eastern Counties Railway Company had been taking traffic during the last week in the parish of Littlington that he had conferred with him thereon and found it was very considerable and that he had requested Mr. Kimpton a Farmer in the parish to take a copy of the particular and amount who had accordingly done so and been with it to Messrs. Nash and Thurralls Office but as the latter Gentleman was not at home he Dr. Webb thought he had better mention the matter to us.

Writing Mr. Drake on the subject accordingly.

July 4th

Having received a letter from Messrs. Bircham & Co. stating that the Lord's amendments would come under discussion in the House of Commons on Tuesday next the 7th instant and begging we would obtain the attendance and support of our Members in favour of the Bill as some opposition was expected on the part of the Eastern Counties Company. Writing Sir Fitzroy Kelly M.P. for the Town of Cambridge stating to him the position of the Bill and begging his support in the house at the time in question.

The like the Honble H. Manners Sutton M.P.

The like Mr. Moffatt M.P.

Writing Messrs. Bircham & Co., in reply to their letter.

6th

Attending Revd. Dr. Webb Master of Clare Hall who called to confer on the decision come to by the Lord's Committee and desired to know what step the Company now intend to take stating his readiness to give any assistance in his power to provide extending the Line granted as far as Cambridge and we begged him at the same time to request the University

Members who were now here on a visit to their Constituents to be in their place on Tuesday and support the amendments in the Commons.

Mr. Sutton having written to inform us he was in his place in the House ready to support the Bill as requested had the opposition not been withdrawn. Writing to thank him for the same.

The bill record ends at this point with a final charge of	£190. 11. 10
Disbursements	64. 12. 10
Total	£255. 4. 8

Appendix IV

Appendix V

PRINCIPALS AND PARTNERS
PRACTISING FULL TIME IN CAMBRIDGE
1789 – 1989

	From	To
Christopher Pemberton	1789	1850
Thomas Fiske	1813	1829
William W. Hayward	1820	1838
William Thrower	1842	1850
Clement Francis	1850	1880
Alfred S. Riches	1861	1878
Thomas Webster	1861	1876
T. Musgrave Francis	1875	1931
Walter H. Francis	1887	1940
Edmund H. Parker	1887	1888
John Collin	1898	1944
Frank Kitchener Peile	1905	1927
Walter M. Francis	1931	1968
Hugh G. Collin	1934	1945
Dudley V. Durell	1937	1972
Kenneth W. Welfare	1948	1951
Bernard W. Cox	1953	1981
Derek G. Hanton	1957	
Peter E. P. Hall	1957	1970
Hugh W. A. Thirlway	1965	1968
A. Timothy Pearce Higgins	1968	-
Christopher E. H. Jackson	1969	-
Clive Sutton	1972	1973
David Anthony Cowper	1976	-
Desmond C. F. Hutchinson	1976	1989
Duncan M. Ogilvy	1979	-
Peter A. J. Hallinan	1983	-
Michael D. T. Barley	1984	-
Michelle G. Cookson	1987	-
John H. R. Carver	1987	-
John W. Knight	1987	1989
Graeme Menzies	1988	-
Roger Bamber	1988	-
Brian Marshall	1988	-
Penelope Elliott	1988	-
Beverley Firth	1989	-
Glynne Stanfield	1989	-

Sources and Further Reading

A. *MANUSCRIPT*

Roll or book of Attornies commencing
Hilary Term 1789 ending Trinity Term
1803, Queen's Bench (plea side) Public Record Office

Chancery Admission Roll 1719–1791 Law Society's Library

The Treasury Register of Bonds given by
Receivers General 1760–1821 Public Record Office

Grove Lodge Lease Documentation
1795–1851 Peterhouse College Library

17–18 Emmanuel Street Leasehold
Documentation 1836–1893 Emmanuel College Library

10 Peas Hill — Title Deeds —in the custody of the
Practice

Romilly's Diary 1850 Cambridge University
Library

Minutes of the Fitzwilliam Museum
Syndicate 1824 Cambridge University
Library

Memoranda concerning the University
solicitor 1858–1862 Cambridge University
Library

Minutes of the Quarter Sessions for the
County of Cambridge 1793–1850 Cambridgeshire County
Record Office

Minutes of the Eau Brink Drainage
Commissioners 1803–1848 Cambridgeshire County
Record Office

Bill Books and Ledgers, Pemberton & Co., Gunning and Francis, Francis & Co. 1821–1924	Cambridgeshire County Record Office
Pemberton & Co. Deeds delivered book 1818–50	—in the possession of the practice
Minutes of the Sex Viri	University Registry
Minutes of the Cambridge Law Society 1839–1866	Cambridgeshire County Record Office
Minutes of the Cambridge and District Law Society 1871–1880	Cambridgeshire County Record Office
Minutes concerning the Proposed Statute No. 54	St. John's College, Cambridge
Correspondence and Counsels' Opinion concerning the Messenger Service	Trinity College, Cambridge

B.   *NEWSPAPERS AND PERIODICALS*

Cambridge Chronicle and Journal 1789–1812
Cambridge Chronicle and Journal and Huntingdonshire
    Gazette 1812–1849
Cambridge Chronicle and University Journal 1849–1931
Cambridge Independent Press 1839–1934
Cambridge Daily News/Cambridge News/Cambridge
    Evening News 1888 to present
Cambridge University Reporter 1850 to present
The Cambridge Review 1928
The Times 1850 to present

C.   *PARLIAMENTARY PAPERS*

Report to the House of Commons from the Select
    Committee on Receivers General, 1821.
Report to the House of Commons from the Select

Committee on the County Rates. 13th July 1934.
An Abstract Return relative to the Clerks and Deputy
Clerks of the Peace for every County of England
and Wales. 28th May 1845.
Report of the Select Committee on the Courts of
Law and Equity, 1848.

D. *BOOKS*

Atkinson T. D. & Clark J. W.	Cambridge Described and illustrated	1897
Baker J. H.	The Order of Serjeants-at-Law	1984
Bury J. P. T. (ed)	Romilly's Cambridge Diary 1832–42	1967
Birks M.	Gentlemen of the Law	1960
Cambridge Historical Register 1910	Reprinted	1984
Clark-Kennedy A.E.	Cambridge to Botany Bay	1983
Cooper C.H.	Annals of Cambridge	1842–1908
Darby H.C.	The Draining of the Fens	1940
Fellows R.B.	London to Cambridge by Train 1845–1938	1976
Francis T.M.	Notes on the Cambridge County Club	c1910
Girouard M.	The Victorian Country House	1979
Gow A.S.F.	Letters from Cambridge	1945
Gray A.B.	Cambridge Revisited	1921
Gray A.	The Town of Cambridge	1925
Grove R.	The Cambridgeshire Coprolite Mining Rush	1976
Gunning H.	Reminiscences of the University Town and County of Cambridge	1854
Hardwicke, Philip Yorke (3rd Earl)	Observations upon the Eau Brink Cut	1793
Hardy G.H.	Bertrand Russell and Trinity	1942
Harraden R.B.	Cantabrigia Depicta	1809
Holden's Triennial Directory		1805–7
Holford W & Wright H.M.	Cambridge Planning Proposals	1950

Howarth T.E.B.	Cambridge Between Two Wars	1978
Jowitt (Earl) ed	The Dictionary of English Law	1959
Larke H.M. &	The Foundation of Edward Storey,	
Shield S.	A History 1693–1980	1980
Lister R.	College Stamps of Oxford and	
	Cambridge	1966
Lysons B and S	Magna Britannia, Cambridge Volume	1808
Maitland Prof. F	Constitutional History of England	1908
Mortlock J.F.	Experiences of a Convict	
	(ed. Wilkes and Mitchell) reprinted	1975
	Eighteen Imaginary Dialogues	1868
	How I came to be a Bankrupt	1868
Murphy M.J.	Cambridge Newspapers and Opinion	
	1780–1850	1977
National Trust	Guide to Wimpole Hall	1979
	Guide to Anglesey Abbey (Robin	
	Fedden)	1972
Pevsner N.	Cambridgeshire (Buildings of	
	England Series)	1954
Pigot	Directory of Cambridgeshire 1823–4 and1839	
Potter H.	Historical Introduction to	
	English Law. 2nd edn.	1943
Reeve F.A.	Cambridge	1964
Riddell &	The Cambridgeshires 1914–1919	
Clayton		1934
Rouse M.	Cambridge in old picture postcards	1984
Royal Commision On Historic Monuments		
	City of Cambridge	1959
	North East Cambridgeshire	1972
Shelford L.	The Law of Railways	1846
Spalding	Handbook to Cambridge	1910
Steers J.A. (ed)	The Cambridge Region 1961–1965	
Stephens E.	The Clerks of the Counties 1360–1960	1961
Strachan H.	History of The Cambridge University	
	Officers Training Corps	1976
Summers D.	The Great Ouse	1973
Taylor C.	The Cambridgeshire Landscape	1973
Tuker M.A.R.	Cambridge	1907

Turner P.	By Rail to Mildenhall		1978
Undrill M.	Cambridge as it might have been		
	(R.I.B.A. catalogue)		1976
Vancouver C.	General View of the Agriculture of		
	the County of Cambridgeshire		1794
The Victoria County History of Cambridgeshire			
	and the Isle of Ely	Vol. 3	1959
		Vol. 6	1960
Watkin D.	The Triumph of the Classical-		
	Cambridge Architecture 1804–1834		
	(Fitzwilliam Museum Catalogue)		1977
Watts Peggy	Stow-cum-Quy through Two Twenty		
	Five year Reigns		1977
White R.J.	Cambridge Life		1960
Willis R &	The Architectural History of the		
Clark J.W.	University of Cambridge		1886
Winstanley D.A.	Later Victorian Cambridge		1947

INDEX